SALZBURG STADT UND LAND

Copyright 2007
Kunstverlag Josef Bühn GmbH
München

ISBN 978-3-932831-00-3

Übersetzungen:
Wayne van Dalsum (englisch)
München

Grafische Gestaltung
und Desktop Publishing:
Grafik Design Zeitlmeir
München

Druck und Bindearbeiten:
Vereinigte Verlagsanstalten GmbH
Düsseldorf

Für die Richtigkeit redaktioneller und bestellter Texte übernimmt der Verlag keine Haftung.

Alle Rechte der Verbreitung behält sich der Verlag vor. Nachdruck, Aufnahme in Online- Dienste und Internet sowie die Vervielfältigung auf digitalen Datenträgern bedarf der schriftlichen Zustimmung des Verlages.

SALZBURG
STADT UND LAND

Wirtschaftsstandort und Kulturraum
Economic Location and Cultural Area

KUNSTVERLAG
JOSEF BÜHN

Inhalt
Contents

Grußworte
Welcome

Salzburg – eine Vorstellung Salzburg – an introduction	*Landeshauptfrau* *Mag. Gabi Burgstaller*	8
Salzburg – eine Quelle der Inspiration Salzburg – a source of inspiration	*Landeshauptmann-Stellvertreter* *Dr. Wilfried Haslauer*	10
Salzburg – ein Standort mit Zukunft Salzburg – a venue with a big future	*Dr. Heinz Schaden* *Bürgermeister der Stadt Salzburg*	12

Willkommen in Salzburg
Welcome to Salzburg
Maja Lenz
Redakteurin
14

Salzburg ist die Hauptstadt von Salzburg
Salzburg is the Capital of Salzburg
Dr. Roland Floimair
Chefredakteur Landespressebüro Salzburg
36

Der Wirtschaftsraum Salzburg – Spitze!
The commercial region Salzburg – in front!
58

Der Wirtschaftsraum Salzburg und die „Marke" auf der Zielgeraden The commercial region Salzburg and the "brand" on the final straight	*Landeshauptmann-Stellvertreter* *Dr. Wilfried Haslauer*	60
Salzburg ist einzigartig Salzburg is one of a kind	*Dipl.-Ing. Rudolf Strasser* *Leiter WirtschaftsService der Stadt Salzburg*	72
Salzburg – ein Wirtschaftsstandort voller Inspiration Salzburg – a commercial venue full of inspiration	*Mag. Gritlind Kettl* *Geschäftsführerin StandortAgentur Salzburg GmbH*	82

**Wirtschaftskammer-Bildung:
Von der Lehre bis zum MBA**
The economic chamber-education:
from apprenticeship to MBA
Kommerzialrat Julius Schmalz
Präsident der Wirtschaftskammer Salzburg
94

Die Paris-Lodron Universität Salzburg als Erfolgsgeschichte eines europäischen Forschungsstandorts
Paris-Lodron University of Salzburg – The success story of a European research venue
Univ.-Prof. Dr. Albert Duschl
Vizerektor für Forschung
Universität Salzburg
100

Inhalt
Contents

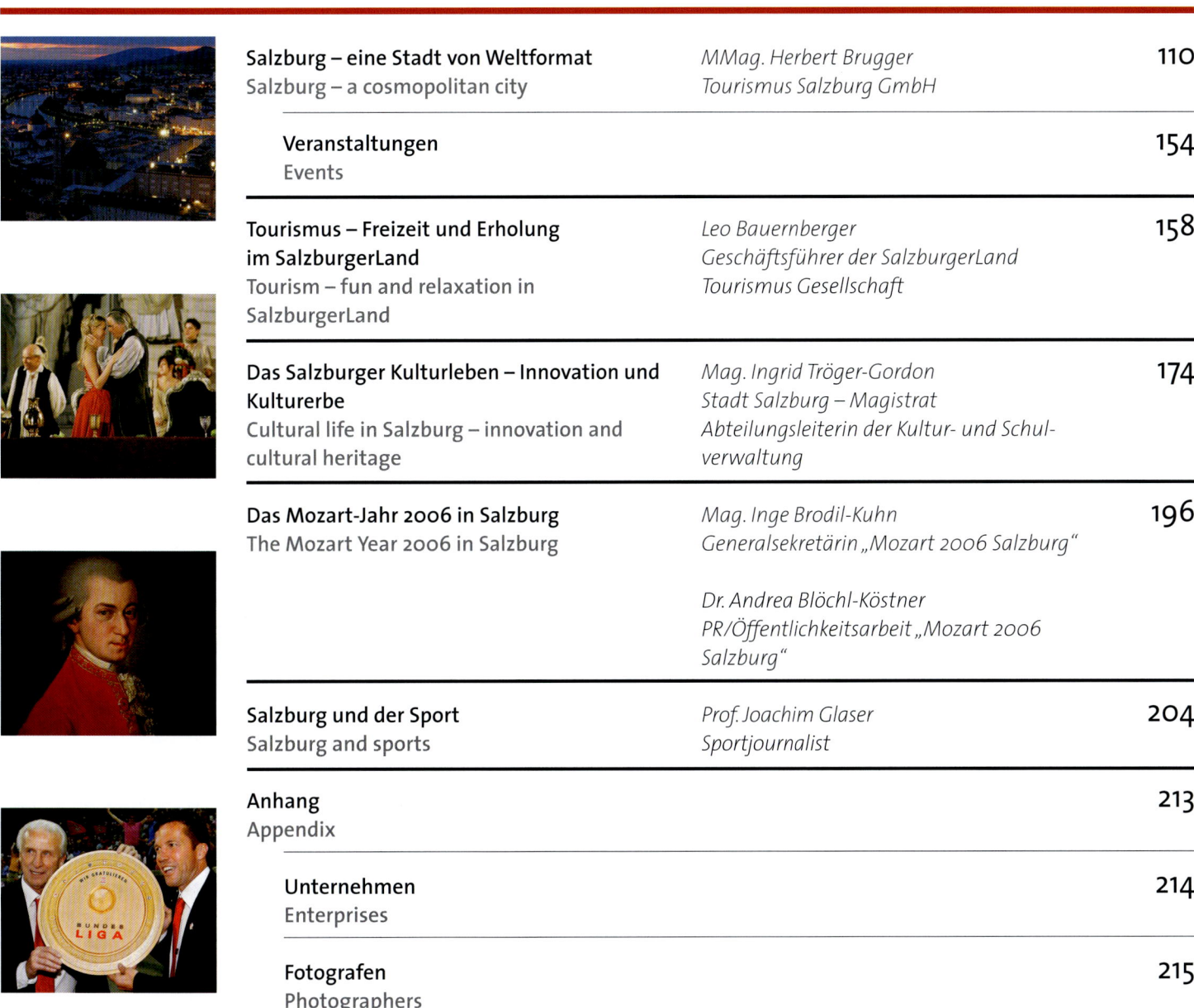

Salzburg – eine Stadt von Weltformat Salzburg – a cosmopolitan city	MMag. Herbert Brugger Tourismus Salzburg GmbH	110
Veranstaltungen Events		154
Tourismus – Freizeit und Erholung im SalzburgerLand Tourism – fun and relaxation in SalzburgerLand	Leo Bauernberger Geschäftsführer der SalzburgerLand Tourismus Gesellschaft	158
Das Salzburger Kulturleben – Innovation und Kulturerbe Cultural life in Salzburg – innovation and cultural heritage	Mag. Ingrid Tröger-Gordon Stadt Salzburg – Magistrat Abteilungsleiterin der Kultur- und Schulverwaltung	174
Das Mozart-Jahr 2006 in Salzburg The Mozart Year 2006 in Salzburg	Mag. Inge Brodil-Kuhn Generalsekretärin „Mozart 2006 Salzburg" Dr. Andrea Blöchl-Köstner PR/Öffentlichkeitsarbeit „Mozart 2006 Salzburg"	196
Salzburg und der Sport Salzburg and sports	Prof. Joachim Glaser Sportjournalist	204
Anhang Appendix		213
Unternehmen Enterprises		214
Fotografen Photographers		215

Salzburg – eine Vorstellung
Salzburg – an Introduction

Muss man Salzburg wirklich erst „vorstellen" – im Sinne von „bekannt machen"? Aus der Außenperspektive gedacht: Gibt es nicht schon jetzt in nah und fern ein überaus facettenreiches „Salzburg-Image", das ein weiteres Sich-Vorstellen praktisch erübrigt? Stimmen denn die bekannten Klischees von der barocken Geburtsstadt des wohl berühmtesten Salzburgers, W.A. Mozart, von den Festspielen, den Salzburger-Nockerl, den wie von liebevoller Hand in eine verträumt anmutige Landschaft gesetzten Gebirgsseen und idyllischen Bergdörfern, von glitzernd weißen Schneehängen, die den Schifahrer zur Rast in tief verschneiten Berghütten einladen usw. Taugen diese und ähnliche vertraute Bilder wirklich noch dazu, dass sich „jedermann" ein richtiges Bild vom heutigen, erst recht vom künftigen Salzburg machen kann? Ja und nein! Denn Salzburg ist all das – aber zugleich noch sehr viel mehr!

Ein näheres Hinsehen weckt freilich Neugierde auf das *andere* Salzburg als eine moderne und dabei sehr erfolgreiche Einheit aus Stadt und Land, die beide stolz den gleichen Namen tragen. Unser wohl mit wenig mehr als 7100 km² und rund 530 000 Einwohnern recht kleines, aber eben auch recht feines Land liegt in der geografischen Mitte Österreichs und – so sehen wir uns aus vielen guten Gründen auch selber gerne – in der Mitte Europas. Die anhaltende Zuwanderung mag auch als ein weiteres Indiz dafür gelten, dass es sich sehr gut leben lässt am überaus dynamischen Wirtschaftsstandort Salzburg. Die stolzen Zahlen dazu – „bench-marks", könnte man heute sagen – liefern alljährlich Wirtschaft und Arbeitsmarkt der Region, mit einer gewissen „Neigung" zu Spitzenplätzen im friedlichen Leistungswettbewerb der Bundesländer untereinander.

Stichwort Dynamik: Bezeichnend, dass gerade im Parade-Dienstleistungsland Salzburg zuletzt das produzierende Gewerbe und eine stark exportorientierte Industrie mit ihren viel beachteten Produktideen, ihren technologischen Innovationen aller Art und den daraus resultierenden Erfolgen in weitem Umkreis besonders von sich reden machen. Auch das „Forschungsland Salzburg" gilt unter Kennern längst als gute Adresse!

Und so gilt auch für Salzburg: Das Ganze ist weit mehr als die Summe seiner Teile! Salzburg *heute* sollte man sich vorstellen als eine gelungene Symbiose aus dem liebevollen Bewahren von regionalen und lokalen Traditionen, aus dem Bewusstsein für ein weltweit beachtetes Kulturschaffen auf der Höhe der Zeit, aus der Pflege einer Dienstleistungsqualität auf höchstem Niveau, aus erstklassigen Nischenprodukten industrieller Fertigung und ganz generell aus der Lust auf Innovation und ein aktives Mitgestalten der Zukunft. Unserer Zukunft!

Dieses Buch möge als weitere Orientierungshilfe dienen beim Kennenlernen des *neuen, zukunftsgewandten* Salzburg, das indessen als Land *und* Stadt – also quasi mit beiden „Beinen" – fest auf den Fundamenten des Altbewährten steht.

Does Salzburg really need an introduction? Doesn't the world already have an impression of the multifaceted "Salzburg image" that makes introductions superfluous? But are these merely clichés of the baroque town where the most famed of all Salzburg's sons W.A. Mozart was born, of the festivals, the Salzburg culinary specialities, the dreamily sculptured mountain lakes and idyllic villages set in breathtaking landscapes, glistening snowy white valleys that entice skiers to take them on and then seek rest in lodges buried deep in snow? Do all these and the other familiar images really give us the right impression of today's or more importantly tomorrow's Salzburg? Yes and no. Because Salzburg is all that, but it is also much more.

A closer look arouses a curiosity to find out more about the *other* Salzburg, the modern and highly successful unity of city and state that both proudly bear the same name. With less than 7,100 km^2 and around 530,000 residents, our state boasts more quality than quantity at the geographic heart of Austria and – as we see it for many reasons – the heart of Europe. The continued immigration into our state also bears witness to the fact that life is very good in the dynamic commercial centre Salzburg. The region's business and labour markets keep delivering the top figures that justify this claim – with a tendency to be among the leaders every year in the friendly competition between federal Austrian states.

And speaking of dynamics: It is significant that in this prime example of a service-oriented economy that Salzburg is, the manufacturing sector and the exporting industries have been making more and more of an impression on a broader scale of late with notable product ideas, all kinds of technological innovations and the successes that these bring with them. Even the "research state Salzburg" has long been discovered as a top address among those in the know!

The whole is far greater than the sum of its parts – and that also applies to Salzburg. Salzburg *today* is a symbiosis between lovingly preserving regional and local traditions, the sensitivity for globally acknowledged, leading-edge cultural activities, a top class service industry, the production of quality industrial niche products and a general desire for innovation, and the active shaping of the future. Our future!

May this book serve as a guide in getting to know the *new, forward-looking* Salzburg, that now stands with both feet – as a state *and* as a city – firmly planted on the foundation of the tried and trusted.

Landeshauptfrau
Mag. Gabi Burgstaller

Salzburg – eine Quelle der Inspiration
Salzburg – a Source of Inspiration

Salzburg ist einzigartig. Salzburg inspiriert. Salzburg gelingt die Symbiose eines attraktiven Wirtschaftsstandorts mit einer enorm hohen Lebensqualität. Zur einmaligen Natur, und einem der vielfältigsten Kulturangebote der Welt kommen noch optimale wirtschaftliche Rahmenbedingungen hinzu.

Internationale Persönlichkeiten und Entscheidungsträger versammeln sich alljährlich zu zahlreichen kulturellen, gesellschaftlichen und wirtschaftlichen Anlässen in der Mozartstadt. Salzburg ist somit nicht nur wegen seiner Festspiele und als Geburtsort von Mozart weltberühmt, sondern wird auch als eine der schönsten Regionen Europas gesehen.

Umso bedeutungsvoller ist ein koordiniertes Vorgehen von Politik und Wirtschaft, um diese außergewöhnliche Stellung zu sichern und zu stärken. Hier ist es Aufgabe der öffentlichen Hand, sich ständig über die derzeitige Position am globalen Markt im Klaren zu sein, gesellschaftliche Entwicklungen und Trends zu verfolgen, Potenziale zu erforschen und die Strategien für die Zukunft darauf auszurichten.

Die Politik nimmt dabei die Rolle des Partners und aktiven Unterstützers ein, indem mit der Wirtschaft die Strategien nicht nur gemeinsam erarbeitet, sondern vor allem die Rahmenbedingungen optimiert sowie die Maßnahmen zur Umsetzung von der Politik initiiert und aktiv unterstützt werden.

Wir gehen von unseren Stärken aus – und zwar einer einzigartigen Landschaft, einem weltweit bekannten Kulturschauplatz sowie einer sehr guten Wirtschaftsstruktur. Wir haben ein Ziel und das heißt Wachstum. Wir haben Chancen, nutzen wir sie.

Salzburg is unique. Salzburg inspires. Salzburg succeeds in nurturing a symbiosis between an attractive commercial venue and a very high standard of living. On top of the breathtaking nature and one of the most diverse cultural programmes that the world has to offer, Salzburg also has an ideal economic infrastructure.

International public figures and decision-makers gather here every year in the Mozart city on numerous cultural, social and commercial occasions. So Salzburg is not only world renowned for its festivals and as the birthplace of Mozart, it is also known as one of the most beautiful regions in Europe.

All the more important it is to have a coordinated interaction between the political and industrial sectors in order to secure and support this extraordinary status that Salzburg enjoys. The public administration has the responsibility of constantly knowing the current position in the global market, keeping abreast of social trends and developments and researching areas of potential so as to orient the strategies for the future on them.

The political sector takes on the role of a partner and active helper by not only designing these strategies together with the industry, but also by optimising the commercial environment in which they are to be realised and initiating and actively supporting their implementation.

We have our strengths – an unparalelled natural environment, a globally famed cultural stage and an excellent base for business. We have a goal – and that goal is growth. We have opportunities – and we make the most of them.

Landeshauptmann-Stellvertreter
Dr. Wilfried Haslauer

Salzburg – ein Standort mit Zukunft
Salzburg – a Venue with a Big Future

Salzburg ist als Kultur- und Festspielstadt international bekannt. Mit den Oster-, Pfingst- und Sommerfestspielen ist Salzburg jährlich der Magnet für viele Besucher, und die Stadt Salzburg wird zum Treffpunkt internationaler Persönlichkeiten und Entscheidungsträger. Bekannt ist Salzburg aber auch für die unvergleichbare Altstadt, die als Weltkulturerbe ausgezeichnet wurde. Aber nicht nur Kultur und Historie kennzeichnen Salzburg, sondern auch Hochtechnologie, Spitzenforschung und Sport. Viele international tätige Firmen haben ihren Sitz in Salzburg gewählt: wegen der Einzigartigkeit Salzburgs, der Überschaubarkeit, wegen der hohen Lebensqualität in einer intakten Umwelt mit hohem Freizeitwert.

Salzburg liegt im Zentrum Europas und zählt zu den innovativsten und wettbewerbsstärksten Regionen Europas. Salzburg besitzt eine sehr gute Verkehrsanbindung sowohl über die Autobahn, wie auch mit der Bahn zu den großen Wirtschaftsräumen um München und Wien. Der Salzburger Flughafen ergänzt dieses Angebot hervorragend.

Die Stadt Salzburg hat eine ausgeglichene Größenstruktur der Betriebe. In über 7 000 Betrieben arbeiten ca. 91 000 Beschäftigte. Als regionales Zentrum dominieren vor allem handelsbezogene Dienstleistungen sowie Handels- und – in geringerem Ausmaß – Produktionsbetriebe. Die Stadt wird zunehmend attraktiver für neue innovative Unternehmungen im Hochtechnologiebereich. So haben etwa der für den Motorsport Leichtbauteilhersteller Carbo-Tech und die für Sicherheit stehende Firma Commend ihre Firmen erfolgreich am Standort Salzburg ausgebaut. Wir unterstützen verstärkt die Forschungstätigkeit, wobei zwei Bereiche für uns große Bedeutung haben. Zum einen der Schwerpunkt Geoinformation und angewandte Computertechnologie in der neuen „Science City" und zum anderen die Gesundheitsforschung mit Biotechnologie.

Intensive Forschungstätigkeit und vor allem Ausbildung wird an der Paris-Lodron-Universität, Universität Mozarteum, der Paracelsus Medizinischen Privatuniversität und der Salzburger Fachhochschule geleistet. Sehr zukunftsweisend ist die Ausbildungskooperation der Universität Salzburg mit der TU München im technischen Bereich. Unsere jungen Menschen haben zudem die Möglichkeit in berufsbildenden Schulen zielgenau auf die Berufstätigkeit vorbereitet zu werden. Die mittelständische Wirtschaft gewährleistet durch ihr Engagement in der Lehrlingsausbildung bestgeschultes und hoch motiviertes Personal.

Die Salzburger genießen eine positive Wirtschaftsentwicklung, ein gutes Arbeitsplatzangebot und hohe Lebensqualität in einem sicheren Umfeld.

Ich freue mich, dass das vorliegende Buch über Stadt und Land Salzburg all diese Facetten anschaulich und ästhetisch aufbereitet und vorstellt. Salzburg BesucherInnen, Wirtschaftstreibende und all jene, die mehr über Salzburg wissen wollen, finden auf den folgenden Seiten wichtige und interessante Informationen über Stadt und Land. Ich hoffe, Sie werden dadurch neugierig auf unsere Stadt und unsere Region!

Salzburg is known around the world as a city of culture and as a home of festivals. With its Easter, Whitsun and Summer Festivals, Salzburg is a magnet for innumerable visitors every year and the meeting point for internationally famous people and decision-makers. But Salzburg is also well known for its incomparable historic town centre – a world heritage site – as well as for high technology, top-level research and sports. Numerous international companies have chosen to locate their headquarters here; because of Salzburg's uniqueness, manageable size, high standard of living and intact environment with many leisure-time options.

Salzburg lies at the heart of Europe and is one of the most innovative and competitive regions on the continent. Its transport connections to Munich and Vienna are excellent by both Autobahn and by train, and Salzburg Airport rounds off the options.

The balance of different sized companies in the city of Salzburg is ideal. Around 91,000 people work here in more than 7,000 companies. As a regional centre, trade related services dominate the commercial landscape, as do retail and to a lesser extent manufacturers. The city is becoming ever more attractive for new, innovative companies in the high-tech field. For example, the motorsports light-component maker Carbo-Tech and the security firm Commend have expanded their activities in Salzburg. We provide support to the research sector, whereby two particular fields are of special significance to us. One of these is geoinformation and applied computer technology in the new "Science City", and the other is healthcare research with biotechnology.

Paris-Lodron-University, Universität Mozarteum, Paracelsus Private Medical University and Salzburg Polytechnic are intensively involved in research and most especially in educating the next generation of researchers. The cooperation between Salzburg University and Munich Technical University in the technical field is exemplary. Our students have the opportunity here to prepare themselves for precisely the profession they choose at our vocational schools. With its commitment to traineeships, the small and medium-sized corporate sector also makes a great contribution to producing well trained and highly motivated personnel.

The citizens of Salzburg enjoy a strong economy, a good range of jobs on offer and a high standard of living in a safe and secure setting.

I am very happy to see how beautifully this book presents all these facets of the city and state of Salzburg. Visitors to Salzburg, commercial players and all those who would like to learn more about Salzburg will find the following pages packed with important and interesting information about the city and its surrounds. I hope it will make you curious to come and see it for yourself!

Dr. Heinz Schaden
Bürgermeister der Stadt Salzburg

„*Die Gegenden von* **Salzburg,** *Neapel und Constantinopel zähle ich zu den schönsten der Erde.*"

Alexander von Humboldt

Salzburger Nockerl

Ein ganz wichtiger Bestandteil der Salzburger Küche sind die Salzburger Nockerl, jener Nachspeisentraum, von dem die Operette singt: „Süß wie die Liebe, zart wie ein Kuss".

Der Legende nach ließ sich der berühmte Salzburger Fürsterzbischof Wolf Dietrich Raitenau damit von seiner Geliebten Salome Alt verwöhnen. Die schöne Bürgerliche gebar ihm 15 Kinder, dafür schenkte er seiner Geliebten Schloss Mirabell. Soweit, so belegt.

Nicht bewiesen ist hingegen die Geschichte mit den Nockerln, denn Ende des 16. Jahrhunderts war es noch nicht möglich, den süßen Traum nach heutiger Rezeptur herzustellen, braucht man doch dazu ein Backrohr mit regulierbarer Hitze, das es erst seit dem 19. Jahrhundert gibt.

The Salzburger Nockerl is a big part of Salzburg cuisine. It is a pancake-like dessert that the operetta refers to as: "As sweet as love, as soft as a kiss".

Legend has it that the famed Salzburg Prince Bishop Wolf Dietrich Raitenau bowed to its temptations in the hands of his beloved Salome Alt. The beautiful commoner bore him 15 children, and in return he made her the gift of his dear Mirabell castle.

That much is true, but the bit about the Nockerls... . After all, at the end of the 16th century it wasn't possible to bake this sweet dream – at least not as we know it today – because the current recipe demands an oven with regulated temperature, and they weren't invented until the 19th century.

Salzburger Nockerl

Zutaten für 3 große Nockerl:
7 Eiklar
100 g Kristallzucker
2 Eidotter
20 g Mehl glatt
1 EL Vanillezucker
Butter zum Bestreichen
Staubzucker zum Bestreuen

Zubereitung:
Eiklar unter ständiger Beigabe von Kristallzucker zu festem Schnee schlagen. Vanillezucker und Eidotter einrühren. Mehl vorsichtig unter die Masse heben. Flache Wanne oder Platte mit Butter bestreichen. Nocken pryramidenförmig daraufsetzen und im vorgeheizten Backrohr backen. Mit Staubzucker bestreuen, sofort servieren.
Backrohrtemperatur: 220°C
Backdauer: 9 Minuten

Salzburger Nockerl

Ingredients for 3 large Nockerl:
7 egg whites
100 g sugar
2 egg yolks
20 g flour
1 tablespoon vanilla sugar
Butter for the baking tin
Icing sugar for dusting

Preparation:
Beat the egg whites until stiff, while gradually adding sugar. Mix in the vanilla sugar and egg yolk. Carefully fold in the flour. Butter a flat baking tin or tray. Place the mixture in pyramids on it and bake for 9 minutes in an oven preheated to 220°C. Dust with icing sugar and serve while still warm.

Mozartkugel

Im Jahre 1890 erfand der Salzburger Konditor Paul Fürst die heute weltberühmte Mozartkugel. Den Namen wählte er, um dem großen Salzburger Sohn Mozart seine Referenz zu erweisen. Mit seiner einzigartigen Rezeptur gewann Paul Fürst im Jahre 1905 in Paris sogar eine Goldmedaille. Die Qualität und der feine Geschmack waren es, die dieser neuen Spezialität einen so großen Erfolg bescherten.

Schon bald kopierten auch andere Konditoren sowie die Süßwarenindustrie die feinen Kugeln, doch bis heute dürfen sich allein die Produkte aus der Konditorei Fürst, die nach wie vor nach den alten, aufwändigen Verfahren hergestellt werden, „Original Salzburger Mozartkugeln" nennen.

The Salzburg confectioner Paul Fürst invented the now world-famous Mozart praline in 1890. He chose the name in honour of Salzburg's greatest son. With the unique recipe Paul Fürst even won a gold medal in Paris in 1905, with the quality and taste of this speciality ensuring the enormous success.

It didn't take long before other confectioners and the confectionary industry were copying these exquisite little spheres, but to this day only those stemming from Konditorei Fürst, which are still made in accordance with the complex, ancient procedure, have the right to call themselves "Original Salzburger Mozartkugeln".

Aufbau und Herstellung der „Original Salzburger Mozartkugel"

Marzipan mit Pistazien auf Holzstäbchen gesteckt wird umhüllt mit feinem Nougat und in dunkle Kuvertüre getunkt anschließend auf Brettchen zum Erstarren gestellt, das Stäbchen wird entfernt und das Loch mit Schokolade verschlossen.

How the "Original Salzburg Mozartkugel" praline is made

A marzipan and pistachio mix is mounted on a wooden skewer, covered with finest nougat and dipped in a dark chocolate coating. This is then placed on a board to set, the skewer is removed and the hole it leaves filled with chocolate.

Kaffeehaus

Zeitung lesen, Kaffee trinken, Leute anschauen – seit dem 18. Jahrhundert ist das Kaffeehaus wichtiger Bestandteil österreichischer Kultur. Seine Glanzzeit erlebte das Kaffeehaus während des Biedermeier. Ausgestattet mit Lüstern, Plüsch und Silbergeschirr war es geschäftlicher, privater und geselliger Treffpunkt von Politik, Wirtschaft, Kunst und Kultur.

Kleiner Brauner, großer Brauner, Melange, Kaisermelange, Mokka, Einspänner, Espresso, Schale Braun, Fiaker, Franziskaner, Maria Theresia.... Der Erfindungsreichtum kennt keine Grenzen. Ob mit Milch, Schlagobers, Rum, Cognac, Orangenlikör, Eidotter, einfach alles kann mit Kaffee gemischt werden. Das Kaffeehaus ist ein Synonym für österreichische Geselligkeit.

Reading a paper, sipping a coffee, watching the people – the coffee shop has been an important part of Austrian culture since the 18th century. Its heyday was during the Biedermeier period. Furnished with voluptuous plush and serving with silver cutlery, it was a business, private and social place to meet for the political, commercial, art and cultural sectors.

The Kleiner Brauner, Großer Brauner, Melange, Kaisermelange, Mocca, Einspänner, Espresso, Schale Braun, Fiaker, Franziskaner, Maria Theresia.... There is no end to the different kinds of coffee you can get in an Austrian coffee shop. Whether milk or cream, rum, cognac, orange liqueur or egg yolk; you can mix nearly anything with coffee. The coffee shop is a synonym for Austrian conviviality.

WOLFERL

Aussehen: „Er war klein, rasch, beweglich und blöden Auges, eine unansehnliche Figur in grauem Überrock" (L. Tieck).
Festanstellungen: 1772-77 Konzertmeister in Salzburg, 1779-81 Hoforganist, 1787-91 k. k. Kammer-Komponist.
Freimaurer: Er tritt 1784 der Wiener Loge „Zur Wohltätigkeit" bei.
Frieselfieber: die Krankheit, die ihn am 5. Dez. 1791 das Leben kostete.
Geld: Mozart kann damit nicht besonders gut umgehen. Lange Zeit regelt der Vater seine Finanzen.
Kinderarbeit: Erstmals hat er bei seinem Auftritt als sechsjähriger in München Geld verdient.
Köchel, Ludwig: Erfindet 1862 das Köchel-Verzeichnis, das 626 Mozart-Werke chronologisch auflistet.
Mama: Maria Anna, eine Bürgerliche aus dem Salzburgischen.
Nannerl: Mozarts Schwester Maria Anna Walburga Ignatia.
Papa: Johann Georg Leopold M. (1719-1787) aus Augsburg, Geiger, Organist, Komponist, Hofgeiger und ab 1763 Vicekapellmeister in Salzburg.
Reisen: Er war erstmals als Sechsjähriger unterwegs, es sollen 3 720 Tage gewesen sein, ein Drittel seines fast 36 Jahre dauernden Lebens.
Requiem: Seine letzte Komposition. Eine Auftragsarbeit für Graf Walsegg-Stuppach. Mozart hat allein den Introitus vollendet.

Appearance: "He was small, quick, nimble and cockeyed; an unsightly figure in a grey bavaroy" (L. Tieck).
Salaried positions: 1772-77 concertmaster in Salzburg, 1779-81 court organist, 1787-91 chamber composer.
Free mason: He entered the Vienna Order "for Benefaction" in 1784.
Severe miliary fever: the malady that cost him his young life on 5 December 1791.
Money: Mozart was not good with money. His father kept control of his financial matters for a long time.
Child labour: He earned money for the first time in is life as a six year-old at an appearance in Munich.
Köchel, Ludwig: Invented the Köchel catalogue in 1862 – a chronological list of 626 works by Mozart.
Mama: Maria Anna, a Salzburg commoner.
Nannerl: Mozart's sister Maria Anna Walburga Ignatia.
Papa: Johann Georg Leopold M. (1719-1787) from Augsburg. Violinist, organist, composer, court violinist and deputy music director in Salzburg from 1763.
Travels: Began when he was six and by all accounts he spend 3720 days on the road – a third of his almost 36 years.
Requiem: His last composition. A commissioned work for Count Walsegg-Stuppach. Mozart only finished the Introitus.

Mozart geht online

**Sämtliche Partituren stehen jetzt gratis im Internet unter:
www.MOZARTEUM.AT**

Mozart goes online

**All of Mozart's scores are now available free of charge at:
www.MOZARTEUM.AT**

NB: Wolferl is the diminutive form of Wolfgang in Austria

Schnürlregen

Sie fahren nach Salzburg? Vergessen Sie bitte nicht Ihren Regenschirm! Er sollte so klein wie möglich sein, in den engen Gassen der Altstadt könnte es nämlich sonst zu Kollisionen kommen. In Salzburg heißt der Regen übrigens „Schnürlregen", weil er in Schnüren vom Himmel kommt. Und er kommt ziemlich häufig, denn atlantische West- und Nordwestwinde führen zu so genannten Nordstaulagen, die zu jeder Jahreszeit feuchte Luftmassen bringen, die sich am Alpenrand stauen, abkühlen und in Form von Regen herabkommen.

Der Theaterkritiker und Schriftsteller Hans Weigel hat einmal die These aufgestellt, Gott habe Kärnten sonnig geschaffen, auf dass es die Menschen anziehe und das Salzkammergut regnerisch, um nicht alle anderen Landstriche zu entvölkern. Die Gerechtigkeit dieser göttlichen Witterungsprävention ist immerhin, dass sie Einheimischen wie Gästen das Leben zeitweise nachhaltig schwer macht.

So ist in Salzburg der Mensch „feucht-fröhlich", wenn er bei Regen trotzdem lacht!

Travelling to Salzburg? Don't forget your brolley! The smaller the better, otherwise you could be in for collisions in the narrow lanes of the old town. Rain in Salzburg means Schnürlregen, "Schnürl" being strings and "Regen" rain. That's how the rain looks when it comes down here, and it does so quite often with Atlantic west and north-west winds causing clouds to get caught up in the mountains, cool off and then head downwards – in strings of rain.

The theatre critic and author Hans Weigel once proposed the theory that God made Kärnten sunny to attract people and the Salzkammergut region rainy so it didn't steal the population from all the other regions. The justice behind this divine preventive weather measure is that it makes life difficult for natives and visitors sometimes.

So people in Salzburg learn to enjoy a good drop – even if it comes in the form of a sudden downpour!

Bosna

Der aus Bulgarien stammende Zanko Todoroff kreierte in der Mitte des letzten Jahrhunderts die bekannte und so beliebte Salzburger Spezialität. Sie bestand damals aus einem aufgeschnittenen Wecken, zwei Schweinsbratwürsten, Zwiebel, Petersilie und einer curryhaltigen Gewürzmischung, alles umwickelt mit weißem Papier. Den Namen „Nadanitza" konnten sich die Salzburger nicht merken, weshalb sie die Köstlichkeit kurzerhand in „Bosna" umtauften.

Schon 1950 konnte sich der findige Bulgare ein eigenes Geschäft in Salzburgs Innenstadt leisten. Seit den 1970er Jahren ist der „Balkan-Grill" im Besitz der Familie Walter. Eine Spezialanfertigung ermöglicht heute in dem zwei Quadratmeter großen Geschäft die Herstellung von bis zu 2 000 Bosnawürsten am Tag.

Neben dem Original gibt es auch die Varianten mit zusätzlich Senf oder Ketchup.

In the middle of the last century, Zanko Todoroff of Bulgaria created the famed and well-loved Salzburg speciality Bosna. It comprised a bread roll cut through the middle, two pork sausages, onions, parsley and a mixture of curry and other herbs and spices, all wrapped in white paper. Where Todoroff comes from this delicacy is called a "Nadanitza", but the citizenry of Salzburg couldn't seem to get their tongue around that, so they simply changed its name to "Bosna".

By 1950 the inventive Bulgarian was already able to afford his own store in the inner city of Salzburg. Since the 1970s the "Balkan Grill" has been in the hands of the Walter family. Nowadays, a special machine enables up to 2,000 Bosna sausages to be produced a day in the 2 square-metre shop.

And in addition to the original there are also versions with additional mustard or ketchup.

Variationen

Die Größe der Bosna variiert. Man kann sie jedoch wie folgt kategorisieren:
- kleine Bosna: üblicherweise eine kleine Bratwurst
- mittlere Bosna: üblicherweise zwei kleine Bratwürste
- große Bosna: je nach Region entweder drei kleine oder eine große Bratwurst

Auch die Zusammensetzung variiert:
- Kafka: bei dieser Form wird anstatt einer Bratwurst eine Käsekrainer (die Bratwurst enthält auch noch Käse) verwendet.
- Teufelsbosna: mit Cocktailsauce, die fein geschnittene Chilischoten enthält.
- Knoblauchbosna: mit Knoblauchsauce
- Käsebosna: der klassischen Bosna wird Käse beigemengt.

Darüber hinaus gibt es noch viele Varianten, die vom jeweilgen Anbieter und dessen Kunden geprägt sind.

Variations

The size of the Bosna varies, but they can be generally categorised as follows:
- Little Bosna: Customarily a small sausage
- Medium Bosna: Customarily two small sausages
- Large Bosna: regionally variable, but either three small or one large sausage

And the composition varies too:
- Kafka: Here a grilled sausage with cheese is used.
- Devil's Bosna: With a cocktail sauce containing finely diced chile peppers.
- Garlic Bosna: With garlic sauce
- Cheese Bosna: Cheese is added to the classical Bosna.

And of course different vendors and customers can put together their very own variations as well.

Janker

Die Trachtenjacke, österreichisch auch Janker genannt, wurde ursprünglich als Schutz unter der Rüstung verwendet. Im 16. und 17. Jahrhundert fungierte sie als Jagdweste und bis in die 1950er Jahre als Hausjacke. Im Laufe der Zeit wurde der Janker von einem funktionellen Kleidungsstück zu einer modischen Ergänzung jeder Garderobe, ganz gleich ob Mann, Frau oder Kind.

Konnte man früher aus Farbe, Verzierung und Schnitt Rückschlüsse auf Herkunft, Beruf oder Stand des Trägers ziehen, so sagt all das inzwischen höchstens noch etwas über dessen Modegeschmack aus.

Man kann heute den Janker zu jedem Zweck tragen: vom ausgedehnten Wandern über das zwanglose Treffen in der Freizeit bis hin zu eleganten Feierlichkeiten.

Gefertigt wird der Janker aus hochwertigem Material wie Loden, Leinen oder Leder und verziert beispielsweise mit Hirschhornknöpfen und aufwändigen Stickereien.

Übrigens: Coco Chanel soll für die Jacke ihres berühmten Kostüms von einem Trachtenjanker inspiriert worden sein.

The traditional jacket known as the Janker was originally worn as protection beneath a suit of armour. In the 16th and 17th centuries it was used as a hunting vest and right up to the 1950s it was considered casual attire for around the house. Over time the Janker developed from being a functional garment to a fashion accessory for every Austrian wardrobe, whether for man, woman or child.

And where it was once possible to draw conclusions about a person's family history, profession or standing in society by looking at the colour, adornment and cut of his Janker, nowadays a Janker at best tells us something about a person's taste in clothing.

People wear Jankers for any number of different purposes nowadays: for hiking, meeting friends or dressing up on occasions demanding evening-wear.

They are made of top-quality materials such as loden, linen or leather and trimmed, for example, with buckhorn buttons and elaborate embroidery.

BTW: It is said that a Janker was the inspiration for the jacket in Coco Chanel's famous skirt suit.

Salzburger Barock

Diese weltberühmte barocke Treppe, genannt die „Engelsstiege", befindet sich in Schloss Mirabell, das Erzbischof Raitenau Anfang des 17. Jahrhunderts der von ihm verehrten Salome Alt widmete. Nach seiner Neugestaltung im 18. Jahrhundert und einem Brand im Jahr 1818 wurde das Schloss im klassizistischen Stil wiedererbaut. Allein das Treppenhaus, gestaltet von Georg Raphael Donner zu Beginn des 18. Jahrhunderts, blieb damals erhalten.

Die Stufen führen zum Marmorsaal, dem man nachsagt, der schönste und atemberaubendste Trauungssaal der Welt zu sein. Wer sie erklimmt, geht vorbei an der weißen Marmorbalustrade, auf der sich pausbäckige Putten tummeln. Ein Klaps auf deren Hinterteil verheißt angeblich ewiges Eheglück.

These world famous baroque steps called the "Engelsstiege" or "Angel's Stairway" can be found in Mirabell Castle, which archbishop Raitenau dedicated to his much adored Salome Alt at the beginning of the 17th century. After its reconstruction in the 18th century and a fire in 1818, the castle was rebuilt in the Classical style. Only the steps, designed by Georg Raphael Donner at the beginning of the 18th century remained.

The steps lead up to the Marble Hall, which is said to be the most breathtaking and beautiful wedding hall in the world. Climbing them one passes the white marble balustrade decorated with playful cherubs. Legend has it that giving them a slap on the bottom ensures everlasting marital bliss for the lucky couple.

Sommerakademie

Als Oskar Kokoschka im Jahr 1953 die Sommerakademie Salzburg gründete, ging es ihm um die Schaffung einer offenen Begegnungsstätte, in der Menschen verschiedenster Provenienz nach den geistigen Verheerungen des 2. Weltkriegs humanistische Ideale wieder beleben und pflegen sollten. Die Jugend war ihm dabei ein besonderes Anliegen. Grundbedingung für seine „Schule des Sehens" war, dass sie für alle offen sein sollte, ungeachtet des Alters, des Geschlechts, der Nationalität und der künstlerischen Vorbildung. In einer unakademischen Umgebung sollten die Menschen in der Begegnung mit der Kunst, im schöpferischen Sehen, innerlich wachsen können.

Die weltweit renommierte Internationale Sommerakademie für Bildende Kunst Salzburg setzt sich seit ihrer Gründung auch über politische, religiöse und kulturelle Grenzen hinweg. So stammten im Jahr 2006 die 500 Studierenden aus aller Welt. Weltweite Partnerschaften garantieren einen Austausch zwischen Studierenden und Lehrenden.

As Oskar Kokoschka founded the Salzburg Summer Academy in 1953, he wanted to create a place where people of every background could meet after the spiritual cataclysm of World War 2 and reanimate and nurture humanistic ideals. Young people were especially important in his considerations. The basic precondition for his "School of Seeing" was that it be open for everyone, regardless of age, gender, nationality or artistic grounding. The people were supposed to be able to grow inwardly through a confrontation with art and seeing creatively there.

The world-renowned International Summer Academy of Fine Arts in Salzburg has always ignored political, religious and cultural borders, as can be seen in the fact that in 2006 the 500 students come from all over the world. Worldwide partnerships ensure an exchange of students and teachers.

Das Programm der Internationalen Sommerakademie für Bildende Kunst vom 16.7. – 25.8.2007

Malerei
Zeichnung
Installation
Medien
Skulptur
Plastik/Modellieren
Fotografie
Illustration
Grafik
Steinbildhauersymposium
Architektur
Design
Schmuckgestalten

www.summeracademy.at

The program of the International Summer Academy of Fine Arts from July 7 to August 25, 2007

Painting
Drawing
Installation
Media workshop
Sculpture
Plastic art/Modelling
Photography
Illustration
Graphic arts
Stone sculpture symposium
Architecture
Design
Jewellery design

www.summeracademy.at

Jedermann

Seit 85 Jahren sind die Salzburger Festspiele untrennbar mit Hugo von Hofmannsthals (1874-1929) Mysterienspiel „Jedermann" verwoben, das im Laufe dieser Zeit beinahe zum Synonym für das Festival wurde. Jedermann: Das ist das Spiel vom Sterben des reichen Mannes, das am 1. Dezember 1911 im Berliner Zirkus Schumann unter der Regie von Max Reinhardt uraufgeführt wurde. Darin treten Gott, der Tod, der Teufel und andere abstrakte Wesen als Personifikationen auf. Der reiche Jedermann wird mit dem unerwarteten Tod konfrontiert, der ihn vor Gott führen will. Weder sein ihm ergebener Knecht, noch seine Freunde, noch sein Geld wollen ihn ins Grab begleiten. Erst der Auftritt seiner Werke und seines Glaubens bringen ihn dazu, sich zum Christentum zu bekennen und als reuiger Bekehrter ins Grab zu steigen.

Die Handlung des Mysterienspiels ist eine Allegorie des christlichen Weltgefüges, vor dem sich der Mensch, also „Jedermann", verantworten muss. Aufgeführt wird das Stück im Freien, vor der Kulisse des Salzburger Doms. Jahr für Jahr pilgern tausende von Jedermann-Begeisterten im Sommer nach Salzburg, um diesem – hochkarätig besetzten – Schauspiel beizuwohnen.

The Salzburg Festival has been inextricably interwoven with Hugo von Hofmannsthal's (1874-1929) mystery play "Everyman" for 85 years, and over time it has even become something of a synonym for the Festival itself. Everyman is a play about the death of a wealthy man that premiered on 1 December 1911 in Berlin's Schumann Circus, directed by Max Reinhardt. In it, God, Death, the Devil and other abstract beings make special appearances as personifications. The wealthy Everyman is unexpectedly confronted by Death, who wants to take him before God. Neither his loyal servant, his friends nor his money want to accompany him into the grave. Not until his Worldy Deeds and his Belief make an entrance is he moved to accept Christianity and accept his fate as a penitent convert.

The story of this mystery play is an allegory of the Christian beliefs, which make every person or "Everyman" answerable for his acts. It is staged outdoors against the background of Salzburg cathedral. Summer after summer, thousands of Everyman fans pilgrimage to Salzburg to see the star-studded show.

Besetzung 2007
Cast of Characters 2007

Regie:
Christian Stückl
Leitung:
Gunnar Letzbor
Bühnenbild Kostüme:
Marlene Poley,
Dorothea Nicolai
Musik:
Markus Zwink

Jedermann:
Peter Simonischek
Teufel:
Norman Hacker
Buhlschaft:
Nina Hoss
Gott der Herr:
Karl Merkatz
Tod:
Ulrike Folkerts
Jedermanns Mutter:
Bibiana Zeller
Jedermanns guter Gesell:
Norman Hacker
Ein armer Nachbar:
Karl Merkatz
Ein Schuldknecht:
Arthur Klemt
Des Schuldknechts Weib:
Susanne Schäfer
Der Hausvogt:
Johann Christof Wehrs
Der Koch:
Olaf Weissenberg
Dicker Vetter:
Heinz Zuber
Dünner Vetter:
Achim Buch
Mammon:
Maximilian Brückner
Gute Werke:
Elisabeth Rath
Glaube:
Elisabeth Schwarz
Knecht:
Gerald Koblinger
Die Spielansager:
Riederinger Kinder

35

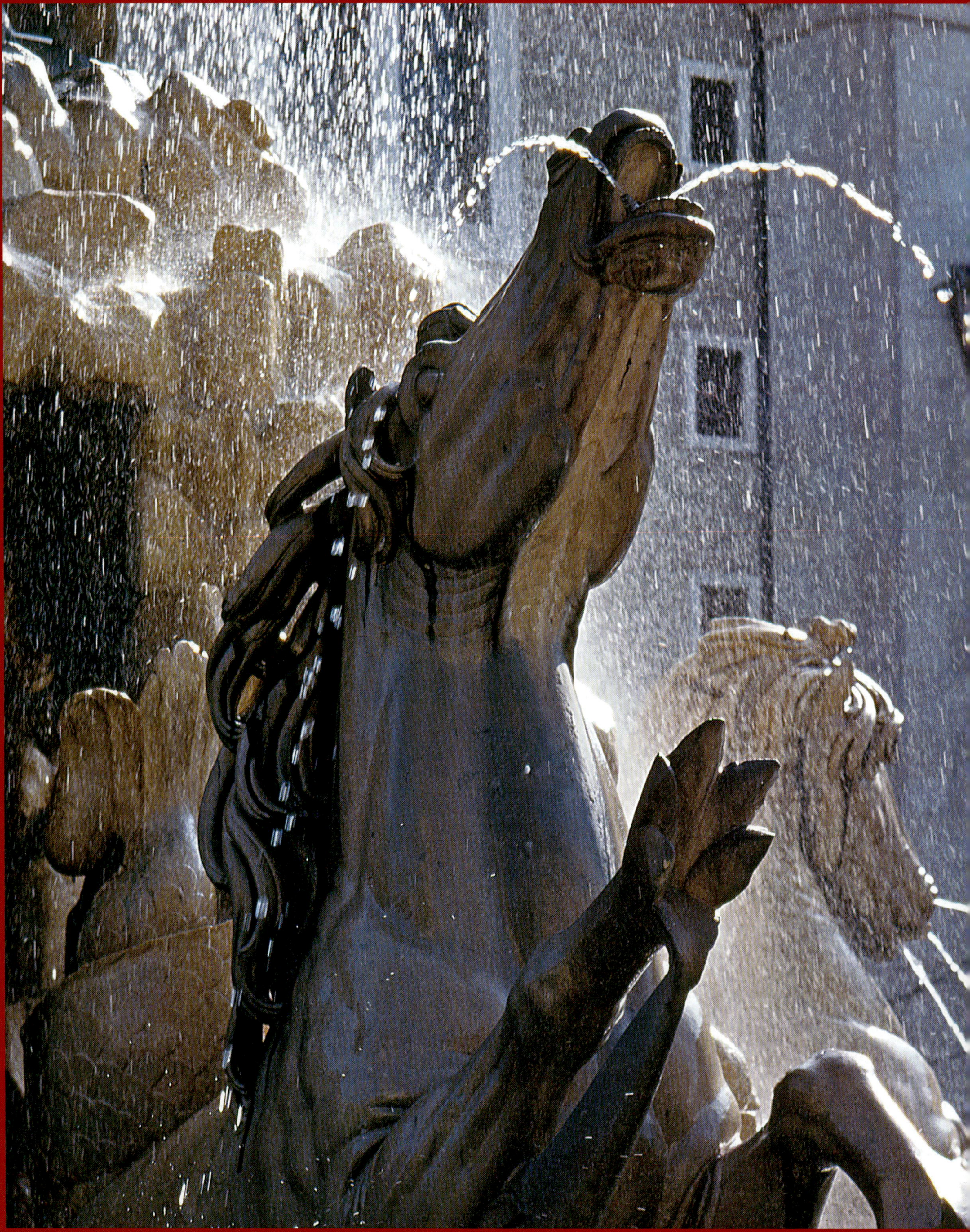

Dr. Roland Floimair
Chefredakteur
Landespressebüro Salzburg

Salzburg ist die Hauptstadt von Salzburg

Salzburg is the Capital of Salzburg

„Bringen Sie mir Salzburg oder gehen Sie!" Eine solche, recht ungnädige Weisung soll seinerzeit Kaiser Franz von Österreich seinem Kanzler Metternich erteilt haben. Die kaiserliche Äußerung gilt zwar nicht als authentisch, doch ist sie durchaus denkbar, denn das jahrhundertelang bestehende, selbstständige geistliche Fürstentum war kurz zuvor (1803) als geistliches Regierungsterritorium aufgelöst worden, hatte anschließend eine Herrschaft unter dem Großherzog von Toskana hinter sich, war 1805 bis 1809 bereits einmal österreichisch und in der Folge nach kurzer französischer Verwaltung von 1810 an bayerisch gewesen. Mit 1. Mai 1816 fiel Salzburg bekanntlich an Österreich; Grenzverlauf und Gestaltung des heutigen Bundeslandes gehen somit auf diesen Zeitpunkt zurück. Beides blieb dann sowohl 1918 als auch 1945 gleich: Die Fläche beträgt 7 155 Quadratkilometer. Seiner Größe nach nimmt Salzburg in der Reihe der neuen Bundesländer die fünfte, bezüglich der Bevölkerungszahl (521 238 Einwohner) die siebte Stelle ein. In der Wirtschaftskraft liegt Salzburg, abgesehen von Wien, an der Spitze der Bundesländer.

Obwohl es historisch zu den jüngeren Ländern Österreichs zählt, nimmt Salzburg Österreichs Mit-

"Get me Salzburg or go!" This is said to be the rather ungracious command that Kaiser Franz of Austria gave his chancellor Metternich once upon a time. It is not considered to be a direct quote, but it is quite conceivable that he would have said something like this, because the centuries-old independent religious principality was dissolved as a government territory shortly beforehand (1803), had just put the rule of the Grand Duke of Tuscany behind it, had already been Austrian once before from 1805 to 1809, to then be Bavarian from 1810 onwards after a brief French period of administration. On 1 May 1816, Salzburg became Austrian. The border and form of today's state go back to this point in time. Both remained unchanged in 1918 and 1945, the total surface area comprising 7,155 square kilometres. Salzburg is the fifth largest of the new Austrian states in terms of geographical size and seventh in terms of population (521,238 inhabitants). In terms of economic power the state of Salzburg is second only to Vienna.

Although it is one of the younger states of Austria from a historical standpoint, Salzburg occupies the centre of Austria. All domestic Austrian transport channels into the two western states lead

Die Natur machte Salzburg zu einem Dreh- und Mittelpunkt, wo Europäer aus allen Ländern einander begegneten

The natural surroundings made Salzburg one of the central spots where Europeans from all countries meet

te ein. Alle inner-österreichischen Verkehrswege in die zwei westlichen Bundesländer führen über Salzburg. Schon allein diese Tatsache gibt dem Bundesland mehr Gewicht, als ihm auf Grund seiner Fläche beziehungsweise der Einwohnerzahl innerhalb des Staates zukommen würde.

Die Natur machte Salzburg zu einem Dreh- und Mittelpunkt, wo Europäer aus allen Ländern einander begegneten. Und die Begegnung so vieler großer Geister gab Salzburg jene Weltoffenheit, die so bedeutende Künstler wie Stefan Zweig, Hermann Bahr, Peter Handke und viele andere anzog.

Salzburgs zentrale Lage, die Naturschönheiten und seine künstlerische Bedeutung – die Stadt ist der Geburtsort des größten Komponisten Wolfgang Amadeus Mozart, im Flachgauer Ort Oberndorf wurde zum ersten Mal das weltweit meist gesungene Weihnachtslied „Stille Nacht, Heilige Nacht" komponiert und aufgeführt – und der Ruf des „Sound of Music-Landes" machen Salzburg so begehrt. Die Stadt und ihr Umland schienen schon dem Schriftsteller Stefan Zweig nicht nur durch ihre landschaftliche, sondern auch geografische Lage als ideal, weil am Rande Österreichs gelegen, „zweieinhalb Eisenbahnstunden von München, fünf Stunden through Salzburg. This fact alone makes the state more important than its size or population alone would afford it.

The natural surroundings make Salzburg one of the central spots where Europeans from all countries meet. And this meeting of so many great minds lent Salzburg that cosmopolitanism that in turn attracted such great creative minds as Stefan Zweig, Hermann Bahr, Peter Handke and many others.

Salzburg's central location, its natural beauty and its artistic significance make Salzburg such an object of desire – history's greatest composer Wolfgang Amadeus Mozart was born in the city, the most widespread and popular Christmas carol "Silent Night" was composed and performed for the first time in the Flachgau town of Oberndorf, and the hills are alive with the Sound of Music (musical). Author Stefan Zweig even thought the city and its surrounds to be ideal, not only because of the nature but also because of its geographic position on the edge of Austria which made it a "veritable centre of Europe, two and a half hours by train to Munich, five hours to Vienna, ten to Zurich and Venice and 20 to Paris".

den von Wien, zehn Stunden nach Zürich oder Venedig und 20 nach Paris, also ein richtiger Abstoßpunkt nach Europa".

Noch bis ins 19. Jahrhundert hinein war allgemein eine recht einfache aber treffende Zweiteilung des Landes üblich. Man sprach vom „Land außer Gebirg" – der Landeshauptstadt, dem heutigen Flachgau und dem Tennengau – also das gesamte Gebiet vor dem Pass Lueg, der eine landschaftliche Grenze bildet, und vom „Land inner Gebirg" – Pongau, Pinzgau, Lungau. Allgemeiner bekannt ist die heutige Gaueinteilung.

Trotz der Kleinheit des Landes kann Salzburg mit Vielgestaltigkeit und landschaftlichem Abwechslungsreichtum aufwarten. Bezogen auf die Fläche ist Salzburg als ausgesprochenes Gebirgsland einzustufen. Hinsichtlich des Lebensraumes seiner Bevölkerung ist es jedoch ebenso ein außeralpines Land, lebt doch ein beträchtlicher Teil der Bewohner im Zentralraum rund um die Stadt Salzburg. Hier im Salzburger Becken vereinigen sich auch die zwei natürlichen Hauptleitlinien des Bundeslandes, das Salzach- und das Saalachtal.

Während es zur Beschreibung des „typischen Münchners" oder des „typischen Wieners" genügend Klischees gibt, fehlen derart griffige Formeln zur Charakterisierung des Salzburgers. Sprachlich ist ihm nicht ohne weiteres beizukommen, wiewohl in den einzelnen Regionen des Landes deutlich ausgeprägte Dialekte gesprochen werden.

Das Land Salzburg wird von außen oft mit der Landeshauptstadt gleichgesetzt. Schon der „rasende Reporter" Egon Erwin Kisch fing sich, wie er im „Marktplatz der Sensationen" schreibt, eine Ohrfeige ein, weil er beim Lernen die banale Tatsache „Salzburg ist die Hauptstadt von Salzburg" laut rezitierte.

In seiner geschichtlichen Entwicklung ist das Land Salzburg von der wechselvollen Vergangenheit der Stadt nicht zu trennen. Zu prägend war zu allen Zeiten die Stellung der Metropole.

Die Landeshauptstadt, am Rand der Alpen und als einzige größere Stadt Österreichs unmittelbar an der Grenze gelegen, ist geprägt durch die Dominanz der Stadtberge Mönchsberg, Festungsberg, Kapuzinerberg und Rainberg. Zur beeindruckenden Kulisse der Stadt tragen darüber hinaus Gaisberg und Untersberg bei. Die Festung Hohensalzburg als Wahrzeichen Salzburgs thront über der Altstadt, die von der UNESCO in den Rang eines Weltkulturerbes erhoben wurde.

Wolfgang Amadeus Mozart: Dem genius loci der Stadt begegnet man auf Schritt und Tritt. Zwar prägte Alexander Humboldts Ausspruch von einer der schönsten Landschaften der Welt wie auch die einzigartige Architektur des „Rom des Nordens" oder gar der vor allem in Übersee so populäre Musi-

**von oben nach unten:
Der Untersberg, unweit der Landeshauptstadt gelegen, ist Salzburgs Hausberg**

Auf dem Heuberg in Salzburg

Franziskischlössl auf dem Kapuzinerberg (638 m)

**rechte Seite:
Blick vom Mönchsberg**

**from top to bottom:
The Untersberg, situated not far from the state capital, is Salzburg's signature mountain**

On the Heuberg in Salzburg

The Franziskischlössl (little Franciscan castle) on the Kapuzinerberg (638 m)

**page right:
View from the Mönchsberg**

Right into the 19th century, a fairly simple but effective splitting of the state was generally accepted. One spoke of the "state outside the mountains" – of the state capital, what we now know as Flachgau and Tennengau – i.e. the entire area ahead of the Lueg Pass, which forms a natural border, and the "state within the mountains" – Pongau, Pinzgau and Lungau. Better known today is the separation into Gaus or administrative districts.

Despite the small size of the state, Salzburg has a plethora of different landscape and structural varieties to offer. Salzburg is a mountain state viewed on the whole, but in terms of the living space for its population, it is also flatland, as many of its inhabitants live in and around the city of Salzburg. Here, in the Salzburg Basin, the two main natural leading lines of the state meet: the Salzach and Saalach valleys.

While there are any number of clichés to describe the "typical Münchner" or the "typical Viennese", there isn't such a clear characterisation for the Salzburgers. The high-German speaker can understand them well, although some strong dialects are spoken in the different regions in the state.

Outsiders often think of the state of Salzburg as being the same thing as its capital city. Even the "Roving Reporter" Egon Erwin Kisch received a clip over the ear, as he describes it in "Marktplatz der Sensationen", because he said the simple fact out loud that "Salzburg is the capital of Salzburg".

In its historical development, the state of Salzburg cannot be separated from its fickle past. Its importance was quite simply too great throughout history.

The capital city, on the edge of the Alps and the only major Austrian city directly on the border, is dominated by Mönchsberg hill, the Festungsberg with its fortress, Kapuzinerberg and Rainberg. The Gaisberg and Untersberg hills also make their contribution to the impressive cityscape. Hohensalzburg fortress watches over Salzburg's old town and has been appointed the ranking of World Heritage Site by UNESCO.

Wolfgang Amadeus Mozart: the genius loci of the city is omnipresent here. Although Alexander Humboldt's dictum of one of the most beautiful landscapes in the world, the incomparable architecture of the "Rome of the north" and of course the "Sound of Music" have made their contributions to the development of Salzburg, without Mozart it would never have become as famous as it is, and without him there would almost certainly not be the internationally renowned festival.

Originally a city of residence for the archbishop, Salzburg was reduced to a provincial town in the first period of Austrian rule and it needed decades if not more than a century to find a new identity.

41

cal-Film „Sound of Music" das Bild Salzburgs, ohne Mozart hätte die Stadt jedoch niemals diese Berühmtheit erlangt, und ohne ihn gäbe es wohl auch nicht die international bedeutendsten Festspiele.

Die in der ursprünglichen Geschichte beachtete bischöfliche Residenzstadt verkam in der ersten Zeit der österreichischen Herrschaft zu einer Provinzstadt und brauchte Jahrzehnte, wenn nicht sogar mehr als ein Jahrhundert, um eine neue Identität zu finden.

Als Stefan Zweig 1919 hierher zog, erschien ihm Salzburg als „ein antiquarisches, schläfriges, romantisches Städtchen am letzten Abhange der Alpen", noch unberührt von der Selbsteinschätzung, wichtig für die ganze Welt zu sein. Diesen Zug nahm Salzburg erst nach Gründung der Festspiele an,

As Stefan Zweig moved here in 1919, Salzburg gave him the impression of being an "antiquated, sleepy, romantic little town on the bottom slopes of the Alps", still untouched in its view of itself as being important for the entire world. However, it wasn't till after the Salzburg Music Festival was founded that it in fact became of interest to an international audience. The characteristic features of Salzburg – magnificent buildings, expansive squares, beautiful villas – were already long present in 1919, however, along with everything that makes "the beautiful city" (Georg Trakl).

Each of the five districts in the state – Flachgau, Tennengau, Lungau, Pongau and Pinzgau – has its own typical landscape form and its own mannerisms of its people, culture and customs.

nachdem die Stadt für ein internationales Publikum interessant geworden war. Die spezifischen Merkmale Salzburgs – prächtige Bauten, weite Plätze, formschöne Bürgerhäuser – aber waren 1919 schon längst ausgeprägt, alles, was „die schöne Stadt" (Georg Trakl) auszeichnet, war vorhanden.

Jeder der fünf Gaue des Landes – Flachgau, Tennengau, Lungau, Pongau und Pinzgau – ist gekennzeichnet durch eine typische Landschaft sowie die Eigenart seiner Bewohner, seiner Kultur und seines Brauchtums.

Viele reizvolle Seen im Flachgau

Der nördlichste Landesteil Salzburgs ist der Flachgau. Aber „so flach wie es sein Name ausdrückt" ist dieser Teil des Landes in Wirklichkeit nicht. Während

Many beautiful lakes in Flachgau

The northernmost district in Salzburg is Flachgau. But it isn't nearly "as flat as its name would suggest" (translator's note: flach means flat in German). During the Ice Age, the glacial masses of the Salzach glacier were pushed in fingers to the north between Bavaria and Salzburg, forming the sub-alpine landscape of Flachgau. The rolling moraine landscape that resulted is surmounted by the Flyschberg mountains, with heights of up to more than 1,000 metres. Hochgitzen, Buchberg, Tannberg, Irrsberg, die Große Plaike, Kolomannsberg and Haunsberg are just some of the mountains that deserve mention in this context.

The fact that the Mozart and festival city of Salzburg is today seen as utterly unique throughout

Die besonderen Merkmale Salzburgs – prächtige Bauten, weite Plätze, formschöne Bürgerhäuser

Salzburg's most special features – magnificent buildings, expansive squares, beautiful houses

FLACHGAU

Geschichte

Seit dem 6. Jahrhundert gehörte das Gebiet des späteren Flachgaus zum „Salzburggau" des Herzogtums Baiern. Mit der Anerkennung der Salzburger Grenzen durch den Baiernherzog im Jahr 1275 trat die Ablösung Salzburgs von Baiern in ihre letzte Phase. Als der Erzbischof Friedrich III. von Leibnitz 1328 eine eigene Landesordnung erlassen hatte, war das Erzbistum Salzburg zum weitgehend eigenständigen Staat innerhalb des Heiligen Römischen Reichs geworden. Bis zum Jahr 1803 dauerte die Herrschaft des Erzstifts Salzburg im „Land vor dem Gebirg". Nachdem das Gebiet im Zuge der Napoleonischen Kriege kurze Zeit vom Königreich Bayern annektiert worden war, kam es 1816 mit der Stadt Salzburg zu Österreich. Die westlich der Salzach gelegenen Gebiete blieben als Rupertiwinkel bei Bayern. Salzburg hatte seine Eigenständigkeit verloren und wurde kurzerhand als Salzachkreis an das Kronland Österreich ob der Enns angeschlossen. Mit der Aufwertung zu einem eigenen Kronland erfolgte 1850 die Herausgabe einer Landesverfassung, die auch eine Neuregelung der Landesverwaltung und die Einführung der Gemeindeordnung mit sich brachte.

Bis in das späte 19. Jahrhundert bildete das Gebiet des späteren Flachgaus eine Einheit mit dem heutigen Tennengau und dem nach 1805 vom Pongau zugewonnenen Lammertal. Mit der Errichtung der Bezirkshauptmannschaft Hallein im Jahr 1896 (Beschluss: 1895) fielen diese Gebiete dem heutigen Tennengau zu. Gleichzeitig begann sich für das übrig gebliebene Gebiet des ehemaligen „Salzburggaus" in Anlehnung an die mittelalterlichen Bezeichnungen des salzburgischen Gebietes Innergebirgs (Pongau, Pinzgau, Lungau) und dem neu entstandenen Tennengau der Name „Flachgau" durchzusetzen.

History

The region that would become known as Flachgau belonged to the Salzburggau district of the Baiern duchy since the 6th century. With the duke of Baiern's recognition of the Salzburg borders in 1275, the separation of Salzburg from Baiern entered its last phase. As archbishop Friedrich III von Leibnitz decreed a system of state government in 1328, the archbishopric Salzburg became a largely independent state within the Holy Roman Empire. The archbishops' rule in Salzburg held until the year 1803 in the "Land before the Mountains". After the region was annexed by the Kingdom of Bavaria during the course of the Napoleonic Wars, the city of Salzburg came to Austria in 1816, while the region to the west of the Salzach river remained Bavarian and known as Rupertiwinkel. Salzburg had thus lost its independence and was joined to the Crown state Austria ob der Enns without further ado. With its raising to the status of its own Crown state, the state constitution was published in 1850, which led to the reorganisation of the state administration and the introduction of a municipal code.

Up until the late 19th century the region later to be known as Flachgau was one with today's Tennengau and Lammertal, which was gained from Pongau in 1805. With the setting up of the Hallein regional administration in 1896 (resolution: 1895) these districts fell to today's Tennengau. At the same time, the name Flachgau began to prevail for the rest of the Salzburggau region, following the Medieval terms for the Salzburg's Innergebirg area (Pongau, Pinzgau, Lungau) and the newly created Tennengau.

---

der Eiszeit haben sich die glazialen Massen des Salzachgletschers fingerförmig zwischen Bayern und Salzburg nach Norden geschoben und die voralpine Landschaft des Flachgaus geformt. Aus der so entstandenen, sanft gewellten Moränenlandschaft ragen die Flyschberge mit Höhen bis über 1 000 Meter hervor. Hochgitzen, Buchberg, Tannberg, Irrsberg, die Große Plaike, Kolomannsberg und Haunsberg sind hier zu nennen.

Dass die Mozart- und Festspielstadt Salzburg heute weltweit als einzigartig gilt, dazu hat wesentlich ihre Umgebung beitragen: Gleichsam als Ouvertüre zur „Oper Salzburg" breitet sich der Flachgau als nördlichster Teil des Bundeslandes vor der Landeshauptstadt aus. Oder, um ein anderes Bild zu gebrauchen: Wie ein Vorgarten eines fürstlichen Hauses umflurt der Flachgau die Salzach-Metropole. Die Spuren der Eiszeit verhelfen dem Flachgau zu einer ungewöhnlichen landschaftlichen Vielfalt: Von schroffen Gebirgsstöcken über waldige Hügelkuppen, sanft wogende Hänge, blühende Wiesen, Felder und Obstbaumkulturen bis hin zu ausgedehnten Sumpfmooren, dazwischen eingebettet eine Vielzahl von Teichen und Seen mit dem Salzkammergut als Herzstück.

the world is in no small part thanks to its surrounds: As if a kind of overture to the "Opera of Salzburg", the Flachgau district spreads out before the state capital as the northernmost part of the state. Or, to use another image: like a front garden to the prince's house, Flachgau borders the Salzach metropolis. The traces from the Ice Age provide Flachgau with an extraordinary variety of landscapes: from craggy massifs to forested hilltops, softly flowing slopes, blossoming meadows, fields and fruit tree plantations, right through to expansive marshlands interspersed with ponds and lakes and the Salzkammergut "salt chamber" at its heart.

Salt as eponym

The Tennengau district say some, reminds one of the fate of Cinderella. Generally underestimated as the smallest Gau and industrial region of the state of Salzburg, a closer look reveals its true splendour. Because looking more closely, Tennengau can easily give rise to rhapsodies and astonishment at the "state records" it holds. For example, beneath Schlenken-Ostgrat, archaeologists discovered tools made of flintstone and bone in a bear's cave that

FLACHGAU

1 Hotel Schloss Fuschl am Fuschlsee nahe Salzburg
2 Die romanische Kirche St. Oswald in Anif bei Salzburg
3 Das Wasserschloss in Anif bei Salzburg
4 Weltberühmt: der Wolfgangsee bei Salzburg
5 St. Gilgen am Wolfgangsee
6 Die Salzburger Seenplatte
7 Tierparadies auf Gut Aiderbichl in Henndorf

1 The Castle hotel Schloss Fuschl on the banks of Lake Fuschl near Salzburg
2 The Romanic St. Oswald church in Anif near Salzburg
3 The moated castle in Anif near Salzburg
4 World famous: Lake Wolfgang near Salzburg
5 St. Gilgen on the banks of Lake Wolfgang
6 The Salzburg lake district
7 Animal paradise at the Aiderbichl estate in Henndorf

Tennengau

1 Golling bei Salzburg
2 Die Salzstadt Hallein ist Bezirkshauptstadt des Tennengaus
3 Franz Xaver Gruber komponierte das Weihnachtslied „StilleNacht"

1 Golling near Salzburg
2 The salt city Hallein is the administrative capital of the Tennengau district
3 Franz Xaver Gruber composed the Christmas carol "Silent Night, Holy Night"

TENNENGAU

Geschichte

Mit der Entstehung eines eigenen Kronlandes Salzburg 1848 erfolgte die Herausgabe einer Landesverfassung, die auch eine Neuregelung der Landesverwaltung und die Einführung der Gemeindeordnung mit sich brachte. Der Bezirk Hallein bildete bis 1896 eine Einheit mit dem heutigen Flachgau. Erst 1895 wurde ein neuer Bezirk mit der Bezeichnung Tennengau zur Entlastung der zu großen Bezirkshauptmannschaft Salzburg genehmigt und ein Jahr darauf mit der Einrichtung der Bezirkshauptmannschaft Hallein vollzogen.

History

With Salzburg becoming its own Crown state in 1848, a state constitution was published that reorganised the state administration and brought with it the municipal code. Up until 1896 the Hallein region was united with what today is known as the Flachgau region. Not until 1895 was a new district called Tennengau authorised to relieve the large Salzburg administration, and then finally consummated a year later as the Hallein district administration was set up.

SALZ ALS NAMENSGEBER

Der Tennengau, so meinen manche, erinnert an das Schicksal des Aschenputtels. Gemeinhin unterschätzt als kleinster Gau und als Industriezone des Landes Salzburg, entpuppt er sich doch als Prachtstück. Bei genauem Hinsehen verleitet einen der Tennengau zum Schwärmen und Staunen über „Landesrekorde" von besonderer Güte. Unterm Schlenken-Ostgrat beispielsweise entdeckten Archäologen in einer Höhle Werkzeug aus Feuerstein und Knochen von Höhlenbären – ungefähr 40 000 Jahre alt. Hier hinterließen die ersten Salzburger ihre Spuren – Neandertalmenschen. Auch die Wiege der Salzburger Industrie und Kultur stand im Tennengau. Auf dem Dürrnberg bauten die Kelten vor fast zweieinhalbtausend Jahren nicht nur Steinsalz ab, sie schufen auch so erlesene Kunstwerke wie die berühmte Schnabelkanne. Schließlich verschaffte das Salz aus dem Tennengau dem Land derartig hohe Einkünfte, dass es ihm nicht nur den Namen gab, sondern die Salzburger Erzbischöfe zu den vier reichsten unter allen deutschen Fürsten zählten.

Die Westgrenze des Tennengaus wird vom mächtigen Massiv des Hohen Göll beherrscht, im Osten führt der Pass Gschütt nach Oberösterreich, und im Süden hat sich die Salzach im Laufe von vielen Jahrtausenden ihr schmales, tief eingeschnittenes Bett durch Hagen- und Tennengebirge gegraben. Die Durchbruchsklamm der Salzach, die so genannten Salzachöfen beim Pass Lueg sowie auch die „Lammeröfen" der Lammer zwischen Scheffau und Abtenau sind touristische Anziehungspunkte.

WELTWEIT GRÖSSTE EISHÖHLE

Der südlich des Tennengaus gelegene Pongau ist im Norden von den Felsmauern der Salzburger Kalkhochalpen, von Tennen- und Hagengebirge abgeschirmt, nur durchbrochen von der Salzach. Im

are around 40,000 years old. It was here that the first Salzburgers left their mark – Neanderthals. And Tennengau is also the cradle of Salzburg's industry and culture. The Celts mined not only salt on the Dürrnberg mountain almost two and a half thousand years ago, they also created exquisite works of art such as the famous spouted pot. Indeed, the salt from Tennengau brought the state such a high income that Salzburg not only took its name from it, it also made the Salzburg archbishops among the fourth most prosperous of all German state rulers.

The western border of Tennengau is dominated by the mighty massif of the Hoher Göll. In the east the Gschütt Pass leads to Upper Austria, and in the south the Salzach has dug itself a narrow, deep bed over the millenia that leads through the Hagen and Tennen mountains. The Durchbruchsklamm gorge of the Salzach river, the Salzachöfen near Lueg Pass and the "Lammeröfen" of the Lammer river between Scheffau and Abtenau are tourist attractions.

WORLD'S LARGEST ICE CAVE

The Pongau, south of Tennengau is shielded from the Tennen and Hagen mountains by the sheer rock walls of the Salzburger Kalkhochalpen and only broken by the Salzach river. In the south it is bordered by the Hohe Tauern and the Radstädter Tauern. In the east the Dachstein group rises above it and in the west the Steinernes Meer and the Hochkönig.

Joseph Mohr (Text) und Franz Xaver Gruber (Noten) sind die Urheber des weltberühmten Weihnachtsliedes „Stille Nacht". Es entstand in Hallein bei Salzburg

Joseph Mohr (German lyrics) and Franz Xaver Gruber (music) wrote the world famous Christmas carol "Silent Night, Holy Night" in Hallein near Salzburg

Pongau

1. Falkenschau auf Burg Hohenwerfen
2–3. Der Kur- und Wintersportort Bad Gastein im Naturpark Hohe Tauern
4. Radonbalnealogie im Gasteiner Heilstollen Böckstein
5. Die Eisriesenwelt in Werfen war bis ins 19. Jahrhundert weitgehend unbekannt
6. Die mittelalterliche Burg Hohenwerfen

1. Falcon show on Hohenwerfen Castle
2–3. The spa and winter sports town of Gastein in Hohe Tauern natural reserve
4. Radon balnealogy in the Gastein underground health spa Böckstein
5. The "World of Ice Giants" in Werfen was almost unknown until well into the 19th century
6. The medieval castle Hohenwerfen

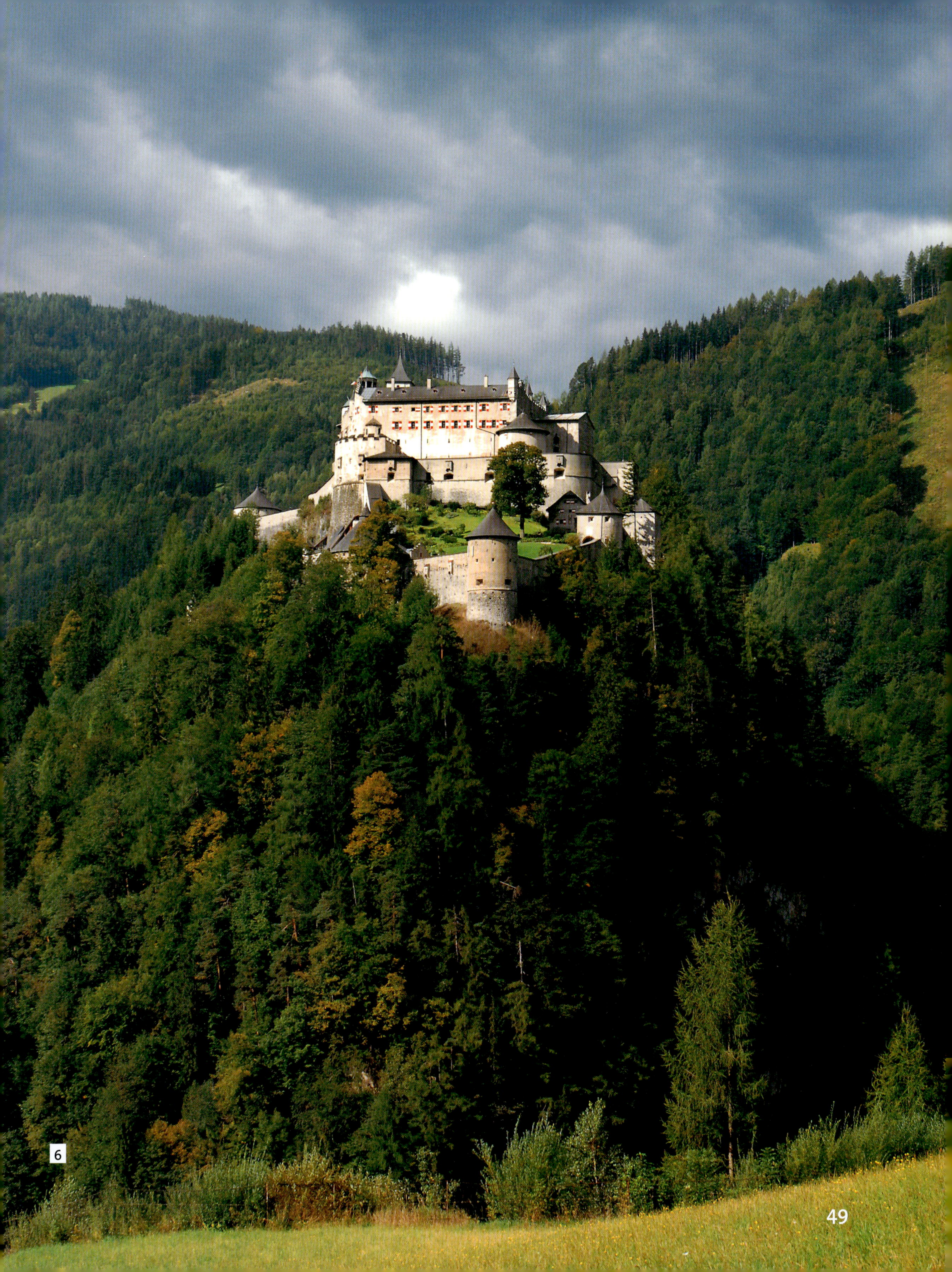
6

PONGAU

Geschichte

Funde deuten auf eine erste Besiedlung des Gebietes in der Bronzezeit ca. 2000 v. Chr hin, speziell die Stollensysteme für den Kupferabbau im „Arthurstollen" und die hölzernen Grubeneinbauten, mit einem durch die Radio-Carbon Methode ermittelten Alter von ca. 3000-3700 Jahren. Die erste Nennung des Namens erfolgte 1074: „ad sanctum Johannem in villa".
Während der Bauernkriege 1525/26 stellt sich St. Johann auf Seite der Protestanten. Im Laufe der Kriege wurde der Ort verwüstet. Im Zuge der Ausweisung von Protestanten aus dem Erzbistum Salzburg, die 1731 ihren Höhepunkt findet, müssen 2 500 Einwohner die Gemeinde verlassen. Das Recht zur Führung eines Wappens erhält St. Johann im Jahr 1929.
Ab 1939 bis zum Ende des Zweiten Weltkriegs heißt die Gemeinde Markt Pongau (Reichsgau Salzburg). Nationalsozialistischer Bürgermeister wird Hans Kappacher (ernannt durch Kreisleiter Josef Kastner). Kappacher wird in den 1950er Jahren erneut Bürgermeister und vom Gemeinderat zum Ehrenbürger ernannt.
Im Juni 2000 wird die Gemeinde zur Stadt erhoben.

History

Archaeological findings point to a first settling of the region in the Bronze again around 2000 BC. The most significant of these were the tunnel systems for the copper mines in the "Arthurstollen" tunnels and wooden mining constructions that have been carbon-dated as being 3000-3700 years old. The name Pongau can first be found in writing in 1074: "ad sanctum Johannem in villa".
During the Peasant Wars in 1525/26, St. Johann fought on the side of the Protestants. The entire site was ravaged throughout the course of the wars. 2,500 people had to leave the community as Protestants were banished from the archbishopric of Salzburg, an act that reached its peak in 1731. St. Johann was awarded the right to a coat of arms in 1929.
From 1939 to the end of the Second World War, the district was called Markt Pongau (Reichsgau Salzburg). The National Socialist mayor was Hans Kappacher (appointed by district governer Josef Kastner). Kappacher then became mayor again in the 1950s and was given the honour of honorary citizen. The township was elevated to a city in June 2000.

Süden begrenzen ihn die Hohen Tauern und die Radstädter Tauern, im Osten ragt steil die Dachsteingruppe auf und im Westen das Steinerne Meer sowie der Hochkönig. Mittendurch fließt die Salzach, in Werfen gekrönt von der wehrhaften Burg Hohenwerfen. Vom Salzachtal zweigen mehrere Seitentäler ab, wie beispielsweise das Klein- und das Großarltal oder das touristisch weltbekannte Gasteinertal. Die Liechtensteinklamm im Großarltal ist eines der berühmtesten Naturdenkmäler Österreichs. Die Eisriesenwelt im Tennengebirge gilt als die weltweit größte Schauhöhle. Die Gipfelketten der Hohen und der Niederen Tauern erheben sich über die wald- und almenreichen Pongauer Schieferberge, die klassisches Bergbauernland sind.

Der Pongau zeigt den Charme einer Landschaft, die in ihrer ursprünglichen Natürlichkeit weitgehend erhalten geblieben ist, obwohl die teilweise technische Erschließung den großen Touristenschwärmen und Schischwüngen im Winter Raum lässt.

Und nicht zuletzt: Am Hochgründeck, etwa auf halber Strecke zwischen Bischofshofen und Wagrain, so heißt es, liege die „Mitte des Salzburger Landes".

SANFTE ALMBÖDEN UND SCHROFFE BERGFLANKEN IM LUNGAU

In der südöstlichsten Ecke des Salzburger Landes liegt der Lungau, dessen Landschaft vielfältig ist: Sanfte Almböden wechseln mit schroffen Bergflan-

And through the middle of them flows the Salzach, crowned in Werfen by the castle of Hohenwerfen. Several smaller valleys branch off from the Salzach valley, such as the Kleinarl valley and Großarl valley and the world renowned Gasteiner valley. The Liechtensteinklamm in the Großarl valley is one of the most famous natural monuments in Austria. The Eisriesenwelt in the Tennen mountains is considered the largest publicly accessible ice cave in the world. The peaks of the Hohe and Niedere Tauern mountain ranges rise above the heavily forested and green-meadowed Pongauer Slate Mountains, which are typical mountain farming land.

The Pongau has the charm of a landscape that has largely retained all its original naturalness, although the partial technical invasion ensures that the flows of tourists and skiiers can hit the slopes.

And not least of all: at Hochgründeck, about half way between Bischofshofen and Wagrain, lies the "middle of the state of Salzburg", or so it is said.

GENTLE MEADOWS AND CRAGGY MOUNTAINS IN LUNGAU

In the south-eastern corner of the state of Salzburg lies Lungau with its varied landscapes: gentle meadows and precipitous mountains, broad mountainsides and narrow valleys. Lungau is an enclosed basin, bordered in the north and east by the Niedere Tauern, in the south by the Nockberg mountains and in the west by the Hohe Tauern. This natural unity not only has its own climate and vegetation,

LUNGAU

1 Einer der schönsten Golplätze in Salzburg: der Golfclub Lungau
2 Die 6er Sesselbahn „Gamskogelexpress" am Katschberg
3 „Lust aufs Mittelalter" verschafft die Erlebnisburg Burg Mauterndorf

1 One of the most beautiful golf courses in Salzburg: Lungau golf club
2 The six-seater chair lift "Gamskogelexpress" on Katschberg mountain
3 Historical Mauterndorf Castle takes you on an exciting journey back to the Middle Ages

LUNGAU

Geschichte
Seit dem 2. Jahrhundert v. Chr. zählte der Lungau zu Norikum, einem keltischen Königreich. 15 v. Chr. wurde der Lungau von den Römern besetzt. 50 n. Chr. wurde er zu einer römischen Provinz. Im 8. Jahrhundert stand der Lungau unter bairischer Herrschaft. Vom 13. Jahrhundert bis zum Jahr 1803 dauerte die Herrschaft des Erzstifts Salzburg. Nachdem das Gebiet kurze Zeit von Bayern annektiert worden war, kam es 1816 mit Salzburg zu Österreich. Mit der Entstehung eines eigenen Kronlandes Salzburg 1848 erfolgte die Herausgabe einer Landesverfassung, die auch eine Neuregelung der Landesverwaltung und die Einführung der Gemeindeordnung mit sich brachte. 1880 wurde der Lungau als „ärmste" Region im Land Salzburg benannt. Grund dafür war seine Abgeschlossenheit. Erst durch den Bau der Tauernautobahn (1974-1976) entwickelte sich die Wirtschaft im Lungau wieder.

History
Lungau belonged to Norikum – a Celtic kingdom – since the 2nd century BC. In 15 BC, the Romans occupied Lungau. In 50 AD it became a Roman province. In the 8th century AD, Lungau was ruled by the Baierns. From the 13th century BC until the year 1803 the archbishops were the worldly leaders of Salzburg. After being annexed by Bavaria for a short period, Lungau then became part of Austria in 1816 together with Salzburg. With Salzburg becoming its own Crown state in 1848, a state constitution was published that reorganised the state administration and brought with it the municipal code. In 1880 Lungau was declared the "poorest" region in the state of Salzburg. The reason it was so poor was its insularity. Not until the Tauern motorway was built (1974-1976) did the economy in Lungau begin to regain its footing.

---

ken, weite Becken mit engen Tälern. Der Lungau ist ein geschlossenes Talbecken, das im Norden und Osten von den Niederen Tauern, im Süden von den Nockbergen und im Westen von den Hohen Tauern begrenzt wird. Diese natürliche Einheit weist nicht nur klimatische und vegetationsgeographische Eigenheiten auf, sie ist auch kulturlandschaftlich ein sehr eigenständiger Teil des Bundeslandes.

Der Lungau liegt nicht „einfach hinten" – wie schon der Schriftsteller Rudi Bayr festhielt – nur weil unkundige Zeitgenossen einen Landstrich als abge-

it is also a highly autonomous part of the state from a cultural point of view.

Lungau is not "simply at the back" as author Rudi Bayr once wrote, simply because people ignorant to its charms call it remote. It is only out the back geographically – behind the Radstädter Tauern and, coming from Kärnten behind the Katschberg mountain.

The two main valleys of the central basin are the Taurach and Mur valleys, with the Taurach valley being the most fertile and densely populated

Wanderwege am Erlebnisberg Großeck-Speiereck in Mauterndorf

Hiking tracks on Großeck-Speiereck mountain in Mauterndorf

legen titulieren. Nur geografisch liegt er hinten, nämlich hinter den Radstädter Tauern und, wenn man von Kärnten kommt, hinter dem Katschberg.

Die beiden Haupttäler des zentralen Beckens sind das Taurach- und das Murtal, wobei das Taurachtal das fruchtbarste und das am dichtesten besiedelte Tal des Lungaus ist. Charakteristisch für diesen Teil des Landes ist auch, dass die Gebirge vom zentralen Becken aus durch fächerförmig angelegte Täler erschlossen werden. Von diesen Nebentälern ist das Zederhaustal hervorzuheben. Durch diesen längsten Teil des Lungaus führt die Tauernautobahn, die dem Lungau zwar mehr Verkehr, aber auch eine bessere Erschließung brachte.

Bekannt ist der Lungau auch für seinen Waldreichtum. Das Klima ist eher kühl, liegt er doch auf einer durchschnittlichen Seehöhe von mehr als 1 000 Metern. Andererseits ist aber gerade der Lungau wegen seiner Abgeschlossenheit und wegen seines Sonnenreichtums beliebt.

Der Pinzgau: Salzburgs grösster Landesteil

Salzburgs größter Landesteil, der Pinzgau, wird in Mitter-, Unter- und Oberpinzgau unterteilt und ist der Gau der Täler. Der Mitterpinzgau schiebt sich wie ein Keil zwischen Tirol und Bayern und ist geprägt durch eine abwechslungsreiche Gebirgslandschaft (Leoganger Steinberge, Dientner Berge, Steinernes Meer) sowie das weite Saalfeldener Becken.

Der Unterpinzgau erstreckt sich zu beiden Seiten der Salzach und ragt ein Stück in die „Zeller Furche" hinein, wo der Hauptort des Pinzgaus, Zell am See, liegt. Auf die Schmittenhöhe bei Zell am See führt seit 1927 die erste Schwebebahn Salzburgs. Vom Salzachtal zweigen das Raurisertal, das Kaprunertal mit dem 3 203 Meter hohen Kitzsteinhorn sowie das Fuschertal mit der Großglockner-Hoch-

valley in Lungau. It is also a characteristic of this part of the country that the mountains can be reached from the basin via a fanned array of valleys. Of these valleys, the Zederhaus valley deserves special mention. The Tauern Autobahn leads through this the longest part of Lungau, bringing with it more traffic, but also better accessibility.

Lungau is also well known for its wealth of forests. The climate here is quite cool, being as it is more than 1,000 m above sea level on average. On the other hand, Lungau is particularly popular for its seclusion and sunshine.

Pinzgau: Salzburg's largest district

Salzburg's largest district, Pinzgau, divides up into Central, Lower and Upper Pinzgau and is the district of valleys. Central Pinzgau projects between Tyrol

Blick auf Zell am See, im Hintergrund das Kitzsteinhorn

A view across Zell am See with the Kitzsteinhorn peak in the background

---

Pinzgau

Geschichte

Im Jahr 923 werden die Grafschaften Ober-, Mittel- und Unterpinzgau in Urkunden erwähnt. Vom 13. Jahrhundert bis zum Jahr 1803 dauerte die Herrschaft des Erzstifts Salzburg. Nachdem der Pinzgau kurze Zeit von Bayern annektiert worden war, kam er 1816 mit Salzburg zu Österreich. Mit der Entstehung eines eigenen Kronlandes Salzburg 1848 erfolgte die Herausgabe einer Landesverfassung, die auch eine Neuregelung der Landesverwaltung und die Einführung der Gemeindeordnung mit sich brachte. Die Bezirkshauptmannschaft war 1850 bis 1854 in Saalfelden untergebracht und kam erst dann nach Zell am See.

History

In 1923 the counties of Upper, Central and Lower Pinzgau were mentioned in official documents. The rule of the Salzburg archbishops lasted from the 13th century until 1803. After briefly being annexed to Bavaria, Pinzgau was then returned to Austria in 1816 together with Salzburg. With Salzburg becoming its own Crown state in 1848, a state constitution was published that reorganised the state administration and brought with it the municipal code. The district administration was based in Saalfelden from 1850 to 1854, after which time it was moved to Zell am See.

Pinzgau

1 Die Großglockner Hochalpenstraße endet vor Österreichs höchstem Berg mit 3 798 Metern
2 Naturlehrweg „Gamsgrube" im Nationalpark Hohe Tauern
3 Mit ihren 380 Metern sind die Krimmler Wasserfälle die höchsten Europas
4 Mooserboden-Stausee mit dem Tauernkraftwerk Glockner-Kaprun

1 The Großglockner alpine road ends at Austria's highest mountain (3,798 metres)
2 The Gamsgrube nature theme trail in Hohe Tauern national park
3 The Krimml Falls are the highest waterfalls in Europe with a drop of 380 metres
4 Mooserboden reservoir with the Tauern power plant Glockner-Kaprun

alpenstraße ab. Österreichs höchster Berg, der Großglockner, liegt zwar nicht auf Salzburger Gebiet, wird jedoch von Salzburg aus durch die 1935 fertig gestellte Großglockner-Hochalpenstraße, eine der schönsten Hochgebirgsstraßen Europas, erschlossen. Im Süden begrenzen die Hohen Tauern den Pinzgau.

Die Dreiheit aus Fels, Stein und Eis, zusammen mit dem verbindenden Element Wasser, sind der besondere Reiz des Pinzgaus, dieser wunderbaren Landschaft inner Gebirg. Mit den ausgedehntesten Gletscherflächen der Ostalpen in den Hohen Tauern, mit den höchsten Wasserfällen Europas in Krimml, durchflossen vom Hauptfluss des Landes der Salzach, von dessen Mitte sich nach Süden federförmig die wanderbaren Tauerntäler in den Nationalpark Hohe Tauern erstrecken. Kahl und zackig die Steinberge, weich und grün die gegenüberliegenden Grasberge. Die Pinzgauer Tauerntäler sind wahre Schatzkammern edler und wertvoller Mineralien. So fanden zwei Bramberger Bergsteiger in den 30er Jahren den größten jemals gefundenen Quarz Einzelkristall der Alpen: er wiegt 618 Kilogramm. Und in Rauris wurde (neben Gastein) jenes Gold geschürft, das Salzburg im Mittelalter den Beinamen „Peru der alten Welt" eintrug.

Im Oberpinzgau reihen sich die Achentäler aneinander, die von den Bergen der Hohen Tauern herunterführen. Sie sind eng und schmal und großteils nur zu Fuß zu erreichen. Erwähnenswert sind das Krimmler Achental, das die höchsten Wasserfälle Europas birgt. Sie haben das Europadiplom, die beiden Sulzbachtäler mit dem Großvenedigermassiv als den größten Gletscherflächen der Ostalpen sowie das längste der Tauerntäler, das Hollersbachtal mit dem „verwunschenen" Kratzenbergsee, dem größten Karsee der Hohen Tauern. Mit 3 674 Metern Seehöhe ist der Großvenediger der höchste Berg des Landes.

1984 wurde der Nationalpark Hohe Tauern – er zählt zu den größten Nationalparks in Europa – gegründet. Bereits 1971 hatten sich die Länder Salzburg, das den weitaus größten Anteil hat, Kärnten und Tirol darauf geeinigt, den Nationalpark Hohe Tauern zu schaffen. Das wesentliche Motiv war und ist, diese Region als einen besonders eindrucksvollen und formenreichen Teil der österreichischen Alpen in ihrer Schönheit und Ursprünglichkeit zu erhalten.

Die Hälfte des Landes von Wald bedeckt

Auf Grund der landschaftlichen, geologischen und klimatischen Situation weist das Bundesland sehr große Unterschiede in der Vegetation auf. Im alpinen Raum ist die vertikale Abfolge der Vegetationszonen charakteristisch: Wald bis etwa 2 000 Meter

and Bavaria like a wedge and is characterised by a varied mountain landscape (Leoganger Steinberge, Dientner Berge, Steinernes Meer) and the broad Saalfeldener Basin.

Lower Pinzgau reaches along both sides of the Salzach and stretches a little into the "Zeller Furche", where the largest town in Pinzgau lies: Zell am See. Salzburg's first suspended railway, in operation since 1927, leads up to Schmittenhöhe near Zell am See. Rauriser valley and Kapruner valley branch off the Salzach valley with the 3,203 meter high Kitzsteinhorn peak and the Fuscher valley with the Großglockner alpine road. Austria's highest mountain, the Großglockner, although not in Salzburg itself, can be reached from Salzburg via the Großglockner alpine road, one of the most picturesque alpine roads in Europe, built in 1935. In the south the Hohe Tauern border the Pinzgau.

The trinity of rock, ice and their binding element water are the special force behind Pinzgau, this wonderful mountainous landscape. With the largest glacial areas in the eastern Alps in the Hohe Tauern, Europe's highest waterfalls in Krimml, through which the main river in the state, the Salzach flows, from the middle of which to the south the Tauern valleys fan out into the Hohe Tauern national park, the stark and bleak Steinberge mountains and the soft, green Grasberge mountains opposite. The Pinzgau Tauern valleys are veritable treasure troves of precious minerals. For example, in the 30s of last century, two mountain climbers from Bramberg found the largest single quartz crystal ever discovered in the Alps, weighing in at 618 kilograms. And it was in Rauris (and Gastein) that the gold was prospected that led to Salzburg being dubbed the "Peru of the Old World" in the Middle Ages.

The Achen valleys form a line in Upper Pinzgau. They reach from the Hohe Tauen mountains, are narrow and steep and mostly only accessible on foot. The Krimmler Achen valley is home to Europe's highest waterfalls. They hold the Europadiplom, the two Sulzbach valleys with the Großvenediger massif, the largest glacier in the eastern Alps and the longest of the Tauern valleys, Hollersbach valley with the "enchanted" Lake Kratzenberg, the largest cirque lake in the Hohe Tauern. At an altitude of 3,674 metres, the Großvenediger is the state's highest mountain.

In 1984, the Hohe Tauern national park – one of the largest in Europe – was founded. As early as 1971, the states of Salzburg, with by far the biggest

Im Naturpark Hohe Tauern: Hier scheint die Zeit stehen geblieben zu sein

In Hohe Tauern nature park – where time seems to stand still

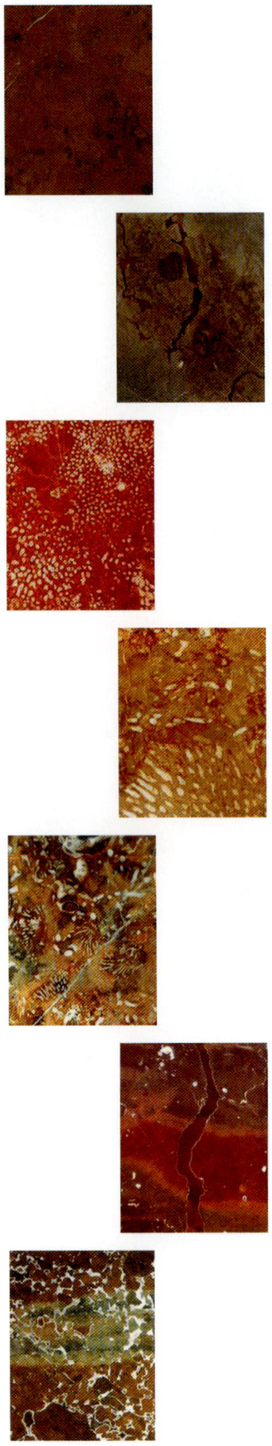

Seehöhe, Almen bis 2 800 Meter und darüber alpines Ödland. Rund die Hälfte des Landes ist von Wald bedeckt. Neben der wirtschaftlichen Bedeutung kommt den Wäldern im Gebirge als Schutz- und Bannwälder eine besondere Rolle für die Sicherung der alpinen Lebensräume zu.

Das kleine Peru der alten Welt

Die Bodenschätze einzelner Gesteinszonen haben Salzburgs Territorialbildung und Staatskasse beeinflusst und Teilen seiner Kulturlandschaft bis heute den Stempel aufgedrückt. Zuvorderst sei das der Stadt, dem Land und dem Fluss den Namen gebende Salz vom Dürrnberg bei Hallein genannt. Der Gold- und Silberbergbau in den Hohen Tauern (Gastein, Rauris, Muhr) hatte zeitweise erhebliche Bedeutung. So wurden die Pongauer und die Pinzgauer Tauern als das „kleine Peru der alten Welt" bezeichnet, als im 15. Jahrhundert „in der Gastein" und in „der Rauris" ein regelrechter Goldrausch einsetzte. Auch verschiedene Fundstätten von Kupfer-, Eisen- und Zinkerzen verdienen Erwähnung.

Der Holzreichtum und die günstigen Transportmöglichkeiten auf den Flüssen waren weitere wichtige Voraussetzungen für die Berg- und Hüttenwirtschaft. Der Salzburger Marmor aus Adnet und vom Nordfuß des Untersbergs hat vielen profanen und weltlichen Bauten ihren besonderen Schmuck und ihre Identität verliehen. Die Lagerstätten der meisten ehemals gefragten Bergbauprodukte sind inzwischen entweder erschöpft oder ihre Ausbeutung ist unwirtschaftlich geworden. Die wirtschaftlichen Interessen sind in Salzburg heute auf Kalk, Gips, Zementmergel, Scheelit, verschiedene Natursteine, Straßen- und Betonschotter gerichtet.

Im weiteren Sinn als Bodenschätze sind die Heilwässer zu nennen. Das darauf basierende Kurwesen, das auch international wegen seines hohen Standards geschätzt wird, hat namentlich in Gastein eine lange Tradition.

Stromlieferant und Touristenattraktion

Österreichs Armut an Kohle hat insbesondere in Salzburg schon ab dem Ersten Weltkrieg zu einem forcierten Ausbau der Wasserkraft für die Elektrizitätsgewinnung geführt. So entstand in den reich vergletscherten Hohen Tauern zwischen 1938 und 1952 das größte Alpenkraftwerk Europas, die Tauernkraftwerke. Diese sind mit den drei Stauseen zugleich unentbehrlicher Stromlieferant und Touristenattraktion. Die Salzach selbst wurde erst spät in den systematischen Ausbau einbezogen, was sich aus landschaftlicher Sicht einerseits für die Planung und Gestaltung als vorteilhaft erwies und andererseits dank des gestärkten Umweltbewusstseins die

share, Kärnten and Tyrol agreed to create the Hohe Tauern national park. The main reason for doing so was and is to retain the beauty and naturalness of this particularly impressive and varied part of the Austrian Alps.

Half of the state covered in forest

Because of the landscape, geological and climatic situation of the state, it exhibits enormous differences in its flora. In the alpine regions the levels are typical: forest up to around 2,000 metres above sea level, meadows up to 2,800 metres and alpine rock above it. Around half of the state is covered in trees. They are important from an economic point of view and as protection for safeguarding the livelihood of the alpine habitats.

The little Peru of the Old World

The natural resources of the rock strata have influenced the formation of Salzburg's territory and coffers, leaving their mark on parts of its cultural landscape until this very day. First and foremost is of course the salt (or Salz) stemming from Dürrnberg by Hallein, which gave the city, the state and the river their names. The gold and silver mining in the Hohe Tauern (Gastein, Rauris, Muhr) was of great importance at various times, with the Pongauer and Pinzgauer Tauern being given the nickname of the "little Peru of the Old World" as the gold rush set in "Gastein" and "Rauris" in the 15th century. The various finds of copper, iron and zinc ore also deserve mention.

The wealth of timber and the excellent transport opportunities on the rivers were further prerequisites in favour of the mining and metalworking industries. The Salzburg marble from Adnet and the northern foot of the Untersberg mountain has provided many special adornments and much of the identity for many a worldly building. The sources of the most popular mining products of the time are now either exhausted or it has become uneconomical to tap them anymore. Salzburg today has its commercial focuses in lime, gypsum, clay, scheelite, various natural stone types and gravel for roads and floors.

Waters can also be considered a natural resource. The spa industry based on water, which is highly esteemed internationally because of its high standard, has a long tradition in Gastein.

Electricity supplier and tourist attraction

Austria's lack of coal forced Austria and in particular Salzburg to expand its hydropower capabilities

Der so genannte Marmor aus Adnet entstand durch Metamorphose aus Kalkstein und ist ausgesprochen dekorativ

Adnet "marble" is born of a limestone metamorphosis and is highly decorative

Aussparung gewisser Abschnitte der Salzach ermöglichte.

Mit dem Hinweis, dass eine Reihe von Verkehrserschließungen im Zusammenhang mit Kraftwerksbauten zustande kam oder dadurch erleichtert wurde, seien nochmals die einleitend erwähnten Verkehrs- und Lagebeziehungen Salzburgs angesprochen. Der Gebirgswall der Hohen Tauern, der seit jeher eine verkehrshemmende Schranke darstellt, erfuhr durch die Tauernbahn am Beginn des 20. Jahrhunderts seine erste Bezwingung. Er konnte dann seit 1935 mit der großartigen Aussichtsstraße der Glocknergruppe wenigstens während des Sommerhalbjahres überwunden werden. Ganzjährig kann der Straßenverkehr dieses Hindernis im Westen auf dem Weg der Felbertauernstraße (1967) und im Südosten, noch bequemer, auf der Tauernautobahn (1975) unterfahren. Eine wichtige Verbindung zwischen Salzburg und Kärnten (Böckstein und Mallnitz) stellt auch die Tauernschleuse dar, durch die Autos per Bahn transportiert werden.

„Dieser harmonischen Landschaft war es vorbehalten, gleich dem Resonanzboden eines Cellos, alle menschlichen Saiten Europas in gemeinsamem Gesang zum Tönen zu bringen… Wie europäisch doch all dies ist! Hier in Salzburg, in dem Winkel zwischen Rhein und Donau, nahe dem Ausgangspunkt dieser beiden Koordinaten Europas, musste es da nicht notwendigerweise zur Verkörperung der kennzeichnendsten europäischen Form des Geistes werden? Hier, genau im Mittelpunkt Europas, bringt jede einzelne der vielen Farben der Palette Europas Eure schöne Landschaft zur Geltung; jede einzelne der Saiten Europas wird über den Resonanzboden des Cellos, das Euer Tal ist, gespannt; die klangvolle der Slawen, die rhythmische der Ungarn, die nachdenkliche der Deutschen, die scharfsinnige der Franzosen und die leuchtende der Italiener, die feurige der Spanier, die subtile der Griechen…, die kriegerische der Türken… Zur Symphonie, aus ihrer aller Zusammenspiel entstanden, fügt Salzburg eine Prise geistigen Salzes hinzu."

Was der Philosoph Salvador de Madariaga in seiner Rede zur Eröffnung der Salzburger Festspiele 1964 formulierte, zieht sich wie ein roter Faden durch das Selbstverständnis Salzburgs und seiner Bevölkerung. „Salzburg, du Kleinod von Österreich" heißt es in der Landeshymne. Man sieht das Land Salzburg als Österreichs geografische Mitte, ausgestattet in verkleinerter Form mit all dem, was auch Österreich der Welt zu bieten hat. ◀

as early as the First World War. Europe's largest alpine power facility was built in the heavily glacial Hohe Tauern between 1938 and 1952, known as the Tauernkraftwerke. With their holding lakes these power stations are both an indispensable electricity provider and a tourist attraction. The Salzach itself was not integrated until the later subsequent expansion of the plants; a fact which proved beneficial for the landscape, as it influenced the planning and design and enabled sections of the river to be excluded from the development.

The transport situation in Salzburg deserves special mention again here, as numerous accesses were built or improved in the context of the building of the power stations. The Hohe Tauern mountain range, which has always been a barrier to travel, was first conquered at the beginning of the 20th century by the Tauern railway track. From 1935 the magnificent scenic road then enabled Glockner group to be passed, at least during the summer months. The Felbertauernstraße allows traffic to pass this barrier in the west since 1967, and to the southwest the Tauernautobahn (1975) makes the passage even easier. The Tauernschleuse is an important connection between Salzburg and Kärnten (Böckstein and Mallnitz), via which cars are transported by train.

"It was reserved for this harmonious landscape to join all the human strings of Europe to sing in unison, like the resonating body of a cello… How very European it all is! Was it not essential that here in Salzburg, in the corner between Rhine and Danube, close to the sources of these two main coordinates of Europe, the European form that characterises the spirit of Europe be embodied? Right here, at the focal point of Europe, every single one of the many colours of this continent complements your beautiful landscape; each of the strings of Europe is drawn over the sounding board of the cello that is your valley: the melodious string of the Slavs, the rhythm of the Hungarians, the pensiveness of the Germans, the keen-witted string of the French, the bright illumination of the Italians, the fire of the Spaniards, the subtlety of the Greeks, the bellicosity of the Turks…, all join together to a symphony with a pinch of salt added by Salzburg."

These words spoken by philosopher Salvador de Madariaga in his opening speech of the Salzburg Festival in 1964 is a self-conception that pervades all of Salzburg and its people. "Salzburg, du Kleinod von Österreich" (Salzburg, you jewel of Austria) says the state anthem. The state of Salzburg is seen as the geographic centre of Austria that has a smaller version of everything to offer the world that Austria itself can boast. ◀

Oberhalb des Kapruner Stausees liegt die Höhenburg, zu Fuß bequem zu erreichen

Höhenburg is easy to get to on foot, just above the Kaprun reservoir

- Oslo 1590 km
- Stockholm 1640 km
- København 1040 km
- Hamburg 940 km
- Amsterdam 970 km
- Berlin 790 km
- Warszawa 1030 km
- London 1250 km
- Bruxelles 920 km
- Frankfurt 550 km
- Praha 370 km
- Paris 950 km
- Wien 290 km
- Bratislava 370 km
- München 140 km
- Budapest 480 km
- Zürich 470 km
- **SalzburgerLand**
- Zagreb 410 km
- Milano 610 km
- Ljubljana 270 km
- Beograd 770
- Barcelona 1640 km
- Roma 990 km

Helsinki
1930 km

Tallinn
1840 km

Riga
1530 km

Moskva
2160 km

nius
0 km

Minsk
1460 km

Kyiv
1680 km

Bucuresti
1430 km

Sofia
1150 km

chubert & Franzke, St. Pölten 2005

Landeshauptmann-Stellvertreter
Dr. Wilfried Haslauer

Dipl.-Ing. Rudolf Strasser
Leiter WirtschaftsService der Stadt Salzburg

Mag. Gritlind Kettl
Geschäftsführerin StandortAgentur Salzburg GmbH

Der Wirtschaftsraum Salzburg – Spitze!

The commercial region Salzburg – in Front!

Landeshauptmann-Stellvertreter Dr. Wilfried Haslauer

Der Wirtschaftsraum Salzburg und die „Marke" auf der Zielgeraden

Salzburg ist es gelungen, sich als dynamische und attraktive Zukunftsregion zu positionieren. Eine Region, die in ihrer gelungenen Kombination aus Wirtschaftsstandort, Bildungs- und Kulturgesellschaft, sozialer Wärme und gesellschaftlichem Engagement ihresgleichen sucht.

Unsere Aufgabe ist es, unser Bundesland hinsichtlich der wirtschaftlichen Dynamik und der Beschäftigung an der Spitze zu halten und diese Spitzenposition nachhaltig abzusichern. Die Voraussetzungen dafür sind denkbar gut: Ein über weite Strecken günstiger Branchenmix, die Innovationsbereitschaft vieler Unternehmer, die hohe Qualifikation, Leistungsbereitschaft und Flexibilität unserer Arbeitnehmer und Arbeitnehmerinnen und eine gut ausgebaute Infrastruktur. Diese Faktoren müssen jene Impulse erhalten, die ihre Zukunftstauglichkeit weiter erhöhen. Die Politik hat hier die geeigneten Rahmenbedingungen zu setzen, die eigentliche Bewährung im internationalen Wettbewerb und die Schaffung und Aufrechterhaltung von Arbeitsplätzen liegen, vorrangig in der Verantwortung der Wirtschaft.

Bildung und Wissenschaft stellen in vielfacher Hinsicht die Basis für den wirtschaftlichen Erfolg – für den Einzelnen ebenso wie für das ganze Land.

The commercial region Salzburg and the "brand" on the final straight

Salzburg has succeeded in positioning itself as a dynamic and attractive region with a promising future; a region that is unparalleled in its perfect balance of commercial venue, educational and cultural society, warmth and commitment to its people.

Our mission is to keep our state at the head of the field with regard to its commercial dynamism and employment opportunities. The background conditions for our success are as good as they could be: a largely favourable industry mix, the willingness of many of our industrialists and entrepreneurs to embrace innovation, our highly qualified, hard working and flexible workforce and a well developed infrastructure. These factors now have to integrate the impulses that will heighten their ability to prevail in the future. The political sector must create the right framework of course, but the economic sector itself bears the main responsibility for ensuring that it remains competitive on the international market and continues to retain and create jobs.

Education and the scientific/academic sector form the basis for commercial success in many ways – both for the state economy as a whole and for the individuals within it. The school of the fu-

Brunnenskulptur von Wanda Bertoni im Eingangsbereich der Naturwissenschaftlichen Fakultät der Paris-Lodron-Universität Salzburg

Hauptgebäude der Naturwissenschaftlichen Fakultät der Universität Salzburg

Fountain sculpture by Wanda Bertoni at the entrance to the Natural Science faculty of Salzburg's Paris Lodron University

The main building of the Natural Science faculty at Salzburg University

Die Schule der Zukunft als eine Schule für die Zukunft agiert nicht bloß nach innen, sondern schließt ihre Umwelt und Mitwelt ein.

Salzburg ist stolz auf seine Universitäten. Mit mehr als 13 000 Studierenden und über 1 400 Mitarbeitern stellen die Salzburger Universitäten nicht nur ein unverzichtbares wissenschaftliches Potenzial für das Bundesland dar, sondern auch einen wichtigen Wirtschaftsfaktor. Hier gilt es, das breite Salzburger Studienangebot zu erhalten und die notwendigen baulichen Maßnahmen zur universitären Standortsicherung voranzutreiben.

Daneben ist Salzburg auch ein Fachhochschulzentrum Österreichs. Das Fachhochschulwesen als zweiter wichtiger höherer Ausbildungsweg wird ständig weiterentwickelt und auch vom Land finanziell gefördert.

Salzburg zeichnet eine große Vielfalt an Natur- und Kulturlandschaft aus, wozu insbesondere auch der Nationalpark Hohe Tauern gehört. Ein sorgsamer Umgang mit dieser Ressource liegt im Interesse der Lebensqualität aller und dient nicht zuletzt auch der heimischen Tourismuswirtschaft als einer der Säulen unseres Wohlstandes.

Von der Weltgeltung Salzburgs darf man ohne alle Anmaßung in kultureller und künstlerischer Hinsicht sprechen. Wenn wir die künftige Größe der Geltung Salzburgs als kulturelles Epizentrum beibehalten, ja ausbauen wollen, dürfen wir nicht bloß uns selbst und dem längst verhallten Applaus von gestern genügen.

Salzburg ist ein Kulturstandort mit internationalem Ruf. Die Salzburger Festspiele als hochkarätiges und weltweit größtes Musikfestival machen die Stadt alljährlich aufs Neue zur Kulturhauptstadt. Mit dem Landestheater, dem Mozarteum Orchester, der vielfältigen und neu gestalteten Museumslandschaft und dem hochwertigen Angebot an klassischer Musik ist und bleibt Salzburg ein kultureller Magnet.

Salzburg als Kulturstandort wird jedoch längst nicht mehr ausschließlich mit seiner Festspieltradition assoziiert, sondern steht auch für eine vielfältige, aktive, moderne und weltoffene Kulturszene. Wir besitzen eine große Palette von Festspiel- und Festivalangeboten in einem weltoffenen und toleranten kulturellen Klima.

Salzburg ist das schönste Bundesland Österreichs. Wir wollen überall die Nummer 1 sein – nicht nur für Millionen Gäste aus allen Teilen der Welt, sondern auch für die Menschen, die Salzburg als Heimat stark machen, hier Ausbildung, Arbeit und Wohnraum gefunden haben und im Land ihren verdienten Lebensabend genießen. Stadt und Land Salzburg sind eine prosperierende Zukunftsregion, die in ihrer Kombination aus Wirtschaftsstandort, Wissens- und Kulturgesellschaft, Schönheit, Lebens-

ture is not introspective but includes its surroundings and contemporaries in its actions.

Salzburg is proud of its universities. With more than 13,000 students and 1,400 staff, Salzburg's universities represent not only an indispensable academic base of potential for the federal state, they are also a key economic factor. Essential here is that we maintain the broad range of academic options available in Salzburg and ensure that all the building necessary for Salzburg's continued consolidation as a university stronghold is done.

Salzburg is also a key centre for technical universities and universities of applied sciences in Austria. The state recognises the great importance of this branch of tertiary education and funds its constant development.

One of Salzburg's most striking features is its multifaceted natural and cultural landscape, to which the Hohe Tauern national park without doubt belongs. Ensuring that this resource is treated with the greatest care lies in our best interests, as it is a big part of our quality of life and a pillar of one of the main sources of our prosperity – our tourism industry.

One can speak of Salzburg's international cultural and artistic standing without any fear of exaggeration. But if we wish to retain and grow this key role as a cultural epicentre in the future, we cannot rest upon our laurels and be satisfied with enjoying yesterday's applause.

Salzburg is a cultural centre of international renown. The annual Salzburg Festival – the world's largest music festival, with top-class performers – helps secure Salzburg's reputation as a global cultural capital time and time again. With its State

Das moderne Kongresszentrum in Salzburg

The cutting-edge congress centre in Salzburg

Fashion Mall Munich –
Ein Orderhaus mit bronce-schimmernder Fassade für die besten Designerlabels

Fashion Mall Munich –
A reseller with shimmering bronze façade for the best designer labels

Franz Fürst entwickelt hochwertige Immobilienprojekte in Österreich, Deutschland und der Schweiz

Franz Fürst develops top-quality real estate projects in Austria, Germany and Switzerland

Fürst Developments –
Innovative Immobilien mit Mehrwert

Fürst Developments, ein Unternehmen mit Salzburger Wurzeln, arbeitet an Projekten zur Stadtentwicklung und hochwertigen Spezial-Immobilien in Österreich, Deutschland und der Schweiz. In der Stadt Salzburg tragen zum Beispiel das Stadtteilzentrum Herrnau und die exklusive Wohnanlage am Fondachhof in Parsch die Handschrift von Franz Fürst. Für die Revitalisierung des historischen Stadtquartiers im Bruderhof wurde der Projektentwickler mit dem renommierten Salzburger Altstadtpreis ausgezeichnet.

Zu Fürsts international wichtigsten Vorzeigeobjekten zählen das Züricher Scenario-Building – heute Firmensitz der Pfizer AG – und die Fashion Mall Munich, ein elegantes Orderhaus für internationale Premium-Modelabels. Mit dem Fashion Mall Konzept, das von Fürst Developments bereits Anfang der Neunziger Jahre in Salzburg erfolgreich umgesetzt wurde, gelang auch ein dynamischer Einstieg in den deutschen Immobilienmarkt. Fürst entwickelt in Deutschland derzeit mehrere Projekte, darunter ein multifunktionales Stadtteil- und Kreativzentrum auf dem Stuttgarter Killesberg.

Fürst Developments –
Innovative real estate with added value

Fürst Developments, a company with its roots in Salzburg, works on urban development and top-quality special real estate projects in Austria, Germany and Switzerland. In the city of Salzburg, for example, the Herrnau district centre and the exclusive residential park at Fondachhof in Parsch both bear the mark of Franz Fürst. Fürst Developments was also awarded the coveted Salzburg Old Town Centre prize for its revitalisation of the historical Bruderhof passage.

Among Fürst's main international projects are the Zurich Scenario Building – today home to Pfizer AG – and the Fashion Mall Munich, an elegant reseller of international premium fashion labels. With this project, the Fashion Mall concept that Fürst Developments began implementing with great success in Salzburg at the beginning of the nineties has also led to a dynamic entry into the German real estate market. Fürst is working on several such projects in Germany at present, one of which is a multifunctional district shopping and creative centre on Stuttgart's Killesberg hill.

**Altstadtquartier Bruderhof –
Ein preisgekröntes Revitalisierungsprojekt in Salzburg**

**Altstadtquartier Bruderhof –
An award-winning revitalisation project in Salzburg**

Neben konzeptiver Intelligenz und professioneller Marktkommunikation in der Projektentwicklung definiert sich Fürst Developments vor allem über die bedingungslose Qualität der Bauwerke selbst. Hochwertige Bau- und Architekturqualität sichern Nachhaltigkeit und Zufriedenheit bei den Nutzern. Fürst arbeitet mit Universitäten, etwa der TU München, mit international bekannten Verkehrs- und Landschaftsplanern und immer wieder mit Toparchitekten wie dem Austrokalifornier Mark Mack, Adolf Krischanitz, Eraldo Consolacio oder Ernst Hoffmann.

Und weil Qualität nicht bei der Übergabe eines Gebäudes an seine Nutzer endet, entwickelt Fürst auch Facility-Managementkonzepte und begleitet eine Reihe von Projekten nach der Realisierung weiter. Dieser ganzheitliche Zugang zu Qualität in der Immobilienentwicklung zeigt sich auch in einer soliden Ertragsrechnung, die den Finanzpartnern von Fürst Developments gute Renditen und hohe Werthaltigkeit sichert. Fürst Developments bietet den Investment-Partnern ein Maximum an Professionalität und Sicherheit, verbunden mit jener Kreativität in der Projektentwicklung, die echte Markenimmobilien ausmacht.

Alongside its exceptional design expertise and professional market communication in the field of project development, Fürst Developments is defined by the uncompromising excellence of its buildings. Top class construction and architectural quality ensure lasting structural integrity and satisfied users. Fürst works together with universities such as Munich Technical University, with internationally renowned traffic and landscape planners and with top architects the likes of the Austro-Californian Mark Mack, Adolf Krischanitz, Eraldo Consolacio and Ernst Hoffmann.

And because quality doesn't end with the handover of a building to its users, Fürst also develops facility-management concepts and continues to accompany a number of projects after their realisation. This holistic approach to excellence in property development can also be seen in the company's solid revenues. These ensure that Fürst Developments' financial partners also enjoy good earnings and lasting value. Fürst Developments offers its investment partners a maximum of professionalism and security combined with that creativity in the project design that sets true premium real estate apart.

**Wohnanlage Fondachhof –
Vier international renommierte Architekten realisierten diese Premium-Wohnanlage im romantischen Park eines ehemaligen Nobelhotels**

Fondachhof residential project – Four internationally renowned architects designed this premium housing estate in the romantic park of what was formerly an exclusive hotel

www.fuerstdevelopments.com

qualität, sozialer Wärme und gesellschaftlichem Engagement ihresgleichen sucht.

Wichtige Bausteine sind der Ausbau des Qualitäts- und Ganzjahrestourismus sowie die Stärkung von Salzburg als Kongress- und Messeregion. Es werden Bildung und Wissenschaft neue Impulse gegeben. Wir setzen auf Integration, neue Technologien, eine Stärkung des Schul-, Fachhochschul- und Universitätsstandorts und regionale Bildungsangebote für alle Altersgruppen.

Salzburg wird sich weiterhin als Begegnungsstätte für Persönlichkeiten aus Politik, Wirtschaft und Kultur sowie als Ort wichtiger internationaler Zusammenkünfte positionieren.

Salzburg – ein pulsierender Wirschaftsstandort

Das Bundesland Salzburg ist als dynamischer und innovativer Wirtschaftsstandort bekannt. In den letzten Jahren konnte die österreichweite Spitzenposition kontinuierlich gefestigt werden. So ist unsere Wirtschaft in den letzten Jahren überdurchschnittlich gewachsen. Die moderne Salzburger Wirtschaftsstruktur gilt außerdem als Anziehungspunkt für zahlreiche renommierte Unternehmen aus dem In- und Ausland. Diese überaus positive Entwicklung kann aber nur dann langfristig beibehalten und abgesichert werden, wenn wir auf unseren Stärken und Bedürfnissen aufbauen und eine zukunftsfähige wirtschaftspolitische Strategie verfolgen. Ganz im Sinne dieser äußerst positiven Entwicklungen gilt es daher vor allem, Salzburg als Land mit höchster Lebensqualität und wettbewerbsstarken, flexibel agierenden Unternehmen sowie neuen und interessanten Arbeitsplätzen im erweiterten Europa zu positionieren. Bei allen künftigen wirtschaftspolitischen Aktivitäten werden also nach wie vor die Steigerung der Salzburger Wirtschaftskraft, die Verbesserung der Situation in den strukturschwächeren Regionen und die Sicherung bzw. Schaffung von Arbeitsplätzen im Vordergrund stehen.

In den nächsten Jahren soll insbesondere die Innovationskraft der Salzburger Wirtschaft durch eine gezielte Weiterentwicklung des regionalen Innovationssystems vorangetrieben werden. Der Aufbau von zusätzlichen Technologiefeldern soll die heimische Wirtschaft ebenso stärken wie die Förderung von Unternehmenskooperationen und -netzwerken. Ziel ist auch, Salzburgs Standortattraktivität durch den lückenlosen Ausbau der modernen Infrastruktur abzusichern und unsere Bildungs- und Qualifizierungseinrichtungen auf höchstem Niveau auf allen Ausbildungsebenen zu unterstützen.

Theatre, the Mozarteum Orchestra, the multifarious and newly restructured museum landscape and the top-quality classical music offering, Salzburg is and remains a cultural magnet.

However, Salzburg's reputation as a major cultural venue has long been associated with much more than just its festival tradition. Salzburg stands for a variegated, active, modern and cosmopolitan cultural scene with a wide range of festivals and other events in an open and tolerant cultural environment.

Salzburg is Austria's most beautiful federal state. And we want to be the Number 1 in every other respect as well – not only for our millions of visitors from all corners of the planet, but also for those people who live here and help make Salzburg what it is; going to school and work here, living here and enjoying their well-earned golden years. The city and state of Salzburg are a prosperous region with a promising future that seeks its peer in terms of the combination it has to offer of commercial venue, educational and cultural society, beauty, quality of life, social security and commitment to its people.

Important building blocks in Salzburg's success are the development of quality and year-round tourism here, and the strengthening of its profile as a congress and exhibition region. Education and the sciences will provide new impulses. We place our emphasis on integration, new technologies, reinforcing the school and tertiary education structures and providing regional education options for all age groups.

Salzburg will continue to position itself as a meeting point for key players from the fields of politics, economics and culture, and as a centre for important international gatherings.

Salzburg – a pulsating commercial centre

The state of Salzburg is well known as a dynamic and innovative commercial location that has further reinforced its leading position in Austria in recent years. Our economy has grown faster than the average in the past years and the modern Salzburg economic structure is a centre of attraction for numerous reputed Austrian and international companies. But we can only be sure to retain and consolidate this very positive trend in the long term if we build on our strengths and pursue a forward-looking political and economic strategy that serves our needs. So it is important that we establish Salzburg as a state that offers an exceptional standard of living, is home to a highly competitive and flexible corporate sector and that offers new and attractive jobs

Gebrüder LIMMERT AG

Die Gebrüder Limmert AG ist ein mittelständisches Elektrogroßhandelsunternehmen, gegründet 1924 von den Brüdern Hermann und Hans Limmert in der Schrannengasse 13 in Salzburg. In der Folge übersiedelte das Unternehmen in die Franz-Josef-Straße 4 und zuletzt in die Samergasse 30-30a.

Durch die 1992 gewählte Betriebsform der AG können Konjunkturflauten aufgefangen, Konkurrenzkämpfe bestanden, wichtige Investitionen getätigt und die Marktführung im Umkreis gehalten werden.

Durch motivierte, fachkundige Mitarbeiter, schnelle und vollständige Lieferung, kompetente Beratung, marktgerechte Preise und gezielte Ausübung der Kreditfunktion an unsere Kunden erreichen wir eine hohe Marktakzeptanz.

Dazu gehören auch ein großes Lager und eine rasche Umsetzung neuer Produkte am Markt sowie die entsprechende Lagerführung. Die schnelle und korrekte Abwicklung so genannter Besorgerartikel hat dabei oberste Priorität.

Als Gesellschafter der in Hannover ansässigen MITEGRO, bestehend aus 26 Großhändlern mit ca. 1,3 Mrd. Euro Umsatz in Deutschland und Österreich, stehen uns Möglichkeiten zur Verfügung, die sonst nur Großkonzerne haben.

Firmendaten 2007: 158 Mitarbeiter, 47 Mio. Euro Umsatz im GJ 2006/07, 9 200 m² Lagerfläche, 3 100 m² Büro-Verkaufsfläche.

Gebrüder LIMMERT AG

Gebrüder Limmert AG is a medium-sized electrical goods wholesaler founded in 1924 by the brothers Hermann and Hans Limmert at Schrannengasse 13 in Salzburg. Since then it has moved to Franz-Josef-Strasse 4 and lastly to Samergasse 30-30a.

Becoming a stock corporation in 1992 has enabled the company to absorb economic downturns, survive competitive battles, make important investments and retain the market leadership in the region.

We enjoy a high market acceptance thanks to our motivated, expert staff, fast and complete delivery, competent advice, fair prices and a judicious use of the credit function extended to our customers.

Part of this success is owed to our large warehouse, a rapid turnover of new products on the market and effective warehouse management. The rapid and accurate handling of supply articles is our top priority.

As a shareholder of the Hanover company MITEGRO, with its 26 wholesalers and Euro 1.3 billion in sales in Germany and Austria, we have options at our disposal that are otherwise only available to major company groups.

Company data 2007: 158 employees, Euro 47 million sales in the 2006/07 business year, 9,200 m² warehouse space, 3,100 m² office sales space.

Betriebsgebäude in der Samergasse 30-30a

Belegschaft mit Gründern anno 1924

The company headquarters at Samergasse 30-30a

Staff and founders in 1924

www.limmert.com

Zudem soll Salzburg eine der wichtigsten Tourismusregionen bleiben und seine starke Umweltorientierung zur Sicherung der Lebensqualität und des hohen Freizeitwerts beibehalten. Ebenso wichtig ist aber auch die Bestandspflege der tausenden Unternehmen, die im Land Salzburg seit Jahren erfolgreich tätig sind und durch kontinuierliches Wachstum und rege Investitionstätigkeit bereits einen entscheidenden Beitrag zur Sicherung der Arbeits- und Ausbildungsplätze leisten. Zur Umsetzung dieser Ziele ist es nötig, die formulierten strategischen Schwerpunktsetzungen konsequent zu verfolgen. Einige wichtige Impulse wurden bereits gesetzt. Und auch die Politik wird ihr Bestes tun, um diesen Prozess weiterhin stetig voranzutreiben.

„Salzburg. feel the inspiration!"

Ein weiterer wichtiger Schritt zu einer noch größeren Wettbewerbsfähigkeit des Standortes Salzburg ist ein gemeinsamer Auftritt nach außen. Salzburg kann sich glücklich schätzen, dass Stadt und Land denselben wohlklingenden Namen haben, der in aller Welt bekannt ist und geschätzt wird. Vor fast 80 Jahren wurden die ersten Versuche gestartet, dies zu betonen und für das In- und Ausland einen gemeinsamen Auftritt zu entwickeln. Ein Projekt über das Jahrzehnte lang diskutiert wurde, ist nun erfolgreich von der Vision zur Markenrealität geführt worden.

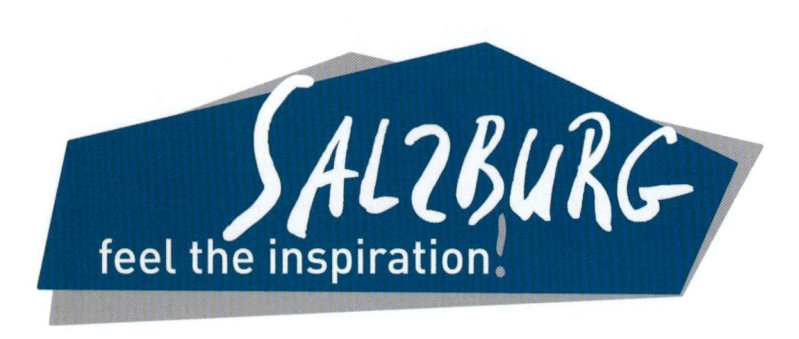

Anfang 2005 startete das Land Salzburg gemeinsam mit der Stadt Salzburg und der Wirtschaftskammer Salzburg die Initiative, das Projekt „Marke Salzburg" umzusetzen. Im Mai 2006 war es dann endlich soweit. Die gemeinsame Marke „Salzburg. feel the inspiration!" wurde der Öffentlichkeit vorgestellt.

Salzburg verfügt damit erstmals über einen gemeinsamen Markenauftritt, der einen entscheidenden Vorteil im Wettbewerb der Regionen verschafft. Mit der neuen Marke Salzburg verfügt die Region über einen einheitlichen Absender, der unser schönes Bundesland in der ganzen Welt noch bekannter macht und klar positioniert. Mit dem neuen Auftritt stellen wir das, was Salzburg so erfolg-

within an expanding Europe. In doing so, our focus will thus remain on raising Salzburg's economic power, improving the situation in the structurally weaker regions and safeguarding and generating jobs.

In the coming years our attention will be directed especially at driving the innovativeness of the Salzburg economy by developing the regional system of innovation. By building up additional technological strengths we aim to strengthen the domestic economy and promote intercompany cooperation and networking. Another goal is to maintain Salzburg's attractiveness as a home to companies by ensuring that our modern infrastructure continues to expand, and by supporting our educational and qualifying institutions at all levels of the educational system.

Salzburg is also to remain one of the main tourist regions, retaining its distinctive environment-friendly orientation to secure the high quality of life and leisure here indefinitely. But it is just as important to us to keep supporting the thousands of companies that already do their business in the state of Salzburg, making a decisive contribution to maintaining the employment and vocational training opportunities here for so many years through their continued growth and commitment to investment. If we are to achieve these goals we will have to pursue the strategic objectives we set ourselves vigorously and systematically. We have already laid some of the ground stones, and the public sector will continue to do its best to drive the process forwards.

"Salzburg. feel the inspiration!"

Another important step in making Salzburg an even more competitive location is its collaborative approach to marketing both city and state. Salzburg can consider itself very fortunate that both the federal state and the city share the same highly agreeable name, known and valued throughout the world. The first steps to drawing attention to this fact were taken almost 80 years ago, and a project that was discussed long and hard for many decades has now developed from a vision into a brand-name reality.

In early 2005 the state of Salzburg, the city of Salzburg and the Salzburg Chamber of Commerce launched the initiative to realise the "Salzburg brand" project. And in May 2006 the joint brand "Salzburg. feel the inspiration!" was presented to the public.

This new approach to marketing Salzburg with a joint brand-name is hoped to give the city and state a decisive edge in the competition between regions. With this new brand, Salzburg now has a

PRIVATINVEST BANK AG, Salzburg

Direkt am Eingang zur Salzburger Altstadt entwickelte sich ein exzellentes Beratungszentrum für Vermögensanlage. Das historische Gebäude, in dem schon seit 1885 die Bank ansässig ist, befindet sich in der Griesgasse 11. In gediegener Atmosphäre und unter Wahrung absoluter Diskretion wird Privatkunden eine breite Palette von Dienstleistungen geboten.

Die Vorzüge der PRIVATINVEST BANK AG liegen insbesondere in der Unabhängigkeit der Beratung und in der langjährigen Erfahrung ihrer gut ausgebildeten Kundenberater. Die Zugehörigkeit zum Allianzkonzern sichert den Kunden einerseits günstige Konditionen, andererseits wird durch die überschaubare Größe der Bank ein besonderes Maß an Service geboten. Ganz nach dem Motto: „Qualität geht vor Quantität!"

Persönliches Engagement, Kompetenz, Verlässlichkeit, Kontinuität und nicht zuletzt ein großes, Vertrauen erweckendes Netzwerk im Hintergrund sind fünf gute Gründe, sein Vermögen in der PRIVATINVEST BANK AG verwalten und vermehren zu lassen.

PRIVATINVEST BANK AG, Salzburg

A top address for asset management was born long ago at the entrance to the historical town centre of Salzburg. The landmark building that the bank has been based in since 1885 can be found at Griesgasse 11. Here, private investors are offered a full range of services in an atmosphere of dignified discretion.

Some of the special advantages of PRIVATINVEST BANK AG are its independence and the many years of experience that its highly trained customer consultants have to offer. Being a company of the Allianz Group, customers are assured the very best terms, and yet the small size of the bank itself means we pride ourselves on our excellent personal service. Our credo: "Quality ahead of quantity!"

Personal commitent to your needs, competence, reliability, continuity and a large, confidence-inspiring network are just five of the many reasons to put the management and multiplication of your assets in the expert hands of PRIVATINVEST BANK AG.

PRIVATINVEST BANK AG am Eingang zur Altstadt. Private Banking mit höchsten Qualitätsansprüchen

PRIVATINVEST BANK AG at the gates to the historical town centre. Top quality private banking

www.privatinvest.com

Geschäftsführer Mag. Ewald Sauerczopf mit seinem Team

General Manager Ewald Sauerczopf with his team

SCOTTS CELAFLOR HANDELSGESELLSCHAFT mbH, Salzburg

Mag. Ewald Sauerczopf und sein Team verantworten von Salzburg aus den wirtschaftlichen Erfolg der Region Zentraleuropa (Österreich, Deutschland, Skandinavien und Osteuropa) für den weltweit tätigen Konzern „THE SCOTTS COMPANY". Wir sind sicher in einem der schönsten Märkte tätig – dem Gartenmarkt. Hier lassen wir unsere beliebten Marken SUBSTRAL, CELAFLOR und NEXALOTTE sprechen, die einen kleinen Beitrag zum schönsten Hobby – dem Garten – stiften.

Mit unseren Qualitätsprodukten in den Bereichen Pflanzendünger, Pflanzenschutz, Erde und Haushaltsinsektizide sind wir Weltmarktführer! Erfolg verpflichtet: Wir entwickeln unsere Produkte den Konsumentenwünschen entsprechend nach Umweltbewusstsein und einfacher Handhabung ständig weiter bzw. bringen neue, innovative Produkte auf den Markt.

SCOTTS CELAFLOR HANDELSGESELLSCHAFT mbH, Salzburg

Ewald Sauerczopf and his team are responsible for the commercial success of the worldwide conglomerate "THE SCOTTS COMPANY" in the Central Europe region (Austria, Germany, Scandinavia and Eastern Europe). Our market is one of the best there is – the garden market. Our highly popular brands SUBSTRAL, CELAFLOR and NEXALOTTE represent us here, making their little contribution to the most natural hobby of all – the garden.

With our top quality products we are the world market leader in the fields of fertilisers, pest management, soil and household insecticides! But we are not resting on our laurels: We are constantly developing and launching new, innovative products to ensure customer satisfaction, conservation of nature and ease of handling.

Speziell der natürliche Pflanzenschutz liegt uns am Herzen: So haben wir heuer unter der Marke CELAFLOR NATUREN einen umweltfreundlichen Pflanzenschutz kreiert, der mit natürlichen, aber bewährten Wirkstoffen ausgestattet ist. Damit werden Schädlinge bekämpft, aber Nützlinge geschont.

Mit unseren Qualitätserden SUBSTRAL NATUREN, die ohne Torf hergestellt werden, kooperieren wir aktiv mit dem WWF und erhalten seit 1994 dafür jährlich das Österreichische Umweltzeichen.

Um den Markt zu beleben, recherchieren und entwickeln wir auf Basis von umfangreichen Marktstudien neue Produkte und Anwendungsmethoden. Eine konsequente Markenpolitik liegt der klaren und unverwechselbaren Positionierung aller Scotts Celaflor Produkte zugrunde. Die Wünsche und Ansprüche der Verbraucher nach Topqualität und Leistung, aber auch nach bedarfsgerechten, sicheren und umweltfreundlichen Produkten haben oberste Priorität.

Unser großer Erfolg ist aber nicht nur in der innovativen Unternehmensphilosophie zu finden, sondern basiert zu einem respektablen Teil auf unseren guten partnerschaftlichen Beziehungen zum österreichischen Handel. Das mit Abstand höchste Werbebudget der Branche nützen wir sowohl für einen starken Werbeauftritt, als auch für attraktive Maßnahmen im Verkaufsraum des Handels: Repräsentative Aufsteller, Informationsbroschüren und selbstverständlich die adäquate Schulung der Handelsmannschaft sind uns ein Bedürfnis.

Auf der Website www.scotts.at finden die Garten- und Pflanzenliebhaber eine Übersicht über das vollständige SCOTTS CELAFLOR Produktsortiment, Anwendungsbeschreibungen und Abbildungen von Schädlingen bzw. von befallenen Pflanzen. Damit wird eine frühe Erkennung der Erkrankung und die Auswahl und Anwendung des richtigen Produkts leicht gemacht. Entsprechend dem Motto „Schöne Gärten für eine schönere Welt" bieten wir sowohl Handel als auch Verbrauchern für jedes Problem in Haus und Garten die richtige Lösung aus einer Hand.

Organic pest management is a very special concern of ours. For example, we have created an environmentally friendly form of pest control that we market under our brand name CELAFLOR NATUREN and that uses only natural and proven ingredients. This means the pests are eradicated while the plant thrives.

With our quality soils SUBSTRAL NATUREN, created without peat, we actively cooperate with the WWF, and have been awarded the Austrian environmental seal of quality every year since 1994.

To keep growing the market, we research and develop new products and applications on the basis of extensive market studies. All Scotts Celaflor products adhere to a strict branding policy and an inimitable positioning. The customers' desire and demand for top quality and performance as well as ideally tailored, safe and environmentally friendly products are our uppermost priority.

But our greatest achievement is not just our innovative corporate philosophy; a large part of our success is due to our excellent partnership with the Austrian retail sector. We use what is by far the largest advertising budget in the industry to ensure a strong advertising presence and attractive measures on the retail sales floor. Attractive promotional displays, information pamphlets and of course well trained sales staff are a must for us.

At www.scotts.at garden lovers will find the entire range of SCOTTS CELAFLOR products, with instructions for use and photos of pests and afflicted plants. This helps recognise diseases in their early stages and select and use the right product to eliminate them. In keeping with the motto "Beautiful gardens for a better world" we offer retailers and consumers the right solution for every problem they may face in their house or garden.

www.scotts.at

Substral Pflanzennahrung mit dem innovativen Kipp & Go Dosierverschluss für die ideale Menge an Nährstoffen und Spurenelementen ist die bequemste Art, Ihre Pflanzen rundum zu versorgen

Substral fertiliser with the innovative Kipp & Go dispenser cap for just the right amount of nutrients and trace elements is the easiest way to make sure your plants are getting everything they need

reich macht, in den Mittelpunkt. Damit wird langfristig der Standort in seiner ganzen Vielfalt gestärkt – und davon profitieren alle, egal ob Wirtschaft, Tourismus, Kultur, Bildung oder der Sport. Der neue Markenauftritt wird Salzburg im In- und Ausland so positionieren, dass seine Attraktivität und Anziehungskraft weiter steigen. Damit wird eine wichtige Basis für zukünftige Investitionen in den Standort Salzburg gelegt, um in Folge neue Arbeitsplätze zu schaffen.

Eine Quelle der Inspiration

Die Markenpositionierung und die kreative Umsetzung beruhen auf zahlreichen Interviews und Befragungen aus dem In- und Ausland. Eine Kombination aus qualitativer und quantitativer Marktforschung war die Grundlage für den neuen Auftritt, der die Stärken Salzburgs aufnimmt und weiterentwickelt.

Die Ergebnisse zeigten, dass Salzburg schon jetzt eine weltweit positiv besetzte Marke ist. Es ging um eine behutsame Ergänzung in Richtung Modernität, Dynamik und Leistung. Die bestehenden „Markenwerte" für Salzburg sind unter anderem: „Hohe Lebensqualität", „Kulturland", „einzigartig" oder „sympathisch". Gemeinsamer Wunsch der Befragten und Fachleute ist nun die Anreicherung dieser bestehenden Markenwerte Salzburgs mit „Dynamik". Vereinfacht könnte man die notwendige Ergänzung so auf den Punkt bringen: „Mozartkugeln und Software", „Weltkulturerbe und Innovationsmanagement" oder „Landschaft und Holztechnik".

Um in der kreativen Umsetzung das Einzigartige und Besondere an Salzburg herauszuarbeiten, wurde danach gefragt, was Salzburg für Mozart, Herbert von Karajan, Max Reinhardt, Thomas Bernhard, für die Gebrüder Obauer, für Dietrich Mateschitz, Hubert Palfinger, Hermann Maier und andere erfolgreiche Salzburgerinnen und Salzburger bedeutet. Für sie alle ist Salzburg eine Quelle der Inspiration. Diese geht gleichermaßen von den Festspielen, von der Natur und Lebenskultur des Landes, von der Kulisse der Stadt, der Architektur und vom sozialen Klima aus. Inspiration ist Grundlage für den Erfolg der Wirtschaft, eine Einladung an Gäste, Basis für kulturelles Schaffen und in der Bildung ebenso wichtig wie im Sport.

In der grafischen Umsetzung wurde ein dynamisches Fünfeck gewählt, das für die fünf Salzburger Bezirke steht: Flachgau, Tennengau, Pongau, Pinzgau und Lungau. Gleichzeit repräsentieren die fünf Ecken auch die fünf Kernwerte von Salzburg: Qualität, Tradition, Kultur, Freizeit, Natur. Die Form stellt auch Assoziationen zum Salzkristall her. Da Inspirationen etwas sehr Persönliches und Indivi-

vehicle charged with further establishing and even more clearly positioning our beautiful state in the eyes of the world. This new approach puts the things that make Salzburg such a huge success at the centre of attention. This will promote us in all our diversity; and that is to the good of everyone, be they in industry, tourism, culture, education or sport. The new brand will make Salzburg even more attractive to people in Austria and abroad, laying an important foundation for future investments in Salzburg and as a result generating more employment opportunities.

A source of inspiration

The brand positioning and creative realisation were built upon the insight gained in numerous interviews and surveys held in Austria and the rest of the world. A combination of qualitative and quantitative market research provided the base for the new image, which picks up on Salzburg's strengths and runs with them.

The research showed that Salzburg already has an excellent image all over the world. Hence, the development of the brand is based on carefully complementing the existing identity with stimuli in the direction of modernity, dynamism and performance. The "brand values" that Salzburg already boasts include "high quality of life", "cultural state", "unique" and "congenial". The mutual wish of the people surveyed and the experts is to now enrich these existing brand values by adding "dynamic". Oversimplified, one could sum it up as "Mozart pralines and software", "world cultural heritage and innovation management" or "landscape and timber processing technology".

In distilling out just what is so unique and special about Salzburg, we asked what Salzburg meant to Mozart, Herbert von Karajan, Max Reinhardt, Thomas Bernhard, the Obauer brothers, Dietrich Mateschitz, Hubert Palfinger, Hermann Maier and other prominent Salzburgers. For all of them Salzburg is a source of inspiration, whether because of the Salzburg Festival, the cityscape, the natural beauty and lifestyle, the architecture or the social climate. Inspiration is one of the keys to the success of the economy, an invitation to guests, a basis for cultural creativity and just as important for education as it is in the sporting field.

A dynamic pentagon was chosen to depict the vision graphically. It represents the five Salzburg districts: Flachgau, Tennengau, Pongau, Pinzgau and Lungau. At the same time the five corners represent the five core values of Salzburg: quality, tradition, culture, leisure and nature, and the form itself also awakens an association to the salt crystal. As inspirations are something very personal and individu-

Seit mehr als 25 Jahren ist das Messezentrum Salzburg das erfolgreichste Messezentrum Österreichs. Jährlich werden rund 35 Fach- und Publikumsmessen veranstaltet

The exhibition centre in Salzburg has been the most successful of its kind in all Austria for more than 25 years. Around 35 fairs are held here every year

duelles sind, wurde für die Gestaltung des Schriftzuges eine Handschrift gewählt. Sie macht das Logo selbst zu einem gelebten Stück Inspiration.

Die neue „Marke Salzburg" wird Stadt und Land Salzburg neuen Schwung verleihen. Mit einer einheitlichen Marke für alle Bereiche stärken wir das gesamte Land. Wir multiplizieren unseren Auftritt im In- und Ausland und profitieren von einer klaren Botschaft. Die „Marke Salzburg" wird langfristig ein Erfolg werden, wenn möglichst viele Unternehmen und Institutionen diese Marke für sich nützen. Die „Marke Salzburg" braucht die Unterstützung möglichst vieler großer, kleiner und mittelständischer Markenträger. Wenn diese „Marke Salzburg" regional wie international eine möglichst hohe Verbreitung und Öffentlichkeit erfährt, wird sie ihre ganze Strahlkraft entfalten.

Die ersten Monate waren sehr viel versprechend. Im März 2007 haben sich bereits über 3 000 Leistungsträger der Region als Markennutzer registrieren lassen. Diese kommen aus den unterschiedlichsten Bereichen und Dimensionen der Region Salzburg: Bildung, Tourismus, Industrie, Körperschaften, Handel und Dienstleistung. Salzburg weckt weltweit positive Assoziationen. Sämtliche Leistungsträger der Region haben nun eine Marke zur Verfügung, die dieses „positive Vorurteil" für sie nutzbar macht. Die Auftraggeber, Land, Stadt und Wirtschaftskammer Salzburg sowie die Tourismusverbände Salzburger Land Tourismus und Tourismus Salzburg setzen die neue Marke ebenfalls in ihrer Kommunikation ein. ◄

al, a handwriting font was chosen for the wording, making the logo itself a work of inspiration.

The new "Salzburg brand" will add new impetus to the state and city. A unified brand will help us power up the whole region. We will multiply our visibility in Austria and abroad and profit from a clear message. The "Salzburg brand" will be a lasting success if as many companies and institutions as possible use it for their own purposes. The "Salzburg brand" needs the support of small and medium-sized multipliers. Only by exposing it to the largest possible market will it be able to radiate its full effect.

The first months of the brand have been very promising. In March 2007 more than 3,000 major players in the region have registered as brand users. They come from the most varied of fields and sizes of enterprises in Salzburg: education, tourism, industry, public bodies, retail and services. Salzburg arouses positive associations in people all over the world, and now all the players in the region have a brand at their disposal that helps them benefit from this "positive prejudice". The initiators: the state, city and commercial chamber of Salzburg, and the Salzburger Land tourism associations and Tourismus Salzburg also use the new brand in their communication. ◄

Dipl.-Ing. Rudolf Strasser
Leiter WirtschaftsService
der Stadt Salzburg

Das baukünstlerische und städtebauliche Optimierungsverfahren für die Gestaltung der S-Bahn-Station „Gnigl - Schwabenwirtsbrücke" wurde von der Stadt Salzburg angeregt. Es hatte zum Ziel, das von den Österreichischen Bundesbahnen (ÖBB) entwickelte Designkonzept für die Gestaltung von Stadtbahn-Stationen im lokalen Kontext zu interpretieren

The architectural and urban optimization of the suburban rail (S-Bahn) station "Gnigl-Schwabenwirtsbrücke" was initiated by the city of Salzburg. The aim was to carry out the design concept of the Austrian railway company (ÖBB) for the local S-Bahn stations

Salzburg ist einzigartig

Salzburg ist einzigartig. Salzburg verbindet Tradition mit Moderne, Natur und Kulturlandschaft mit Städtebau und Architektur. Salzburg ist laut und weltstädtisch und trotzdem überschaubar und kleingliedrig. Salzburg bietet unvergleichliche Höhepunkte in Sachen Musik, ist Fremdenverkehrsdestination von Weltrang. Die Altstadt von Salzburg wurde als Weltkulturerbe ausgezeichnet, die Stadt Salzburg ist aber auch Standort unterschiedlichster Unternehmen von internationalem Rang. Salzburg ist Zentrum einer der attraktivsten Regionen Europas, einerseits des Landes Salzburg und andererseits der Euregio Salzburg, Berchtesgadenerland, Traunstein, verbindet also auch Salzburg mit Bayern, Österreich mit Deutschland.

Salzburg – die Mozartstadt

Salzburg ist mit dem Namen Mozart untrennbar verbunden. Der wohl berühmteste Sohn der Stadt ist Ursprung für die musikalische Tradition, lebt fort in der Universität Mozarteum Salzburg und in den weltberühmten Salzburger Festspielen. Heute aber bietet die Stadt ein weit darüber hinaus gehendes reichhaltiges Konzert- und Theaterangebot, vom Orchester- bis zum Rockkonzert, vom Schauspiel bis zum Kabarett bis hin zum Volkstanz. Vom Jazzfestival bis zum Straßenfest.

Sport ergänzt die Kultur

Der Sport ergänzt inzwischen das Profil der Stadt Salzburg. Die Austragung der Straßen-Rad-Weltmeisterschaften im Sommer 2006 stellt den bisherigen Höhepunkt dieser Entwicklung dar. Salzburg Stadt bewirbt sich aber auch um die Austragung der Olympischen Winterspiele 2014. Als Host-City ist die Landeshauptstadt auch in die Fußball-Europameisterschaften 2008 eingebunden. Hervorragende Sportstätten für den Leistungs-, aber vor allem auch den Breitensport zählen zu den Vorzügen Salzburgs.

Landschaft, Städtebau und Architektur

Über das schon erwähnte Weltkulturerbe Altstadt Salzburg hinaus pflegt die Stadt seit Jahrzehnten die aktuellen Fragen des Städtebaus und der Architektur. Ein internationaler Gestaltungsbeirat sorgt für ein hohes Niveau der Bautätigkeit. Salzburg ist heute ein Ziel für Freunde und Kenner moderner Architektur. Ebenso ambitioniert arbeitet die Stadt an der Erhaltung ihrer Stadtlandschaften, deren Qualitäten entscheidend zu ihrem Erscheinungs-

Salzburg is one of a kind

Salzburg is unique. Salzburg joins tradition with modernity, and nature and cultural landscapes with urban development and architecture. Salzburg is loud and cosmopolitan and yet at the same time somehow diminutive. Salzburg has incomparable highlights to offer in the field of music and is a tourist destination of global renown. The old town centre of Salzburg is a World Heritage Site, but the city of Salzburg is at the same time home to a wide variety of world-ranking companies. Salzburg is the midpoint of one of the most attractive regions in all of Europe: on the one hand of the state of Salzburg and on the other of the Euregio Salzburg, Berchtesgadenerland, Traunstein region linking Salzburg with Bavaria and Austria with Germany.

Salzburg – the Mozart town

Salzburg is inseparably tied to the name Mozart. The town's undoubtedly most famous son is the origin of its musical tradition; a tradition that lives on in the Salzburg Mozarteum University and the world-famous Salzburg Festival. But that is far from all. Today the town's musical variety goes way beyond that, offering a wide range of concerts and theatres, orchestras, rock concerts, stage plays, cabaret, folk dance, from jazz festival to street festival.

Sport complements the culture

Sports also embellish the profile of the city of Salzburg. The road cycling world championship held here in the summer of 2006 was an interim highpoint in the city's sporting development. But it has hopes of eclipsing this success with a winning bid to host the 2014 Winter Olympics. The city of Salzburg is also involved in the European soccer championship Euro 2008 as a host city. Outstanding sporting venues for professional and amateur sports are among Salzburg's prime assets.

Landscape, urban development and architecture

In addition to the World Heritage Site Salzburg Old Town, the city has also occupied itself with questions of urban development and architecture for decades. An international design council ensures that building activity in Salzburg is kept to a very high standard. Salzburg is today a destination for friends and connoisseurs of modern architecture. The city itself is working hard to maintain the beauty of its streetscapes, the qualities of which make

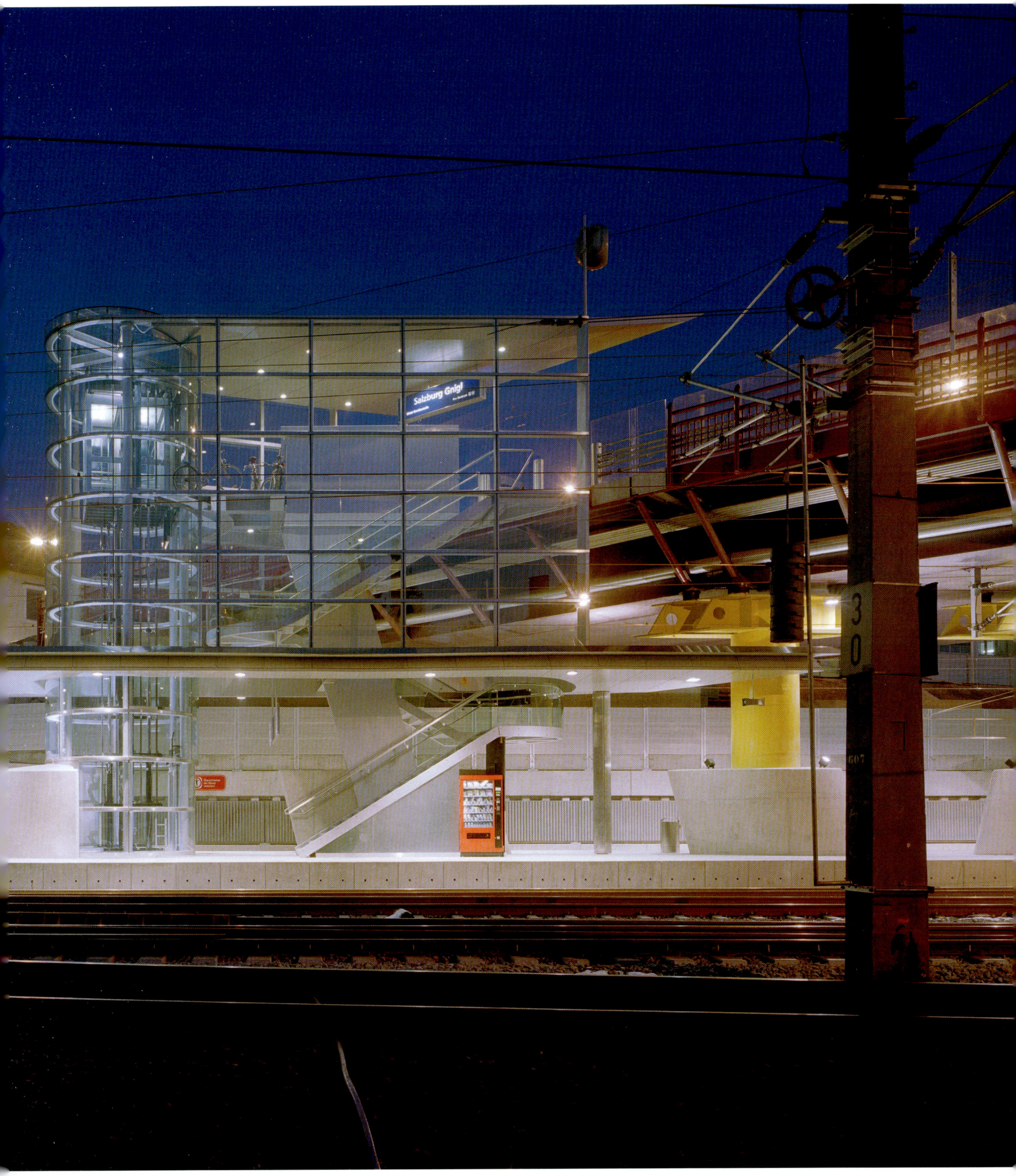
Salzburg Gnigl

bild, wie auch zu ihrer Lebensqualität im Allgemeinen entscheidend beitragen.

Top Wirtschafts- und High-Tech-Standort

Rund 7 300 Betriebe mit rund 91 000 Beschäftigten haben in der Stadt Salzburg ihren Sitz. Als Landeshauptstadt und regionales Zentrum dominieren naturgemäß die unternehmensbezogenen Dienstleistungen sowie die Handels- und – in geringerem Ausmaß – die Produktionsbetriebe. Die Arbeitslosenquote wird 2007 unter 5% fallen und liegt damit signifikant unter dem Österreich-Durchschnitt (knapp über 7%). Die Kaufkraft liegt über dem österreichischen Durchschnitt.

Nicht nur die Mozartkugel wird in Salzburg produziert, auch der Kranbau-Weltmarktführer Palfinger ist hier zu Hause. Kaum ein schwieriges Bauwerk kommt ohne das Know-how der Gleitbau aus, Sicherheitstechnik der Commend findet man in aller Welt, kein Formel I-Rennen wird ohne Carbon-Komponenten der Carbo-Tech bestritten. Damit seien nur einige Beispiele herausgegriffen.

In Salzburg-Itzling liegt das Herzstück des österreichweit größten Technologiezentrums. Ein neuer Technologie- und Forschungsschwerpunkt, die „ScienceCity", wird im räumlichen Anschluss daran an important contribution to their appearance and to the quality of life here in general.

Top commercial and high-tech centre

Around 7,300 companies with 91,000 people on their payrolls are based in the city of Salzburg. As state capital and regional centre, corporate services are of course the dominating force, as are retailers and to a lesser degree manufacturing companies. Unemployment will fall below 5% in 2007, which puts it significantly below the Austrian average (around 7%), and the buying power here is above the national average.

Not only the Mozart chocolates are produced in Salzburg. The world's market leading crane builder Palfinger is at home here. As good as no complex construction can be completed without the company Gleitbau's know-how, Commend safety engineering can be found all over the world, and no Formula 1 race is run without carbon components from Carbo-Tech. And these are just a few examples.

The heart of Austria's largest technology centre lies in Salzburg-Itzling. And a new technology and research facility – "ScienceCity" – will be added to it soon. It will be focused on the fields of geoinformatics and applied computer technology.

Sorgfältige Analysen der experimentellen Daten geben Aufschluss über die Qualität neu entwickelter biologischer Substanzen

Careful analyses of the experiment data shed light on the quality of newly developed biological substances

Mit Palfinger, Salzburgs einzigem börsenotierten Unternehmen, geht es steil aufwärts

Business is on the rise for Palfinger, Salzburg's only listed company

Palfinger bewegt die Welt

Dass die Stadt Salzburg immer mehr zur internationalen Trendstadt wird, liegt nicht nur an der zauberhaften Landschaft, der einzigartigen Architektur und dem vielseitigen Kulturangebot. Es liegt auch an den Konzernen, die von Salzburg aus die Welt erobern.

Als führender Hersteller hydraulischer Hebe-, Lade- und Handlingsysteme hilft Palfinger seinen Kunden und Anwendern weltweit, tonnenschwere Lasten zu bewegen und logistische Meisterleistungen zu vollbringen. Einen der wichtigsten Erfolgsfaktoren bilden dabei die Forschung und die Weiterentwicklung der vielseitigen Produkte. Vom flexiblen Knickarmkran über hochwertige Containerwechselsysteme bis hin zu kraftvollen Ladebordwänden: Palfinger bietet für jedes noch so schwere Problem eine innovative und zuverlässige Lösung und verschafft seinen Kunden tagtäglich einen immensen Wettbewerbsvorteil. Der Blick in die Zukunft ist ähnlich vielversprechend: Durch den kontinuierlichen Aufbau des weltweiten Netzwerks und der ständigen Verbesserung des Kundenservices wird die Palfinger AG auch in den kommenden Jahren ein wichtiger und zuverlässiger Partner für logistische Abläufe und kompetente technische Lösungen sein.

Palfinger moves the world

The enchanting landscapes, unique architecture and multifarious cultural offering are not the only things that make the city of Salzburg one of the trendy places to be on the international map. Another reason lies in Salzburg's companies, that use this town as their launching pad to the rest of the world.

As the leading manufacturer of hydraulic lifting, loading and handling systems, Palfinger helps its customers and users all over the globe to move heavy loads and master tough logistical challenges. Among the main contributors to Palfinger's success are its research work and development of a wide range of products. From the highly versatile knuckle-boom loading crane through top-quality container transfer systems to powerful tail lifts, Palfinger has an innovative and reliable solution for every situation and provides its customers with an enormous competitive advantage, every working day. And the future looks just as promising: By continuously expanding its global network and constantly improving its customer service, Palfinger AG will remain an important and reliable partner for logistical processes and expert technical solutions in the years to come.

www.palfinger.com

Fachhochschule Salzburg, Puch/Urstein

Salzburg technical university, Puch/Urstein

Alpine Mayreder Bau GmbH
Kompetenznetzwerk für Bauprojekte der Superlative

Der Alpine Konzern ist eines der Top-Bauunternehmen Österreichs. Die Aktivitäten umfassen das gesamte Spektrum des Baugeschehens auf nationaler wie auf internationaler Ebene. Alle Geschäftsfelder und Beteiligungen sind in der Alpine Mayreder Bau GmbH mit Hauptsitz in Salzburg zusammengefasst.

Die Geschäftstätigkeit umfasst alle Sparten der Bau- und Dienstleistungen: Hochbau, Straßen- und Ingenieurtiefbau, Tunnel- und Spezialtiefbau, Kraftwerksbau, Projektentwicklung, Gleis- und Bahnbau, Deponien und Umwelttechnik sowie die Spezialbereiche Rohstoffgewinnung, Ziegelproduktion, Asphalt- und Betonerzeugung, Eisenbiegerei und Prüflabor. Mit der Tochtergesellschaft Alpine Energie verfügt der Konzern über einen leistungsstarken Bereich in den Wachstumssparten Energieversorgung, Freileitungsbau und Kommunikationstechnik.

Beispiele für prominente Großprojekte der letzten Jahre:
Basistunnel St. Gotthard als längster Eisenbahntunnel der Welt, Allianz Arena in München, zwei

Alpine Mayreder Bau GmbH
Expert network for superlative construction projects

The Alpine Group is Austria's top construction company. Its activities span the entire range of the building industry, both in Austria and internationally. All the business units and subsidiaries are joined together in Alpine Mayreder Bau GmbH with its headquarters in Salzburg.

The business activities encompass all construction services, from structural engineering, road construction, underground engineering, tunnel construction, special civil engineering, power station construction, project development, rail and track construction and the special fields of raw materials extraction, tile production, asphalt and concrete manufacture, iron bending through to its testing laboratory. In its subsidiary Alpine Energie the group has a high-performance unit in the growth sector of energy supply, overhead lines and communication engineering.

Some of the major projects in recent years:
The St. Gotthard base tunnel; the longest railway tunnel in the world, the Allianz Arena in Munich,

EM-Stadion EURO 2008, Salzburg Wals

EURO stadium 2008, Salzburg Wals

große Baulose der U-Bahn in Singapur, Autobahn Ninghbo in China, Wasserkraftwerke Ermenek in der Türkei, Tsankov Kamak in Bulgarien, Save Brücke „Domovinski Most" nahe Zagreb, FH Salzburg, das UKH (Unfallkrankenhaus) und der Wissensturm in Linz. Aktuell hat die Alpine den Zuschlag für das PPP-Projekt Nordautobahn/Wien bekommen. Um solche Projekte zu realisieren, setzt die Alpine auf Wachstum. Mit einer Gesamtleistung von über 2 Mrd. Euro konnte die Bauleistung seit dem Jahr 2000 mehr als verdoppelt werden, der Auslandsanteil wurde dabei fast verdreifacht und beträgt mittlerweile rund 40 %.

Spitzenposition in Europa
Durch die strategische Verschränkung mit der FCC befindet sich die Alpine unter den Top-Playern im europäischen Umfeld und am Weg zum Global-Player. Mit der FCC und deren rund 70 000 Mitarbeitern werden in der Gesamtgruppe ca. 12 Mrd. Euro Jahresumsatz erwirtschaftet. Die Alpine wird auch mit neuer strategischer Ausrichtung stets von ihrer Konzernphilosophie getragen: Erfahrung nutzen – Verantwortung tragen – Zukunft gestalten.

two major units of the underground in Singapore, the Ninghbo motorway in China, the Ermenek hydro-power stations in Turkey, Tsankov Kamak in Bulgaria, the "Domovinski Most" bridge over the Save near Zagreb, Salzburg technical college, the emergency hospital and the Terminal Tower in Linz. Alpine has also just won the call for tenders for the PPP project to build the Vienna Northern Motorway. To be able to realise projects of this magnitude, Alpine is prepared for growth. With a total order volume of over Euro 2 billion it has more than doubled its turnover since the year 2000. The international share of the company's business has almost tripled during this period and currently accounts for around 40 % of Alpine's sales.

Leading position in Europe
Through its strategic merger with FCC, Alpine is now one of the top players in the European construction landscape and well on its way to becoming a global player. With FCC and its approx. 70,000 staff, the group generates around Euro 12 billion in consolidated sales. And with its new strategic orientation, Alpine remains driven by its group philosophy: use our experience – take responsibility – shape the future.

www.alpine.at

entstehen. Inhaltliche Schwerpunkte sind durch die Bereiche Geoinformatik und angewandte Computertechnologie vorgezeichnet.

Ein weiterer Schwerpunkt in Bezug auf Gesundheit wird in Verbindung mit den Landeskrankenanstalten und der Paracelsus Medizinischen Privatuniversität das Thema Biotechnologie bilden. Ein diesbezüglicher Technologiepark soll 2007 die Konzeptionsphase erreichen.

STANDORT FÜR BILDUNG, WISSENSCHAFT UND FORSCHUNG

Salzburg und Umgebung sind Standort der Paris Lodron Universität Salzburg, der Universität Mozarteum, der Paracelsus Medizinischen Privatuniversität. Die Fachhochschule Salzburg umfasst Lehrgänge für Informationstechnologien, Wirtschaft und Tourismus, Medien & Design, Gesundheit & Soziales, Holz & biogene Technologien. Weitere berufsbegleitende Studiengänge, aber auch sechs weitere Berufsschulen, 29 mittlere und höhere Lehranstalten und eine Vielzahl von Berufsschulen ergänzen das Ausbildungsspektrum. Für das Angebot bestens qualifizierter Arbeitskräfte ist damit gesorgt.

Another focus will be on biotechnology within the field of healthcare, together with the state hospitals and Paracelsus Medical University. This technology park is to go into the design phase in 2007.

VENUE FOR EDUCATION, SCIENCE AND RESEARCH

Salzburg and surrounds are the home of Paris Lodron University Salzburg, the Mozarteum University and the Paracelsus Private Medical University. Salzburg Technical College offers courses in information technology, economics and tourism, media and design, health and social welfare, wood and biogenous technologies. Other courses of study for professionals, six other vocational training schools, 29 institutes of higher education and numerous trade schools round off the educational spectrum and ensure that there is no shortage of well qualified people on the market.

A cooperation has been in place with Munich Technical University since 2006, and the Academy of Sciences has also opened another institute (geoinformatics) in the city of Salzburg. The Christian-Doppler labs bridge the gap between research and development in the industrial sector.

Hoch motivierte StudentInnen und junge WissenschafterInnen stellen eine treibende Kraft für die Forschung an der Universität Salzburg dar

Highly motivated students and young scientists are a driving force for research at Salzburg university

40 Jahre Böhm Schweißtechnik – Familienunternehmen und Fachbetrieb

Je größer die Großen werden, desto mehr Möglichkeiten haben kleine flexible Unternehmen. Mit dieser Strategie ist Böhm Schweißtechnik als Familienunternehmen seit 40 Jahren erfolgreich. Als eine der ersten Frauen im harten Männer-Business des Maschinenhandels gründete Ernestine Böhm das Unternehmen 1967. Ihr Sohn Franz Xaver Böhm errichtete 1988 den neuen Firmensitz am heutigen Standort in Salzburg-Schallmoos.

Mit dem Auslieferungslager in Innsbruck und einem Vertriebsnetz in ganz Österreich ist Böhm Schweißtechnik heute ein hoch spezialisierter Partner von Industrie, Gewerbe und Landwirtschaft. Beratung und Schulung, Anlagen, Service und Materialien – Böhm Schweißtechnik bietet mit seinen 14 Mitarbeitern Komplettlösungen. Und die konsequente Weiterentwicklung des Angebots: So hat Löten etwa im Karosseriebau und bei Blech-Reparaturen zahlreiche Vorteile. Dazu gehören vor allem der deutlich reduzierte Aufwand für die Nacharbeit und größere Energie-Effizienz. Technische Gase vervollständigen seit einigen Jahren das Angebot von Böhm Schweißtechnik – auch hier wieder als umfassender Service bis hin zur Feinverteilung der Gasflaschen direkt zum Anwender in Unternehmen, Krankenhäusern und bei Veranstaltungen.

40 years of Böhm welding – Family company and certified specialist

The bigger the big get, the more opportunities smaller, flexible companies have. The family-owned welding company Böhm Schweißtechnik has been successful with this strategy for 40 years now. Ernestine Böhm founded the company in 1967 as one of the first women to get involved in the tough men's business of machine trading. Her son Franz Xaver Böhm established the new company headquarters at its current site in Salzburg-Schallmoos in 1988.

With its warehouse in Innsbruck and a sales network that spans all Austria, Böhm Schweißtechnik is today a highly specialised partner to industry, trade and agriculture. Consulting and training, plants, service and materials – Böhm Schweißtechnik offers complete end-to-end solutions with its 14 employees, and it is constantly and systematically expanding its range. For example soldering has many benefits in car body construction and in repairing sheet metal. These include the much lower costs and reduced effort involved in finishing and greater energy efficiency. Technical gases round off the Böhm Schweißtechnik product range, and here too the services cover the entire spectrum, right through to dispersing the gas bottles directly to the users in companies, hospitals and at events.

KR Franz Xaver Böhm engagiert sich in Wien und Brüssel für seine Branche

KR Franz Xaver Böhm is committed to helping his industry in Vienna and Brussels

Tel: +43 662-87 00 29-0

Seit 2006 wird mit der TU-München kooperiert und hat die Akademie der Wissenschaften wieder ein Institut (Geo-Informatik) in der Stadt Salzburg eröffnet. Die Christian-Doppler-Labors stellen die Brücke zu Forschung und Entwicklung im industriellen Bereich her.

Salzburg – im Herzen Österreichs, im Zentrum Europas

Schon in alten Zeiten kreuzten sich die Verkehrswege – vor den Alpen von Ost nach West und durch die Alpen von Nord nach Süd – in Salzburg. Heute sind es die Autobahnen und Bahnlinien, welche diese Funktion übernehmen. In Zukunft soll auch die europäische Hochleistungsbahn durch Salzburg laufen. Der zweitgrößte Flughafen Österreichs, der Wolfgang Amadeus Mozart-Airport, ergänzt diese hervorragende Qualität der Erreichbarkeit. Viele Logistikfirmen, aber auch Handelsniederlassungen, nutzen diesen Standortvorteil. So hat die zweitgrößte Handelsfirma Österreichs, die Firma SPAR, ihre Zentrale in Salzburg errichtet.

Salzburg – Leben und arbeiten, wo andere Urlaub machen

Trotz Betriebsamkeit und weltstädtischem Gehabe, trotz Lärm, Verkehr und Bautätigkeit ist Salzburg eine kleine Stadt mit allen Vorteilen der Kleingliedrigkeit, Überschaubarkeit und sozialen Sicherheit geblieben. Die Nähe zur und die enge Verflechtung mit der Landschaft und den mannigfachen Grünräumen in und um die Stadt bieten hervorragende Rahmenbedingungen für ein Leben in Salzburg. In wenigen Minuten erreicht man weitläufige Grünbereiche; die Berge und Seen des Alpenvorlandes und des Salzkammergutes liegen in Griffweite. Wandern, Rad fahren, Biken, Bergwandern, Klettern, Schwimmen, Segeln, Golfen…, all das ist in kürzester Zeit erreich- und erlebbar.

Der Freizeitwert der Stadt und ihrer Umgebung ist kaum zu überbieten. Dazu kommen das reichhaltige Kultur- und Vergnügungsangebot und nicht zuletzt die Einkaufsmöglichkeiten von internationalem Standard.

Qualitätvolles Salzburg

Nicht nur der Standort an sich, sondern auch die hier erbrachten Produkte gewährleisten Qualität auf allen Ebenen. Salzburg sieht sich als eine Quelle der Inspiration. Inspirierend sind die Festspiele, inspirierend sind die Natur, die Kulisse der Stadt, die Architektur der historischen wie der modernen Stadt und nicht zuletzt das soziale Klima. Es hat seinen Grund, dass ein Mozart, ein Karajan, ein Max

Salzburg – at the Heart of Austria, in the Centre of Europe

Salzburg has always been the point where the old trading roads came together – along the Alps from east to west and through the Alps from north to south. Today it is the motorways and railway lines that plays this role for. In the future, the European high-performance railway is to run through the state. The second-largest airport in Austria, Wolfgang Amadeus Mozart Airport, rounds off this outstanding quality of accessibility. Many logistics companies and trading offices exploit this location advantage, such as Austria's second-largest trading company SPAR, which has its head office in Salzburg.

Salzburg – Living and Working where others go on Vacation

Despite the busy hustle and cosmopolitan carryings-on, despite noise, traffic and construction activity, Salzburg has always remained a little town with all the advantages of simplicity, visibility and social security that small towns have to offer. The proximity to and close interrelationship with nature and the innumerable park areas in and around the city make living in Salzburg a pleasure. Expansive green belts are just minutes away and the mountains, lakes, foothills and the Salzkammergut region are only a little further afield. Hiking, cycling, mountain biking, mountaineering, climbing, swimming, sailing, golf… it is all just around the corner to be enjoyed.

The leisure-time options are second to none in this city. And then there are the rich cultural and amusement offerings and the shopping opportunities of international standing that help make Salzburg an excellent place to be.

Salzburg Quality

Not only the location itself, but also the products it gives birth to ensure top quality. Salzburg is a source of inspiration. The Festival is inspiring, the nature is inspiring, the city, the architecture – historical and modern – and not least of all the social scene. There is good reason why people like Mozart,

Reinhardt, ein Christian Doppler, ein Dietrich Mateschitz oder Hubert Palfinger hier zu Hause waren bzw. sind. Salzburg steht heute für Begriffe wie sympathisch, einzigartig, international, lebendig, laut, geschmackvoll, traditionell, reich, für Lebensqualität, Paradies und Kultur. Diese Werte sollen gepflegt und erhalten werden.

Weitere Attribute wie jung, bunt, sportlich, vielseitig, fortschrittlich sollen gezielt entwickelt und verfolgt werden. Der Standort Salzburg verspricht dem Touristen einen angenehmen und interessanten Urlaub, dem Unternehmer einen Firmenstandort, an dem Großes entstehen kann, dem Studenten erstaunliche Bewusstseinserweiterungen, dem Kulturliebhaber unvergessliche Kunstgenüsse und dem Bewohner ein Leben in einer intakten und vielseitig nutzbaren Umwelt. ◀

Karajan, Max Reinhardt, Christian Doppler, Dietrich Mateschitz and Hubert Palfinger chose or choose to live in Salzburg. For it is a city that today stands for words like lovable, unique, international, lively, loud, good taste, traditional, rich, quality of life, paradise and culture. And these are all values that Salzburg aims to nurture and maintain.

In addition, it also aims to promote attributes such as young, colourful, sporty, multifaceted and progressive. Salzburg promises its tourists a pleasant and fascinating holiday, its industrialists a place to base their companies where great things can happen, students an astounding broadening of horizons, culture fans unforgettable arts and residents a life in a healthy environment that can be benefited from and used in many ways. ◀

„magazin" heißt das gastronomische Konglomerat am und im Salzburger Mönchsberg, das u.a. eine Accessoiresboutique rund um Küche, Tisch und Liftstyle umfasst

"magazin" is the name of the gastronomic conglomerate on and around Salzburg's Mönchsberg. It encompasses, among other things, a boutique for kitchen, table and lifestyle accessories

Mag. Gritlind Kettl
Geschäftsführerin
StandortAgentur
Salzburg GmbH

Salzburg – ein Wirtschaftsstandort voller Inspiration

Salzburg und seine Wirtschaft sind ein Gespann, das seit vielen Jahren für positive Schlagzeilen sorgt. Der Wirtschaftsstandort Salzburg floriert; ein Blick auf die Wirtschaftsdaten zeigt das ganz deutlich. Salzburg zählt zu den innovativsten und wettbewerbsstärksten Regionen Europas und ist in den wichtigsten Wirtschaftbereichen Spitzenreiter im nationalen und internationalen Vergleich. So befindet sich Salzburg seit Jahren in punkto Beschäftigung, Kaufkraft und Ausbildungsstandards im Ranking der Bundesländer on Top und präsentiert sich somit als überregionaler Vorzeige-Standort.

Eine ausgeglichene Größenstruktur der Betriebe, technisch anspruchsvolle Spezialprodukte, Exportorientierung, eine günstige Verkehrslage und gute Infrastruktur sowie verlässliche und kompetente Mitarbeiter und eine intakte Umwelt sind einige der Erfolgsfaktoren des Wirtschaftsstandortes Salzburg.

SALZBURG ALS ATTRAKTIVER STANDORT

Heute konkurrieren nicht nur einzelne Unternehmen auf den internationalen Märkten; in den vergangenen Jahren hat der Wettlauf der Standorte und Regionen immer mehr an Bedeutung gewonnen. In diesem Wettlauf hat Salzburg ausgezeichnete Karten. Die Zentrallage zwischen den Wirtschaftszentren München und Verona sowie die hervorragende Verkehrsanbindung sprechen ebenso für den Standort Salzburg wie auch das Angebot an Aus- und Weiterbildung. Fachhochschulen und Universitäten decken den Bedarf an Hightech-Arbeitskräften ab. Zahlreiche internationale Universitäten offerieren Bildungsangebote in Salzburg, und eine Vielzahl an öffentlichen und privaten Bildungsstätten stellen hochwertige Programme im Bereich der postgradualen Ausbildung zur Verfügung. All das erfolgt immer in Abstimmung mit der regionalen Wirtschaft und deren Bedürfnissen.

Salzburg verfügt über ein über die Grenzen hinaus bekanntes Image. So bieten Stadt und Land Salzburg nicht nur eine einmalige Natur und einen außergewöhnlich hohen Erholungswert, sondern eines der vielfältigsten Kulturangebote der Welt. Internationale Persönlichkeiten und Entscheidungsträger versammeln sich alljährlich zu zahlreichen kulturellen, gesellschaftlichen und wirtschaftlichen Anlässen in der Mozartstadt.

Salzburg – a commercial venue full of inspiration

Salzburg and its commercial sector are a team that has been making great headlines for many many years. The commercial venue Salzburg is flourishing; one glance at its economic data shows this very clearly. Salzburg is one of the most innovative and competitive regions in Europe and a national and international leader in the most important economic fields. For example, in terms of employment, buying power and educational standards, Salzburg has been the top of the rankings ahead of the other Austrian states for years, making it an international showpiece.

A balanced size structure of the companies, technically qualitative special products, an export orientation, a favourable location for transport, a strong infrastructure, reliable, expert human resources, and a healthy natural environment are just some of the success factors of this commercial location.

SALZBURG IS AN ATTRACTIVE COMMERCIAL VENUE

Today, not only individual companies compete on the international markets. In recent years the race between the cities and regions has become ever more important. Salzburg is a good bet for a win in this race. Its central position between the commercial centres Munich and Verona and its excellent traffic connections speak for Salzburg, as does the education and vocational training offering here. Colleges and universities produce enough high-tech staff for the market. Numerous international universities offer training courses in Salzburg, and numerous public and private educational institutes provide top-quality post-graduate training pro-

links:
W&H Dentalwerk Bürmoos –
Werk II

unten:
Synea LS Schnittmodell –
Schnellläufer

left:
W&H Dentalwerk Bürmoos –
Plant II

bottom:
Synea LS cutaway model –
high-speed machine

W&H – Im Mittelpunkt steht der Mensch

Mit einem Exportanteil von über 95% in über 80 Länder zählt das Familienunternehmen W&H Dentalwerk Bürmoos GmbH zu den weltweit bedeutendsten Anbietern zahntechnischer Präzisionsgeräte. 3 Produktionsstätten, 13 Vertriebsgesellschaften in Europa sowie vier internationale Sales Manager machen W&H zu einem der innovativsten Unternehmen in der Dentalwelt.

Die Produkte, deren Schwerpunkt bei rotierenden Bohrantrieben für die Zahnbehandlung liegt, kommen in Zahnarztpraxen, Zahnkliniken, Dentallabors und in der Mikrochirurgie zur Anwendung.

Viele Patente und Erfindungen beweisen qualitatives Niveau und Kompetenz. W&H arbeitet gemäß dem hohen Anspruch eines Qualitätsmanagement-Systems nach Anhang II der Richtlinie 93/42/EWG, ISO 13485 und erfüllt den Qualitäts-Standard GMP (Good Manufacturing Practice).

Export in 80 Länder der Welt

Verantwortung, Teamgeist und Harmonie sind die Grundpfeiler des Unternehmens W&H. Das perfekt organisierte Vertriebsnetz garantiert den Kunden in allen Ländern zuverlässige Betreuung und technischen Service.

W&H – The person is the focus

With an export share of over 95% to more than 80 countries, the family-owned company W&H Dentalwerk Bürmoos GmbH is one of the world's largest suppliers of precision dental appliances. 3 production sites, 13 sales companies and four international sales managers make W&H one of the most innovative companies in the dental world.

The products – predominantly rotating drill motors – are used in dental practices, dental clinics, dental laboratories and microsurgery.

Numerous patents and inventions bear witness to our high levels of quality and expertise. W&H employs a quality management system pursuant to Annex II of Guideline 93/42/EEC, ISO 13485 and fulfils the GMP (Good Manufacturing Practice) standard.

Exports to 80 countries

Responsibility, team spirit and harmony are the pillars of W&H. The perfectly organised sales network guarantees the customer reliable support and technical service all over the world.

www.wh.com

Salzburg ist auf den Weltmärkten zu Hause

Eine starke Exportorientierung, eine boomende und wettbewerbsstarke Salzburger Wirtschaft sowie enorme jährliche Exportzuwachsraten kennzeichnen die dynamische und international aktive Wirtschaft unseres Landes.

Die produzierende Industrie befindet sich an der Spitze der Warenexporte, wobei Nahrungsmittel und Getränke, Holz, Papier und Holzprodukte, Maschinen, Anlagen, KFZ-Zubehör, Medizin-Technik sowie Elektro/Elektronik die exportstärksten Branchen Salzburgs darstellen.

Hohe Produktivität und Innovation, verbunden mit der starken Exporttätigkeit der heimischen Wirtschaft, lassen den Konjunktur- und Beschäftigungsmotor gehörig brummen.

Salzburg nützt perfekt seine Chancen, spielt auf dem internationalen Parkett mit und ist auf den Weltmärkten zu Hause.

Salzburg setzt auf persönliche Betreuung

Salzburg ist ein Standort, der offen ist für jede Neu-Investition, die einen wirksamen Know-how-Transfer und Innovationsschub ermöglicht und gewährleistet. Diese Offenheit und Flexibilität spiegeln sich auch in der serviceorientierten Betreuung von Investoren aus dem In- und Ausland wider.

Gute Wirtschaftsdaten, hervorragende Infrastruktur, eine wirtschaftsfreundliche Verwaltung und eine ebensolche Wirtschaftspolitik, eine außergewöhnliche Lebensqualität: Salzburg ist ein guter Boden für Investitionen – ein Boden, der gepflegt werden will.

Salzburg bietet deshalb Unternehmern und Investoren – schnell und unkompliziert – professionelle, individuell abgestimmte Unterstützung an. Eine gemeinsame Betriebsansiedlungs- und Standortmarketing-Gesellschaft von Stadt und Land Salzburg (www.salzburgagentur.at) begleitet Interessenten am Standort als zentrale Koordinationsstelle durch den gesamten Investitionsprozess, knüpft Kontakte, bereitet Informationen bedarfsgerecht auf, gibt wichtige Tipps, vermittelt Experten im Förder-, Innovations- und Steuerwesen und vieles andere mehr. Als Informations- und Service-Drehscheibe bietet sie interessierten in- und ausländischen Unternehmen einen „Rundum-Service" bei der Ansiedlung von Betrieben bzw. bei ihrer Investitionstätigkeit oder bei der Suche nach Kooperationspartnern in Salzburg. Das Leistungsangebot ist kostenlos und steht inländischen wie ausländischen Unternehmen gleichermaßen zur Verfügung.

grammes. And all this is coordinated to fit the human resource needs of the regional economy.

Salzburg's image crosses borders. The city and the state of Salzburg not only offer a unique natural environment and an extraordinary quality of leisure time activities, but also one of the most varied cultural offerings in the world. International celebrities and decision-makers gather in the Mozart city every year at numerous cultural, social and economic occasions.

Salzburg is at home on the markets of the world

A strong export orientation, a booming and highly competitive economy and enormously high export growth rates are features of the dynamic and internationally active economy of our state.

The manufacturing industry is at the forefront of goods exports, with foods and beverages, wood, paper and wood products, machines, plant engineering, automotive accessories, medical technology and electrical/electronic goods representing the biggest export sectors in Salzburg.

High productivity, innovation and the strong export activity in the domestic economy are keeping the economic and employment motor humming.

Salzburg makes the most of its chances, is a player on the international stage and is at home on the world's markets.

Salzburg is personal

Salzburg is open to any new investment that makes effective know-how transfer and innovative progress possible. This openness and flexibility is reflected in the service orientation towards domestic and international investors.

Good economic data, excellent infrastructure, a commerce-friendly administration and political economic policies that support it and an outstanding quality of life: Salzburg is a sound foundation for investments – and one that we want to build on.

Which is why Salzburg offers companies and investors fast, uncomplicated, professional and individual support. A commercial settlement and location marketing company initiated by the city and state of Salzburg (www.salzburgagentur.at) accompanies enterprises interested in moving to Salzburg through the investment process, makes contacts, provides tailored information, gives important tips, recommends innovation, promotion and tax experts and much much more besides. As an information and service hub it offers interested domestic and international parties a full service when moving

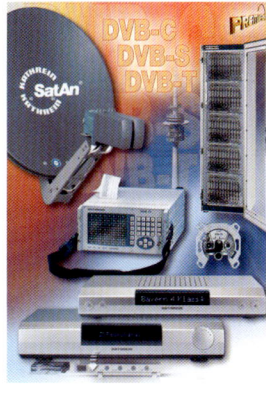

oben:
KATHREIN Parabolantenne, Receiver, Messgerät und UFO compact-Aufbereitung

links:
Professionelle Sendetechnik und Systemkomponenten für die Automobilindustrie

above:
KATHREIN dish antenna, receiver, measurement device and UFO compact format

left:
Professional transmission technology and system components for the automobile industry

KATHREIN – Qualität macht ihren Weg

Die KATHREIN Vertriebsgesellschaft m.b.H., ein selbstständiges Tochterunternehmen der KATHREIN-Werke in Rosenheim, ist seit mehr als 35 Jahren in Österreich erfolgreich tätig. Mit den Niederlassungen in Wien/Innsbruck/Gratkorn und der Zentrale in Salzburg ist es KATHREIN gelungen, sich als der Partner für den österreichischen Fachhandel und Installateur zu profilieren. Weiters zählen zum Kundenkreis Kabelnetzbetreiber, GSM/UMTS-Netzbetreiber sowie Institutionen wie Rettung, Feuerwehr und Polizei.

KATHREIN-Produkte sind heute Inbegriff für Qualität und Zuverlässigkeit. In folgenden Produktbereichen sind wir am Markt ganz vorne zu finden: Satellitenempfangsanlagen für alle Bereiche, CATV-Produkte für den Kabelnetzbetreiber, hochwertige Messgeräte, Autofunkantennen sowie Funkantennen für GSM und UMTS.

KATHREIN weltweit

Die KATHREIN-Firmengruppe beschäftigt heute weltweit ca. 7 000 Mitarbeiter und ist in 70 Ländern positioniert. In den 57 KATHREIN-Gesellschaften sind allein in den letzten 2 Jahren mehr als 2 000 Arbeitsplätze geschaffen worden. Der Gruppenumsatz erreichte 2006 ca. € 1,3 Milliarden. An der Spitze dieses erfolgreichen Unternehmens steht mit Prof. Dr. Anton Kathrein der persönlich haftende geschäftsführende Gesellschafter der KATHREIN-Werke KG.

KATHREIN – Quality prevails

The marketing company KATHREIN Vertriebsgesellschaft m.b.H., an independent subsidiary of KATHREIN-Werke in Rosenheim, has been active on the Austrian market for more than 35 years. With branches in Vienna/Innsbruck/Gratkorn and its head office in Salzburg, KATHREIN has succeeded in becoming the partner of preference for specialist traders and technical firms in Austria. Also among its customers are cable network operators, GSM/UMTS network providers and institutions such as emergency rescue services and the police and fire departments.

KATHREIN products are the embodiment of quality and reliability. We are among the market leaders in all the following product fields: satellite receivers, CATV products for cable network operators, high-precision measurement devices, auto radio antennas and radio antennas for GSM and UMTS.

KATHREIN worldwide

The KATHREIN group of companies employs around 7,000 staff in 70 countries. In the last two years alone, more than 2,000 jobs have been created in the 57 KATHREIN companies. The consolidated sales were € 1.3 billion in 2006. Prof. Dr. Anton Kathrein, the personally liable managing shareholder of KATHREIN-Werke KG, is at the head of the enterprise.

www.kathrein-gmbh.at

SYSTEM STANDBAU –
Individualität ist Kopfarbeit

Rudolf Angermayr, Geschäftsführer von Österreichs führenden technischen Veranstaltungs-Dienstleistern SYSTEM STANDBAU und EXPOXX, setzt das in die Tat um, was andere möglicherweise gerade erst andenken: one-to-one-Dienstleistungen auf oberstem Niveau vom Erstkontakt bis zur Übergabe des fertigen Produkts.

Stoff aus dem Erfolge sind
Die Entwicklung der SYSTEM STANDBAU gleicht einer beispiellosen Erfolgsstory: Als Kleinunternehmen im Jahre 1974 gegründet, verweist das Unternehmen inzwischen auf eine mehr als 30-jährige Entwicklung. Heute sorgen die rund 155 Spezialisten dafür, dass alles wie am Schnürchen läuft: von der CAD-Planung bis hin zur schlüsselfertigen praktischen Umsetzung.

Rudolf Angermayr und seine Teams können in Salzburg, Wien, Wels und Düsseldorf unangefochten ihre nationale Führungsposition bzw. internationale Relevanz ausbauen.

Eine kurze Reaktionszeit von der Marktanalyse bis hin zur Marktanpassung und Neupositionierung eines Geschäftsfeldes ist ein entscheidender Faktor, um im Geschäft erfolgreich zu sein! „Dabei kann nicht nur small, sondern auch big beautiful sein, nämlich dann, wenn dadurch die Leistungsbreite des Angebots für unsere Kunden zunimmt. Individualität und Wendigkeit des Kleinen, gepaart mit der Dienstleisterpotenz des Großen, und dies zu einem überaus attraktiven Preis-/Leistungs-Verhältnis – das ist die Mischung, aus dem Geschäfts-Erfolge heute gesponnen werden", skizziert SYSTEM STANDBAU/EXPOXX-Chef Rudolf Angermayr die entscheidenden Bausteine. Wie ein roter Faden zieht sich dabei der Faktor Qualität durch den gesamten Kundenkontakt. Dies betrifft nicht nur die handwerkliche Qualität in der praktischen Umsetzung, sondern auch das Know-how der einzelnen Mitarbeiter, die natürlich mit der modernsten Präsentationstechnik auf „Du und Du" sind.

Wir liefern alles
Natürlich sind die Ausstattungsprofis von SYSTEM STANDBAU und EXPOXX nicht nur die richtigen Ansprechpartner bei speziellen Einzellösungen, sondern auch bei Komplettlösungen von Veranstaltungen wie Kongressen und Events, also abseits vom Messemarkt. „Den Zeichen von morgen mit der Technik von heute schon gestern gefolgt zu sein", so Rudolf Angermayr, „das macht eben die entscheidende Stärke unseres Unternehmens aus."

www.systemstandbau.at
www.systemstandbau.eu
www.expoxx.at

SYSTEM STANDBAU –
Individuality is achieved first in the mind

Rudolf Angermayr, general manager of Austria's leading technical event service companies SYSTEM STANDBAU and EXPOXX, already provides what others are just starting to contemplate doing: top quality one-to-one services from the first contact to the delivery of the finished product.

The things success is made of
SYSTEM STANDBAU is an unparalleled success story: founded as a small company in 1974, it now has 30 years of experience behind it, and today around 155 specialists keep it running smoothly – from CAD planning through to turnkey implementation.

Rudolf Angermayr and his teams in Salzburg, Vienna, Wels and Düsseldorf are uncontested in their position as national market leader and are building up international relevance.

Rapid reaction times from market analysis to the adjustment and repositioning of a business field are decisive factors if one wants to be successful in this business! "And not only small can be beautiful here. When being big means a better range of services for our customers, it can be attractive too. The individuality and manoeuvrability of a small company coupled with the service potency of a large one, and good value for money, are the building blocks on which successful business are constructed these days", says SYSTEM STANDBAU/EXPOXX boss Rudolf Angermayr. Quality is the key; not only in the craftsmanship but also in the know-how of each team member and expertise with the latest presentation technologies. It spans the entire contact with the customer.

We deliver everything
Of course the professionals at SYSTEM STANDBAU and EXPOXX are not only the right people to contact for special individual fair solutions, they can also organise entire congresses and other events that go way beyond trade conferences. As Rudolf Angermayr puts it: "The decisive strength of our company is in having already used today's technology yesterday to follow the signs of the future."

1 Fa. Linde-Gas auf der „VIENNATEC", Gesamtfläche 100 m²

2 Fa. Lohberger auf der „INTERNORGA", Gesamtfläche 77 m²

3 Fa. Philips auf der „FUTURA", Gesamtfläche 548 m²

4 Fa. Doppelmayr auf der „SAM", Gesamtfläche 432 m²

---

1 Linde-Gas at the "VIENNATEC", total area 100 m²

2 Lohberger at the "INTERNORGA", total area 77 m²

3 Philips at the "FUTURA", total area 548 m²

4 Doppelmayr at the "SAM", total area 432 m²

87

Salzburg als Filmland

Salzburg ist nicht nur durch seine Schönheit und Historie ein idealer Schauplatz für viele TV- und Filmproduktionen, sondern auch Standort von namhaften Filmunternehmen und einer Fachhochschule als Ausbildungszentrum, die das Profil des Filmstandortes abrunden. Um diese Position und die Salzburger Filmwirtschaft zu stärken, wurde in der StandortAgentur Salzburg eine Filmlocation eingerichtet. Diese Service- und Beratungsstelle bietet als erste Anlaufstelle für kommerzielle Film- und Fernsehproduktionen mit internationalem Vertrieb gebündelte Hilfestellungen und Dienstleistungen aus einer Hand an. Von Serien oder Filmen, die über das Fernsehen ein Millionenpublikum erreichen, profitiert der Standort Salzburg in mehrfacher Hinsicht. Neben der Werbewirkung, die für den Salzburger Tourismus entsteht, stellen Filmproduktionen als eine Art temporäre Betriebsansiedlungen einen wichtigen Wirtschafts- und Beschäftigungsfaktor für die Region dar und bieten Geschäftsmöglichkeiten für die zahlreichen Salzburger Unternehmen der IT-, Medien- und Filmwirtschaft.

Salzburg verbindet

In Salzburg redet man miteinander. Die Wirtschaft in Salzburg setzt auf ein starkes Miteinander. Früher war das Bild des Unternehmers das eines Einzelkämpfers, der auf sich allein gestellt durch stürmische Wirtschaftswasser segelte. Heute gewinnt die Erkenntnis Oberhand, dass Wirtschaft viel mit Teamsport zu tun hat. Ganz nach dem Motto: Jeder bringt seine Stärken ein, denn gemeinsam sind wir nun einmal stärker. So lebt erfolgreiches Standortmanagement davon, den Finger am Puls der Zeit zu haben und die Bedürfnisse der Beteiligten optimal zu bedienen. Heute die Trends von morgen erkennen: Diese Devise steht ganz weit oben, wenn es darum geht, Salzburg auch in Zukunft als attraktives Ziel für Investoren zu etablieren und die richtigen Leute zusammen zu bringen. ◄

their business here, when investing or when looking for cooperation partners in Salzburg. The services are free of charge and available to Austrian and foreign enterprises alike.

Salzburg the film land

Salzburg is not only an ideal setting for many TV and film productions due to its natural beauty and history, it is also the home of renowned film companies and a film academy for young aspiring filmmakers. To support this industry here, a film location has been set up at the StandortAgentur Salzburg. This advisory service is the first stop for commercial film and television production companies, and offers international sales assistance and services. Salzburg profits in many different ways from series and films that reach large audiences via television. In addition to the advertising effect these have for Salzburg's tourism, film productions are a kind of temporary company settlement that drive employment and further the economy, providing business opportunities for the many Salzburg companies in the IT, media and film industry.

Salzburg unites

People talk with each other in Salzburg. The Salzburg economy is built on a strong sense of togetherness. There was a time in which the entrepreneur was seen as a lone warrior, sailing solo against the stormy winds of commercial competition. Today people are becoming aware that commerce has a lot to do with teamwork. Everyone brings their strengths into the mixture and together we are stronger. And so, location management thrives on having its finger on the pulse of the times and precisely serving the needs of the market participants. We aim to recognise tomorrow's trends today; and this is paramount when it comes to establishing Salzburg as an attractive place for investors and bringing the right people together. ◄

IFK – als Allroundprofi bei Kabel, Leitungen und Rohren

Als mittelständisches Familienunternehmen stellt die IFK Firmengruppe seit über 35 Jahren eine fixe Größe in der Elektrobranche dar. Im Bereich der **Verlege- und Pflügetechnik** gelten wir sogar als europaweiter Technologieführer. Mit unserem eigenen **Kabelverlegepflug** stellen für uns selbst Spezialitäten wie das Einpflügen von Kabeln und Rohren bis 500 mm Durchmesser oder das Verlegen von bis zu 40 Rohr- und Kabelelementen in einem Arbeitsschritt kein Problem dar. Die maximale Verlegetiefe liegt bei 2,25 m. Wir liefern auf Wunsch auch die Dokumentation der Verlegedaten bis hin zum fertigen Katasterplan.

Unsere großzügigen Lagerflächen an unserem Hauptstandort **Salzburg** ermöglichen die umfangreiche Lagerung von **Kabeln, Leitungen und Zubehör**. Wir sind bekannt für kurze Reaktionszeiten und das prompt verfügbare vielfältige Kabelsortiment. Unsere Kunden schätzen besonders unsere Flexibilität und partnerschaftliche Zusammenarbeit. Zu unseren Handelswaren zählen: **Kabel und Leitungen** aller Art bis hin zu **Hochspannungskabeln** sowie sonstige Produkte rund ums Kabel wie z.B. **Schrumpfmaterial, Kabelabdeckplatten, Trassenwarnbänder, Klemmen, LWL-Rohre, Isolatoren, Klebebänder** u.v.m. Unsere Kunden sind u.a. Energieversorger, Windparkbetreiber, Elektrogroßhandel, Industrie- und Bauunternehmen, Gemeinden u.dgl.

FreshFX – New Media Spezialist

Zur Firmengruppe gehört auch die Medienproduktionsfirma FreshFX Media GesmbH, die bereits zahlreiche nationale und internationale Preise gewonnen hat. Diese junge und innovative Firma ermöglicht durch ein modernst ausgestattetes Tonstudio sowie ein eigenes Filmteam außergewöhnliche, kreative und hochwertige Produktionen im Bereich **Film & Video, 2D/3D Animationen, Visualisierungen, special FX, DVD authoring** u.v.m.

IFK – the all-round professional for cables, wires and tubing

As mid-sized family company, we have enjoyed a major position in the Austrian electrical industry for over 35 years now. We are even considered the leading European company in the **cable plow technology**. Using our own **cable plow equipment**, we can take on special underground projects such as the trenching work for cables and tubes up to 500 mm in diameter or the plowing of up to 40 tube and cable elements in a single step with no problem at all. The maximum plowing depth is 2,25 meters. If required we can provide detailed documentation of the project data including blue prints for the local authorities.

Our spacious warehouse at our headquarters in **Salzburg** provides an extensive storage area of ready-stock **cable, wire and accessories.** We have excellent reputation for short notice delivery as well as for a wide selection of immediately available warehouse-stocked cable. Our customers particularly appreciate our flexibility and collaborative partnership. We have all kinds of **cables and wires** up to high voltage cables, **heatshrink cable** accessories, cable protection covers, **warning tapes, fittings, optic fiber pipes, insulators, tapes** and much more besides. Our clientele includes energy suppliers, wind park operators, wholesalers, industrial and construction companies, municipalities etc.

FreshFX – new media specialist

Also a member of the company group is the media production company FreshFX Media GesmbH which has won numerous national and international awards. With its state-of-the-art sound studio and its own filmmaking team this young and innovative company ensures extraordinary, creative high-quality productions in the field of **film & video, 2D/3D animations, visualisations, special FX, DVD authoring etc.**

Hauptstandort Salzburg (Bürogebäude)

IFK Kabelverlegepflug FSP 20

IFK Hochregallager Salzburg

Headquarters Salzburg (office building)

IFK cable plow FSP 20

IFK High rack warehouse

---

www.ifk.at
www.freshfx.at

Als potenter Investor in den letzten zehn Jahren hat der Flughafen Salzburg Investitionen von mehr als 110 Millionen Euro aus eigens erwirtschafteten Mitteln getätigt um Kunden Komfort in angenehmer Umgebung zu bieten

---

Over the last ten years, Salzburg Airport has invested more than Euro 110 million of its own capital into ensuring its customers a comfortable airport experience in pleasurable surroundings

Flughafen als Wirtschaftsmotor

Womit punktet der Salzburger Flughafen in der Publikumsgunst? Im Linienverkehr sind es vor allem die Billigfluglinien, die mit günstigen Preisen locken. Salzburg wird von Ryanair (London, Dublin), TUIfly (Hamburg, Köln, Hannover, Berlin, Leipzig, Düsseldorf), Niki (Palma) und Thomsonfly (Manchester, Coventry) angeflogen. British Airways fliegt seit Dezember 2006 neu von London-Gatwick nach Salzburg. Reiseveranstalter bieten im Sommercharter mehr als 40 attraktive Ziele rund um das Mittelmeer an.

Der Wunsch der Salzburger, der Wirtschaft und des Fremdenverkehrs nach mehr Anbindung zu den wichtigsten europäischen Zielorten und Wirtschaftszentren konnte in den letzten Jahren zum Großteil erfüllt werden. Die Anbindung Salzburgs wird ständig verbessert. Dies ist für einen Regionalflughafen eine erfreuliche Entwicklung und ein Qualitätsmerkmal, das in einer vernetzten Welt für die Attraktivität der Region Salzburg von hoher Bedeutung ist.

Der Flughafen beschäftigt in seinem Nahbereich und mit seinen Partnern fast 1 200 Mitarbeiter. Er

The airport as an economic driving force

That makes Salzburg Airport so popular? One factor is certainly the discount airlines that land here and attract customers with low prices. Ryanair (London, Dublin), TUIfly (Hamburg, Cologne, Hanover, Berlin, Leipzig, Düsseldorf), Niki (Palma) and Thomsonfly (Manchester, Coventry) all stop in Salzburg. Since December 2006, British Airways has added a connection from London-Gatwick to Salzburg. Tour operators offer more than 40 highly attractive destinations all around the Mediterranean.

The desire of the Salzburg populace, commercial sector and tourist industry for a better connection to the key European destinations and economic centres has largely been fulfilled in recent years. Salzburg's air connection to the rest of the world is improving constantly; a particularly pleasing trend for a regional airport and an attribute that contributes greatly to the attractiveness of the Salzburg region in a closely networked world.

Together with its partners the Airport employs almost 1,200 people in the field of short-haul traffic. As a financially strong investor it has reinvested

Nur im Winter wird Amadeus terminal 2 als Wintercharterhalle verwendet, die restliche Zeit des Jahres wurde für Salzburg mit terminal 2 eine neue Event-Location geschaffen

Amadeus terminal 2 is only used as a charter terminal in winter. For the rest of the year it acts as an event venue

TUIfly (Hapagfly und Hapag Lloyd Express wurden zusammengeführt) bietet von der Mozartstadt aus gute Anbindungen an die deutschen Destinationen Berlin-Tegel, Düsseldorf, Hamburg, Hannover, Köln-Bonn und Leipzig-Halle an

TUIfly (Hapagfly and Hapag Lloyd Express have merged) offers flights from the Mozart town to the German airports Berlin-Tegel, Düsseldorf, Hamburg, Hanover, Cologne-Bonn and Leipzig-Halle

Niki Luftfahrt GmbH – kompetenter Partner von Air Berlin – beförderte 2006 mehr als 1,3 Millionen Passagiere. Von Salzburg aus bedient Niki Las Palams, Palma (Drehkreuz), Ibizza, Teneriffa, Thessaloniki, Rhodos, Heraklion, Kos, Antalia und Hurghada

Niki Luftfahrt GmbH – expert partner to Air Berlin – transported more than 1.3 million passengers in 2006. From Salzburg Niki flies to Las Palmas, Palma (hub), Ibiza, Tenerife, Thessalonika, Rhodes, Heraklion, Kos, Antalia and Hurghada

Der Salzburg Airport W. A. Mozart beschäftigt mit seinen Tochtergesellschaften (100% Tochter S.A.S Salzburg Airport Services – Handling Agent und 85%ige Tochter CARPORT – Parkverwaltung) rund 350 Menschen. Mehr als 1 200 Arbeitsplätze werden dem Flughafen insgesamt mit seinen Partnern und den ansässigen Firmen zugerechnet

Salzburg's W. A. Mozart Airport and its subsidiaries (100% subsidiary S.A.S Salzburg Airport Services – handling agent and 85% subsidiary CARPORT – parking management) together employ around 350 people. Together with its partners and the companies with offices here, the airport has a payroll of more than 1,200

hat als potenter Investor in den letzten zehn Jahren Investitionen von mehr als 110 Millionen Euro aus eigens erwirtschafteten Mitteln getätigt. Eine Untersuchung der Universität Salzburg hat in einer Studie den Sekundärnutzen des Flughafens für die Region mit 250 Millionen Euro erhoben. 43,6 Millionen Euro an Steuernutzen werden direkt durch die Aktivitäten des Flughafens ausgelöst.

Allein in den letzten Jahren investierte der Flughafen kräftig, z.B. für Sicherheitsmaßnahmen wie die neue 100% Großgepäckskontrolle. Der Salzburg Airport W. A. Mozart gehört zu 25% der Stadt Salzburg, zu 75% dem Land Salzburg. Für den Flughafen und seine Tochtergesellschaften arbeiten rund 350 Menschen. Darunter fallen auch die Arbeitsplätze der 100%igen Tochtergesellschaft S.A.S. (Handling Agent: Salzburg Airport Services) und 85%igen Tochtergesellschaft CARPORT (Parkverwaltung). Mit Behörden und ansässigen Firmen werden dem Flughafen insgesamt mehr als 1 200 Arbeitsplätze zugerechnet.

Während der Wintersaison werden regelmäßig zur Bewältigung des Flugverkehrsaufkommens etwa 140 Aushilfskräfte, vorwiegend an Samstagen, eingesetzt. Der Frauenanteil liegt bei ca. 30% der Gesamtbeschäftigten.

more than Euro 110 million of its own earnings over the last decade. In addition, a study by Salzburg University calculated the secondary benefit of the Airport for the region to be Euro 250 million. Euro 43.6 million in taxes are produced directly through the Airport's activity.

In the last years the Airport has invested heavily. For example in security installations such as the new 100% large luggage check. Salzburg's W. A. Mozart Airport is owned to 25% by the city of Salzburg and 75% by the state of Salzburg. Around 350 people work for the Airport and its subsidiaries. These include the payrolls of the 100% subsidiary S.A.S. (handling agent: Salzburg Airport Services) and 85% subsidiary CARPORT (parking management). Counting the public authorities and private companies based here, the Airport is considered to provide more than 1,200 jobs.

And during the winter season, around 140 extra helpers are called upon, mostly on Saturdays, to help cope with the extra passenger volumes. Around 30% of the employees are women.

Erfolgreiches Air Traffic Management: Austro Control (ACG) sorgt mit modernsten Technologien und professioneller Manpower für sichere Luftstraßen. Rund 3 000 Luftfahrzeuge werden täglich von den Fluglotsen in Österreich betreut

Successful air traffic management: Austro Control (ACG) keeps airways safe with cutting-edge technologies and professional staff. Air traffic controllers in Austria guide around 3,000 aircraft every day

Am Anfang stand bei Red Bull die Idee, einen Platz der Phantasie und der Begeisterung an Stelle eines pragmatischen Zweckbaus zu schaffen – einen erhebenden Ort, an dem einander die Liebe zur Fliegerei und zur Kunst begegnen... es entstand Hangar 7

It all started with an idea at Red Bull; of creating a place of imagination and enthusiasm in lieu of a pragmatic, purely functional building. An uplifting place where the love of flying and of art could meet. The result is Hangar 7

www.salzburg-airport.com

93

94

Kommerzialrat Julius Schmalz
Präsident der Wirtschaftskammer Salzburg

Wirtschaftskammer-Bildung: Von der Lehre bis zum MBA

The Economic Chamber-Education: from apprenticeship to MBA

WIFI Gebäude

WIFI building

Das WIFI ist der größte, Anbieter von berufsbezogener Aus- und Weiterbildung im Bundesland Salzburg

The WIFI, or Institute of Economic Development, is the largest vocational training institute in the state of Salzburg

Aus- und Weiterbildung von jährlich mehr als 40 000 Menschen im Bundesland Salzburg – so die beeindruckende Bilanz von „Wirtschaftskammer-Bildung". Unter dieser Dachmarke vereint die Wirtschaftskammer Salzburg alle Ausbildungsstufen von der Lehre bis zum Postgraduate-Studium und ist damit größter nichtstaatlicher Anbieter von Bildungseinrichtungen im Bundesland.

Das Angebot reicht von der Berufs- und Bildungsberatung über das Lehrlings- und Prüfungswesen bis zur berufsorientierten Aus- und Weiterbildung. Dazu kommen (Hoch-)Schul- und Postgraduate-Ausbildung sowie der Bereich Wissenschaft und Forschung.

Mit „Wirtschaftskammer-Bildung" leistet die WK Salzburg einen wichtigen Beitrag zur Standortqualität. „Das große Engagement der WKS in diesem Bereich wird auch von den Unternehmen honoriert", betont WKS-Präsident KommR Julius Schmalz. In einer aktuellen Umfrage haben mehr als 80% der Salzburger UnternehmerInnen das Bildungsengagement der WKS als „sehr wichtig" bzw. „wichtig" eingestuft.

The education and vocational training of more than 40,000 people in the state of Salzburg every year: that is the impressive statistic of the "Economic Chamber-Education". Under this brand name the Salzburg Economic Chamber brings together all educational levels, from apprentice-ships to post-graduate degrees, making it the largest non-government provider of educational facilities in the state.

Its services range from vocational and educational counselling through to trainee and examination administration, and on to vocation-oriented education and further vocational training. On top of that it also offers secondary, tertiary and post-graduate schooling and it is involved in science and research.

With the Economic Chamber-Education, the Salzburg Economic Chamber makes a major contribution to the quality of this commercial location. "This organisation's great commitment to this field is also appreciated and rewarded by the corporate sector", says Chamber president Julius Schmalz. In a recent survey, more than 80% of Salzburg's indu-

Grösstes berufliches Aus- und Weiterbildungsinstitut

Das WIFI der Wirtschaftskammer Salzburg ist mit über 20 000 TeilnehmerInnen jährlich das größte berufliche Aus- und Weiterbildungsinstitut in Salzburg. Das umfangreiche Aus- und Weiterbildungsangebot des WIFI Salzburg verteilt sich auf fünf verschiedene Standorte im gesamten Bundesland. Im vergangenen Jahr wurden mehr als 1,3 Millionen (!) Teilnehmerstunden verbucht und von 1 000 Lehrenden aus der Praxis mehr als 1 700 Veranstaltungen durchgeführt.

Top-Anbieter auch im (Hoch-) Schulwesen

An den renommierten Tourismusschulen der Wirtschaftskammer Salzburg an den drei Standorten Kleßheim, Bad Hofgastein und Bischofshofen erwerben derzeit über 1200 SchülerInnen Wissen für eine Karriere im Tourismus.

Die Fachhochschule Salzburg in der neu errichteten Campus FH in Salzburg-Urstein und am strialists considered the Chamber's involvement in education and training to be "important" or "very important".

Largest institute of vocational education and training

With more than 20,000 students every year, the WIFI (institute for economic furtherance) of the Salzburg Economic Chamber is the largest vocational training institution in Salzburg. WIFI Salzburg's enormous educational offering is shared among five locations throughout the state. Last year more than 1.3 million (!) student hours were counted and more than 1,700 classes were held by the 1,000 teachers.

Top schooling player

More than 1,200 students are presently gaining the education they will need for a career in tourism at the renowned tourism schools of the Economic Chamber in Kleßheim, Bad Hofgastein and Bischofshofen.

Das neu errichtete Gebäude der FH-Salzburg in Salzburg-Urstein bietet beste Voraussetzungen fürs Hochschulstudium

The newly erected building belonging to the Salzburg University of Applied Sciences in Salzburg-Urstein has the best facilities on offer for a tertiary education

Standort Kuchl (Holz) wird von rund 1770 Student-Innen besucht. Die 13 angebotenen Studiengänge werden im Herbst 2007 noch um zwei weitere im Gesundheitsbereich – Ergotherapie und Radiologietechnologie – erweitert.

UNIVERSITY OF SALZBURG BUSINESS SCHOOL

Neu zu Wirtschaftskammer-Bildung zählt seit Herbst 2006 die University of Salzburg Business School (SMBS). Die SMBS ist die Spitzeneinrichtung am postgradualen Bildungssektor im Wirtschafts- und Managementbereich in Salzburg mit regionaler, nationaler und internationaler Ausrichtung.

BERATUNG, AUSBILDUNG UND PRÜFUNG

Fast 8 000 Personen suchen jährlich Beratung bei der AHA!-Bildungsberatung der WKS. Die Lehrlingsstelle ist Anlauf- und Servicestelle für mehr als 10 000 Lehrlinge und 3 500 Ausbildungsbetriebe und hält rund 4 000 Lehrabschlussprüfungen ab. In der Meisterprüfungsstelle gibt es rund 600 TeilnehmerInnen bei Meisterprüfungen, 900 bei Befähigungsprüfungen und 250 bei Unternehmerprüfungen, die zur selbstständigen Führung eines Betriebs befähigen. ◂

The Salzburg Polytechnic on the new FH Campus in Salzburg-Urstein and at Kuchl (Holz) is attended by around 1,770 students. And with the addition of Ergotherapy and Radiology Technology, the 13 courses of study currently on offer here will be expanded again in autumn 2007.

UNIVERSITY OF SALZBURG BUSINESS SCHOOL

The University of Salzburg Business School (SMBS) is a new addition to the Economic Chamber's range of educational options since autumn 2006. The SMBS is the leading institution for post-graduate economic and management training in Salzburg, with a regional, national and international curriculum.

COUNSELLING, EDUCATION AND EXAMINATION

Almost 8,000 people come to the AHA!-vocational counselling centre of the Salzburg Economic Chamber every year for help in starting their career. The trainee centre is a contact and service point for more than 10,000 trainees and 3,500 training companies, and it holds around 4,000 final traineeship examinations. At the master craftsman examination centre there are around 600 master examination applicants, 900 for qualifying examinations and 250 for business administration examinations that give successful candidates the qualification to manage their own company. ◂

Der Schulstandort der Tourismusschulen-Salzburg in Kleßheim

The Salzburg Tourism School campus in Kleßheim

Das Grand Park Hotel wurde kürzlich im Spa-Bereich großzügig ausgebaut

The spa centre of the Grand Park Hotel has recently been considerably enlarged and improved

Wirtschaftskammer Salzburg: starke Interessenvertretung, Bildungsträger und Standortfaktor

Die Wirtschaftskammer Salzburg ist die gesetzliche Interessenvertretung aller Salzburger Unternehmen. Ein umfangreiches Service- und Beratungsportfolio – von der Rechtsberatung bis zum Umwelt-Coaching, vom Gründer-Service bis zur Innovations- und Förderberatung – macht die WKS zu einem enorm wichtigen Info-Partner für Salzburgs Wirtschaft.

Seit jeher ist die WK Salzburg aber auch als starker Bildungsträger im Bundesland Salzburg positioniert. Mit ihren Bildungseinrichtungen Fachhochschule Salzburg (eine 50%-Beteiligung), den international bekannten und erfolgreichen Tourismusschulen in Kleßheim, Bad Hofgastein und Bischofshofen, mit dem WIFI als größtem Weiterbildungsinstitut und anderen Beteiligungen wie der „Salzburg Management Business School" (SMBS) bietet die WKS zukunftsorientierte Qualifikation für die Salzburger Wirtschaft an.

Nicht weniger wichtig für die Standortqualität Salzburgs ist das Messezentrum, das gemeinsam von Stadt, Land und WKS betrieben wird.

The Salzburg Economic Chamber: strong representation of interests, educational promoter and location factor

The Salzburg Economic Chamber is the state lobby for all Salzburg companies. An extensive service and consulting portfolio – from legal counselling to environmental coaching, from a company founding service to innovation and sponsorship consulting – makes the Economic Chamber an eminently important partner to Salzburg's economy.

The Salzburg Economic chamber has also always been an important educational promoter in the state of Salzburg. With its educational institutions such as the Salzburg Polytechnic (50% shareholder), the internationally renowned and highly successful tourism schools in Kleßheim, Bad Hofgastein and Bischofshofen, the WIFI vocational training institute and participations in other facilities such as the Salzburg Management Business School (SMBS), the Salzburg Economic Chamber provides forward-looking qualifications for the present and future needs of the Salzburg economy.

And no less important for the quality of the Salzburg venue is the conference centre that the city, state and Chamber run together.

Bild oben:
Die WK-Salzburg bietet ein umfangreiches Service- und Beratungsportfolio

Die Wirtschaftskammer Salzburg – das Kompetenzzentrum für Salzburgs UnternehmerInnen

Picture above:
The Salzburg Chamber of Commerce offers an extensive service and consulting portfolio

The Salzburg Chamber of Commerce – the competence centre for Salzburg's entrepreneurs

www.wko.at/sbg

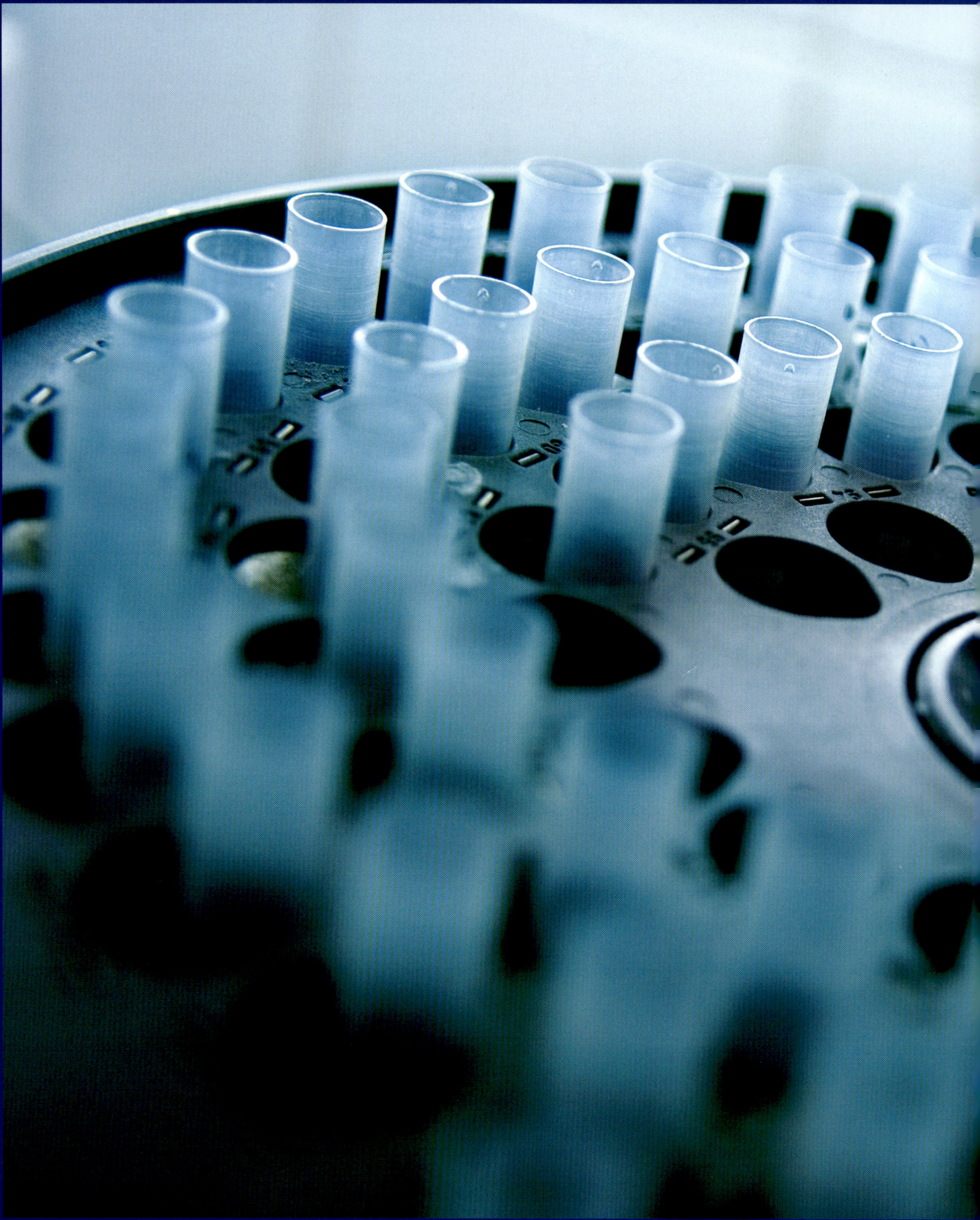

Univ.-Prof. Dr. Albert Duschl
Vizerektor für Forschung
Universität Salzburg

Die Paris-Lodron Universität Salzburg als Erfolgsgeschichte eines Europäischen Forschungsstandorts

Ein modernes Profil für die Paris-Lodron Universität und die Forschungsregion Salzburg

Paris-Lodron University of Salzburg – the success story of a European Research Venue

A modern profile for Paris-Lodron University and the research region Salzburg

Jahrzehntelang galt Salzburg international fast ausschließlich als Wiege des österreichischen Tourismus, bedingt durch Mozart und die Festspiele. Dass sich Salzburg in den letzten Jahren auch als erfolgreicher Wissenschaftsstandort etabliert hat (und damit als wesentlicher Wirtschaftspartner), ist maßgeblich der Paris-Lodron Universität zu verdanken.

Mit dem Abschluss des sechsten EU Rahmenprogramms für Forschung und Entwicklung wurde eine beeindruckende Bilanz vorgelegt – die Universität Salzburg konnte zwischen 2002 und 2006 mehr als doppelt so viele erfolgreiche Projektbeteiligungen vorweisen wie im Vergleichszeitraum zuvor. Ähnlich erfreulich haben sich die Zahlen auch in anderen Bereichen entwickelt, was in Summe dazu führt, dass im Jahr 2006 knapp 14 Millionen Euro von nationalen und internationalen Geldgebern für Forschungsprojekte an die Universität Salzburg geflossen sind. Dies zeigt die hohe Qualität von Wissenschaft und Forschung sowie die Wettbewerbsfähigkeit der Paris-Lodron Universität. Da diese eingeworbenen Gelder hauptsächlich in Stellen für den wissenschaftlichen Nachwuchs fließen, ermöglicht die aktive Forschung auch eine effiziente Nachwuchsförderung.

Die Universität möchte ihren Studierenden nicht nur möglichst gute Bedingungen für das Studium bieten, sondern ihnen auch eine Ausbildung mitgeben, mit der sie später auf dem Arbeitsmarkt

For decades, due to the overwhelming reputation of Mozart and the Salzburg Festival, the world considered Salzburg to be more or less merely the home of Austrian tourism. But, largely thanks to Paris-Lodron University, Salzburg has also established itself as an important scientific and educational venue in recent years (and thus as a key economic partner).

The completion of the sixth EU Framework Programme for research and technological development brought with it some impressive results – Salzburg University was able to boast more than twice as many successful project participations between 2002 and 2006 than during the same previous period. And the improvement in the numbers in other segments has been similarly pleasing, which ultimately means that in 2006, national and international investors pumped around Euro 14 million into Salzburg University for research projects. This bears witness the quality of the education and research at Paris-Lodron University and just how competitive this university is. As this money mainly goes towards helping young academics, the active research done here also helps produce new young high-potentials.

The university not only wants to provide its students with the best possible conditions for their education, it also wants to ensure that the education they gain gives them the best possible chances for subsequent success on the labour

Bibliothek und Landeskarten-Saal in der Juridischen Fakultät

The library and map room at the faculty of Laws

beste Chancen haben. Die dynamische Wechselwirkung zwischen den Zielen von Lehre und Forschung einerseits und den Anforderungen der Wirtschaft an Absolventinnen und Absolventen andererseits wurde 2006 besonders eindrucksvoll mit der Errichtung eines Bachelor Studiums der Ingenieurwissenschaften verwirklicht. Das Studium wird in Kooperation mit der TU München angeboten, die in Deutschland als eine von drei Eliteuniversitäten ausgezeichnet worden ist. Die Industriellenvereinigung hat – wie auch Land und Stadt Salzburg – dieses neue Studienangebot erheblich unterstützt und konnte durch eine von ihr durchgeführte Umfrage die Nachfrage nach technisch-naturwissenschaftlichen UniversitätsabgängerInnen im gesamten Raum Salzburg bestätigen. Mit dem Entwicklungsplan der Universität 2005-2010, bei dem einzelne technische Disziplinen gestärkt werden sollen, nähert sich der gesamte Standort Salzburg dem so genannten Lissabon-Ziel der EU, das eine Anhebung der F&E Quote von einem Prozent vorsieht.

Die Schwerpunktsetzung der Universität erweist sich als besonders vielversprechend für den Standort Salzburg

Mit gezielten Schwerpunktsetzungen wurden und werden Stärken der Paris-Lodron Universität Salzburg gestärkt und somit Synergien gefördert. Bei-

market. The dynamic reciprocity between the goals of education and research on the one hand and the demands that the economic sector places on graduates on the other was accounted for impressively in 2006 with the establishment of a Bachelor degree in engineering. This degree is offered in cooperation with Munich Technical University, which has been named one of three elite universities in Germany. Together with the state and city of Salzburg the Industrialists' Association has provided considerable support for this new degree, and was able to confirm the demand for technical/scientific university graduates in the Salzburg region in a survey it held. With the university's development plan for the years 2005-2010, which provides for an intensification of specific technical disciplines, Salzburg as a whole moves closer to the EU Lisbon objective of raising the R&D quota by one percent.

The focuses that the university has chosen are proving to be very promising for Salzburg

The special strengths of Paris-Lodron University have been further improved and synergies created by setting specific focuses. For example, the Computer Science and Communication Science departments work together with a focus on ICT&S (Information and Communication Technolgies & Society). These are two disciplines that acted largely

Substanzen, die in Zukunft in der Allergietherapie ihren Einsatz finden sollen, werden von Salzburger WissenschafterInnen mit modernsten molekularbiologischen Techniken entwickelt

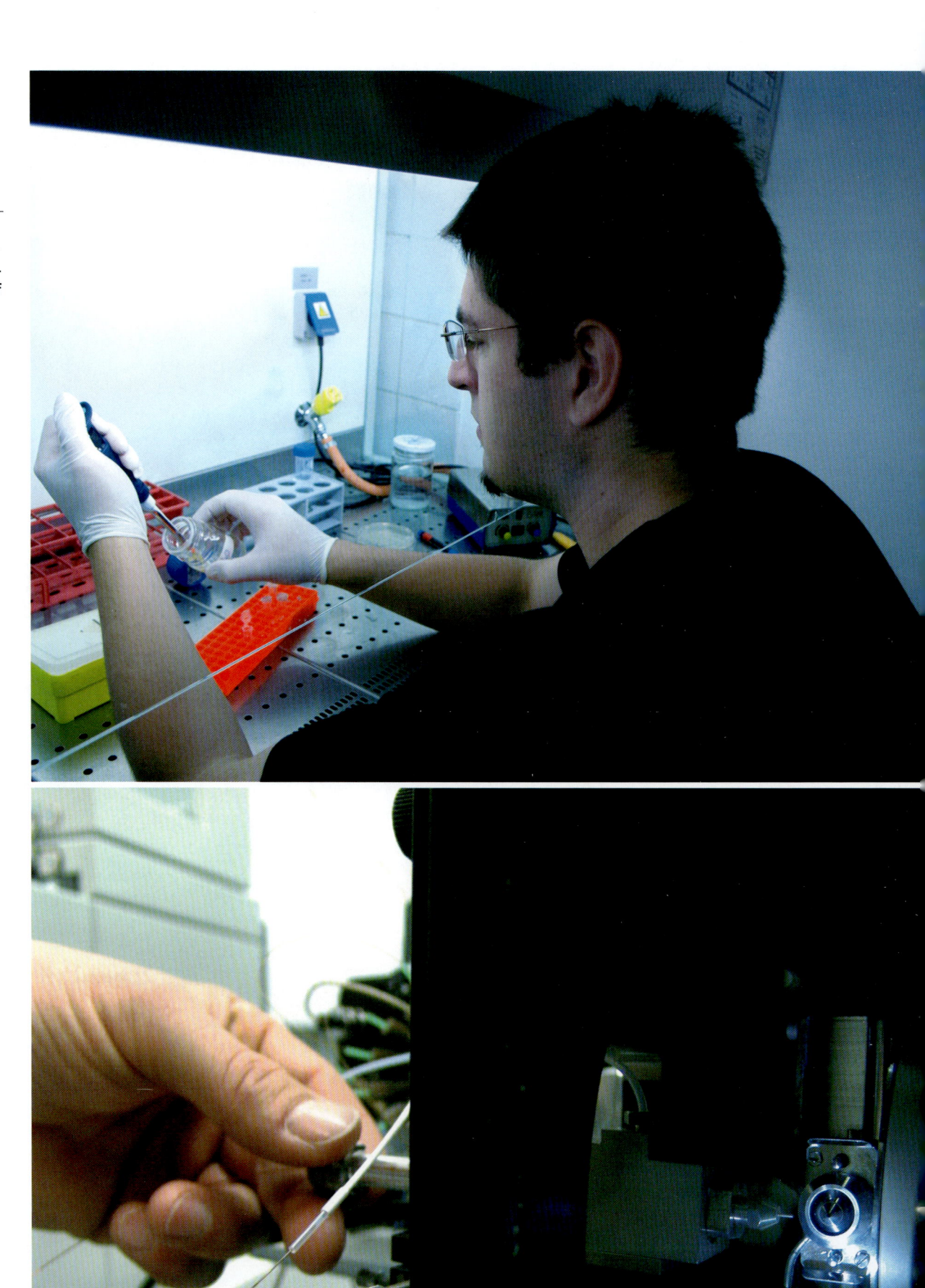

Salzburg scientists use cutting-edge molecular biology technologies to develop substances for use in the field of allergy therapy

spielsweise arbeiten im Schwerpunkt ICT&S (Information and Communication Technolgies & Society) Computer- und Kommunikationswissenschaften zusammen, zwei Disziplinen, die in den vergangenen Jahren weitgehend autonom gehandelt haben, obwohl es in der Praxis wichtige Verbindungen gibt, etwa unter den Schlagwörtern eGovernment oder Kommunikation im öffentlichen Raum. Die Arbeit in diesen zukunftsträchtigen Bereichen wurde ausgebaut, und es wurde eine Plattform geschaffen, die es auch anderen ermöglicht, daran teilzuhaben. Der Fokus des ICT&S Schwerpunktes ist die Beschäftigung mit den Auswirkungen der digitalen Technologien wie beispielsweise des Internets auf unsere Gesellschaft. Mit einer Professur für Usability, bekleidet durch Prof. Manfred Tscheligi, stellt der Schwerpunkt ICT&S einen enormen Mehrwert für Wirtschaftspartner aus der Region dar. Die Möglichkeit, Produkte auf ihre Nutzerfreundlichkeit zu testen, wird von vielen Firmen in der Region in Anspruch genommen, so beispielsweise von der Fa. Ruwido, einem Hersteller von Fernbedienungen. Derartige Kooperationen sind besondes nützlich, wenn sie in nationale wie internationale Forschungsprojekte münden, wie im Falle von ICT&S und Ruwido in ein so genanntes BRIDGE Projekt – ein Brückenschlagsprogramm der FFG, welches Grundlagenforschung unterstützt, die wiederum in ein angewandtes Forschungsthema mündet.

Die Christian Doppler Labors der Paris-Lodron Universität Salzburg

Nie zuvor ist es in der Geschichte der österreichischen Universitäten einer Hochschule gelungen, in einem Jahr drei Christian Doppler Labors zu etablieren, jene Einrichtungen, die als renommierteste technisch-wissenschaftliche Forschungsinstitutionen Österreichs in Zusammenarbeit mit der Wirtschaft gelten und längst über unsere Grenzen hinaus wahrgenommen werden. Ziel der Kooperation zwischen Wissenschaft und Wirtschaft ist es, Erkenntnisse der Grundlagenforschung dem Partner aus der Wirtschaft zugänglich zu machen und die Forschungsergebnisse in der Entwicklung neuer Technologien anzuwenden.

Vorreiter und Begründer des Christian Doppler Labor-„Booms" an der Universität Salzburg ist Prof. Erich Müller. Seine langjährige Kooperation mit der Fa. Atomic mündete 2004 in das erste Christian Doppler Labor in Salzburg: „Biomechanics in Skiing".

Prof. Fatima Ferreira gelingt es als zweiter Frau in Österreich überhaupt, mit dem CD Labor „Allergiediagnostik und Therapie", gemeinsam mit der Pharmafirma Biomay, wichtige Akzente im Kampf gegen die Volkskrankheit Allergie zu setzen. Prof. Wolfgang Pree – gemeinsam mit AVL List – entwick-

autonomously in the past, although there are im-portant connections between them in professional practice, for example in the fields of e-government and communication in public spaces. The work in these forward-looking fields has been expanded and a platform set up that also enables others to take part. The focus of ICT&S is learning about the effects of digital technologies like the Internet on our society.

With a professorship for Usability, held by Prof. Manfred Tscheligi, the ICT&S activities represent an enormous added value for commercial partners from the region. Many companies in the region take the chance to test products for their user-friendliness, for example the company Ruwido, which makes remote controls. Cooperations like these are especially beneficial when they result in national research projects. In the case of ICT&S and Ruwido a so-called BRIDGE project has arisen, a bridging programme of the FFG that supports fundamental research that leads to an applied research topic.

The Christian Doppler laboratories of Paris-Lodron University of Salzburg

Never before in the history of Austrian universities has an institute of tertiary education succeeded in establishing three Christian Doppler loaboratories within the space of one year. These facilities are viewed as the most renowned technical-scientific research institutions in Austria formed together with the commercial sector, and they have long been well known beyond Austria's borders. The goal of the cooperation between the academic and commercial sectors is to make knowledge gained from fundamental research accessible to the commercial partner and to use the results of the research to develop new technologies.

The pioneer and founder of the Christian Doppler laboratory "boom" at Salzburg University is Prof. Erich Müller. His cooperation of many years' standing with the company Atomic brought about the first Christian Doppler lab in Salzburg – Biomechanics in Skiing – in 2004.

With her CD lab "Allergy Diagnostics and Therapy", made together with the pharmaceuticals company Biomay, Prof. Fatima Ferreira succeeded in setting important accents in the fight against the

Prof. Fatima Ferreira gelingt es als zweiter Frau in Österreich überhaupt, mit dem CD Labor „Allergiediagnostik und Therapie", gemeinsam mit der Pharmafirma Biomay, wichtige Akzente im Kampf gegen die Volkskrankheit Allergie zu setzen

Prof. Fatima Ferreira was the second woman in Austria to make key steps in the fight against allergies, with her Christian Doppler laboratory "Allergy Diagnostics and Therapy" and working together with the pharmaceuticals company Biomay

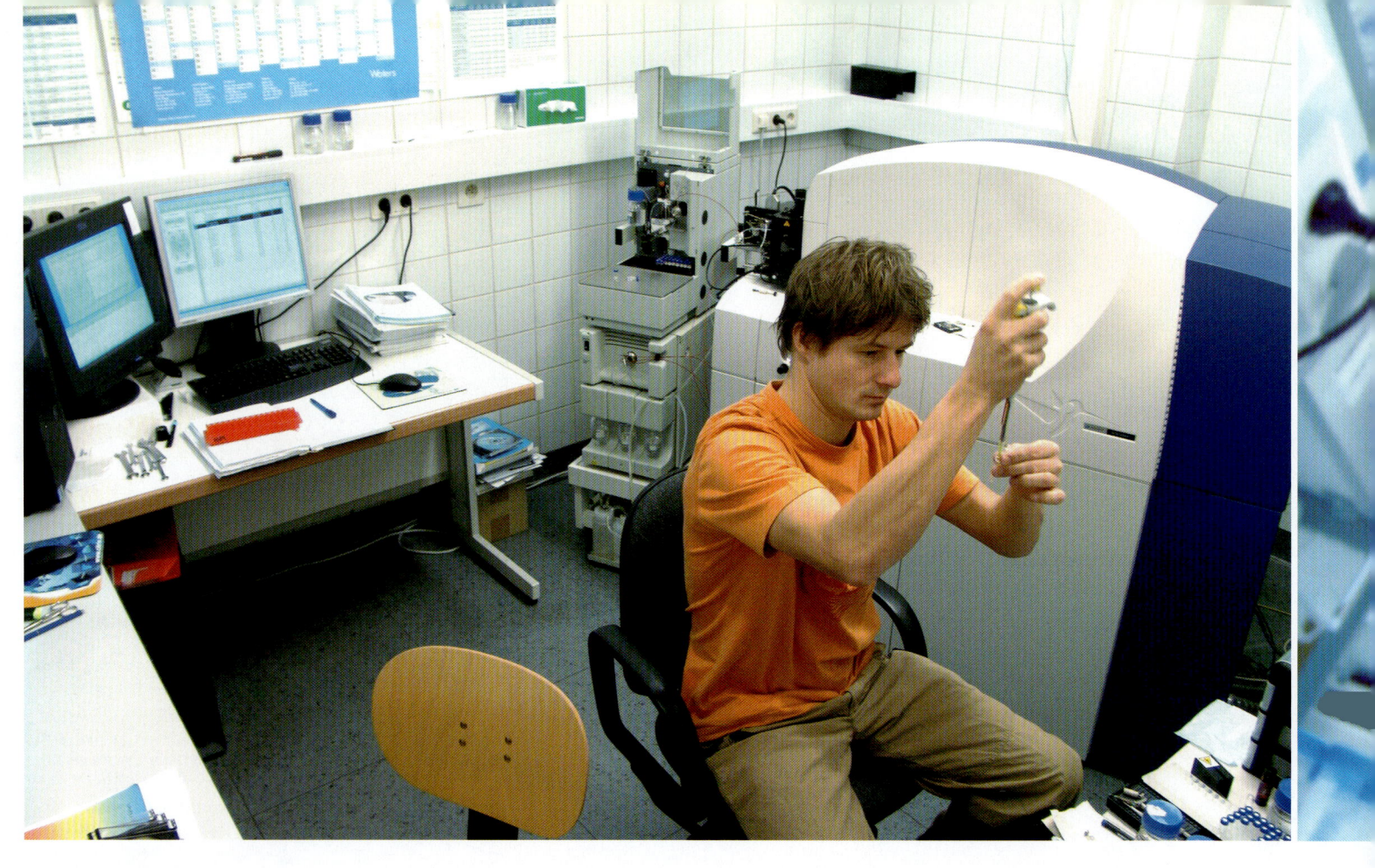

Im Labor für Allergiediagnostik und -therapie werden künstlich hergestellte Therapeutika in ihre Bestandteile zerlegt und deren Eigenschaften genauestens analysiert

In the laboratory for allergy diagnostics and therapy, artificial therapeutic agents are broken down into their component parts and their characteristics analysed in detail

elt mit dem CD Labor „Embedded Software Systems" am Fachbereich Computerwissenschaften innovative, mobile Steuerungselemente für Fahrzeuge. Prof. Herbert Dittrich hat mit dem Prozessanlagenhersteller von Mikrochips SEZ AG das CD Labor „Anwendung von Sulfosalzen in der Energiewandlung" am Fachbereich Materialforschung und Physik aufgebaut.

Was aber haben alle diese Initiativen gemeinsam? Der hohe Innovationsgehalt in der Forschung der beteiligten Arbeitsgruppen ist nicht nur für Fachwissenschaftler interessant, sondern auch für die Wirtschaft, in vielen Fällen im Raum Salzburg angesiedelt, oft aber auch über die Landesgrenzen hinaus. Dazu kommt, dass Christian Doppler Labors einen hohen Wahrnehmungsfaktor aufweisen und es in Folge zu zahlreichen weiteren Kooperationen mit anderen wissenschaftlichen Arbeitsgruppen, aber auch mit Wirtschaftspartnern, kommt.

Awareness und Steigerung der Kooperationen Wissenschaft und Wirtschaft im Raum Salzburg

In den letzten Jahren hat sich gezeigt, dass Sichtbarkeit und positive Wahrnehmung des Forschungsstandortes Salzburg auch ein wesentlicher Faktor für die Verbesserung des Wirtschaftsstandortes selbst sind. Langfristige Kooperationen zwischen Wissenschaft und Wirtschaft ergeben sich in der Regel nur auf Grund von positiven Erfahrungen

widespread problem of allergies. Prof. Wolfgang Pree and AVL List have developed innovative, mobile control elements for motor vehicles with the CD lab "Embedded Software Systems" in the Computer Science department. Prof. Herbert Dittrich has built up the CD lab "The Application of Sulphosalts in Energy Conversion" with the process plant maker of microchips SEZ AG in the Materials Research and Physics department.

But what do all these initiatives have in common? The high level of innovation in the research of the work groups involved is not only interesting for scientists, but also for the economy, both here in Salzburg and right out to beyond the national borders. In addition, the Christian Doppler labs are very well known and they lead to numerous further co-operations with other scientific work groups and commercial partners.

Awareness and intensifying the cooperation between science and commerce in the Salzburg region

In recent years it has become apparent that the visibility and positive perception of the research venue Salzburg are a key factor for the improvement of the commercial venue as a whole. Lasting cooperations between science and commerce generally only arise if both sides have had good experiences in such collaborations in the past. All the more important it is for getting these processes up and running to

auf beiden Seiten. Um diese Prozesse in Gang zu bringen, ist es umso notwendiger, die Forschungsprojekte der Universität zum einen sowie die Anforderungen der Wirtschaft zum anderen sichtbar zu machen.

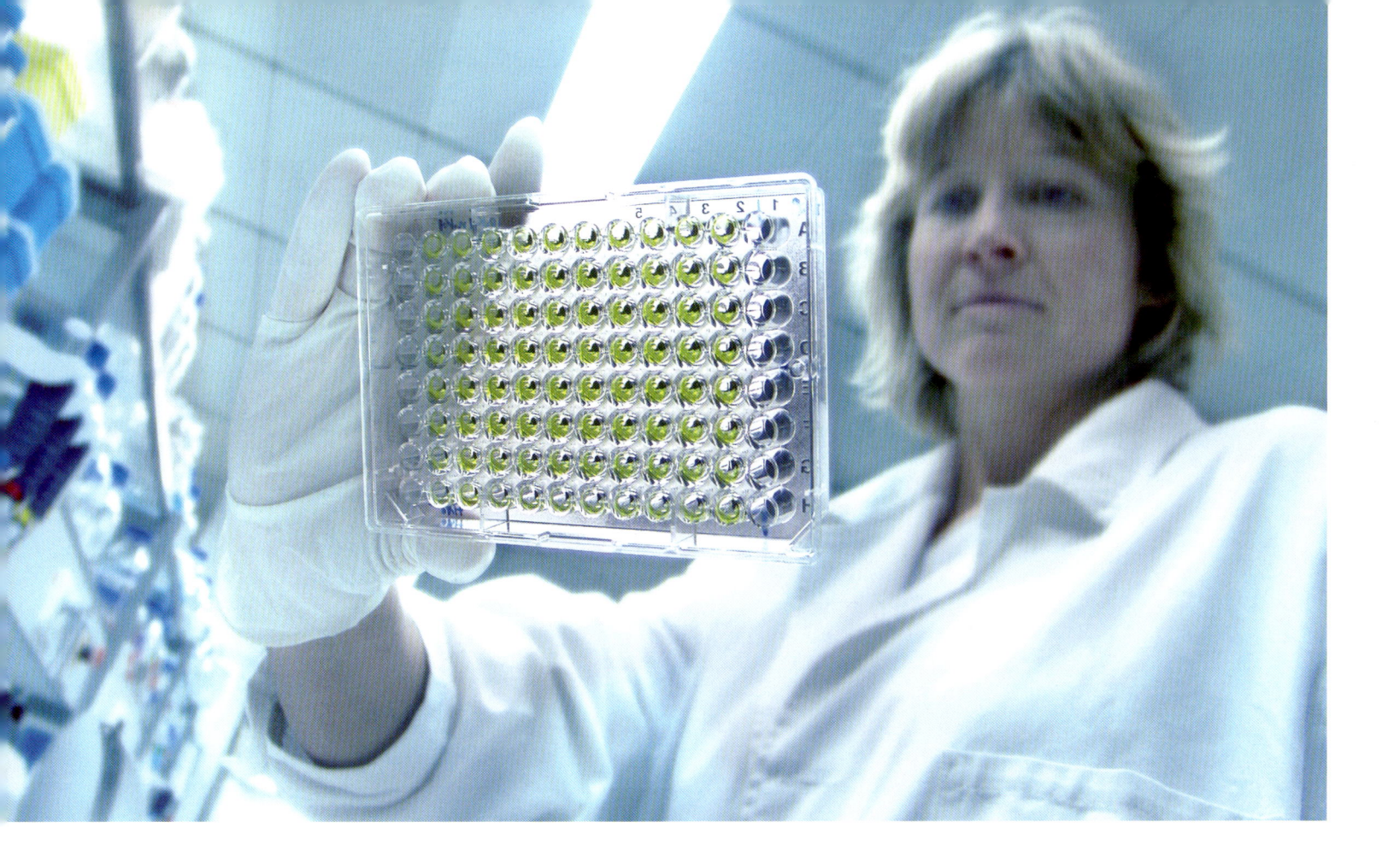

Mit University meets Business setzt die Paris-Lodron Universität neue Akzente, um die Zusammenarbeit zwischen den beiden Welten Wissenschaft und Wirtschaft anzukurbeln und neue Projekte zu generieren. An Hand von drei ausgewählten Projekten werden exzellente Kooperationen einem Publikum von Entscheidungsträgern aus Wirtschaft und Politik vorgestellt. 2006 waren dies das Zentrum für Geoinformatik (Prof. Strobl), gemeinsam mit der Salzburger Firma WiGeoGis, der Schwerpunkt Biowissenschaften und Gesundheit (Prof. Brandstetter) mit der Firma Bruker Austria sowie der interfakultäre Fachbereich für Sport- und Bewegungswissenschaft (Prof. Erich Müller) mit der Firma Atomic.

Die Unterstützung seitens der Industriellenvereinigung Salzburg, des Austria Wirtschaftsservices und zahlreicher anderer Partner aus Wirtschaft und Politik zeigt, wie richtig die Universität Salzburg mit dieser Initiative liegt – und wie günstig dies auch für die Salzburger Wirtschaft ist.

Die Veranstaltungsreihe uni:hautnah funktioniert nach einem ähnlichen Prinzip, sie richtet sich aber in erster Linie an eine breite Öffentlichkeit. Im November jeden Jahres wird der Europark für drei Tage zu einer wissenschaftlichen Erlebniswelt.

make sure the university's research projects and the economy's requirements are visible.

With "University meets Business" Paris-Lodron University is providing new impulses to stimulate cooperation between the two worlds of science and commerce and to generate new projects. Three selected projects are being used to present excellent cooperations to an audience of decision-makers from the economic and political sectors at present. In 2006 these were the Centre for Geoinformatics (Prof. Strobl) together with the Salzburg company WiGeoGis, Biosciences and Health (Prof. Brandstetter) with the company Bruker Austria and the interfaculty department for Sports and Movement Science (Prof. Erich Müller) with Atomic.

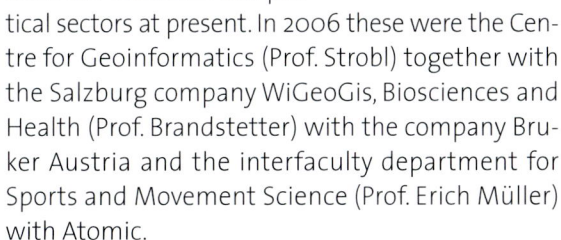

The support from the Salzburg Industrialists Association, the Austria Commercial Service and numerous other partners from industry and politics shows that Salzburg University is on the right track with this initiative, and how good this is for Salzburg's economy.

The event series "uni:hautnah" (uni:upclose) works on a similar principle, but it is aimed princi-

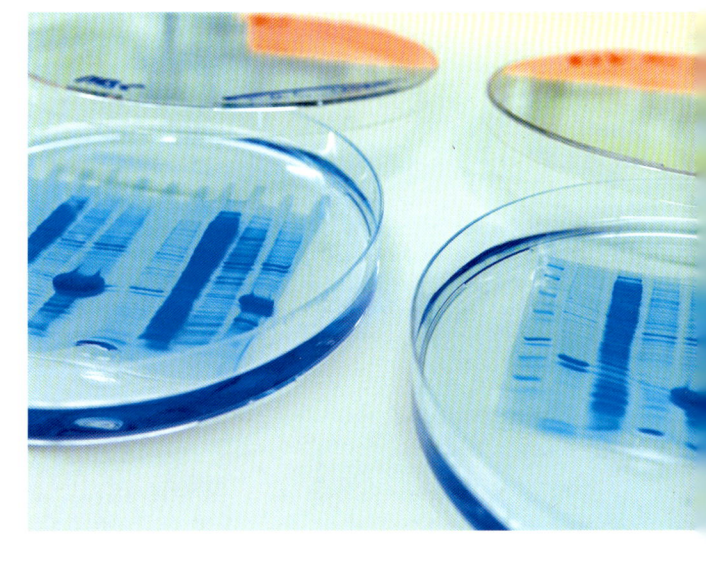

Besucherinnen und Besucher des größten Salzburger Einkaufszentrums haben die Möglichkeit, an wissenschaftlichen Versuchen selbst mitzuarbeiten – die vorgestellten Projekte bieten Wissenschaft zum Anfassen. Dass sich diese Attraktion rasch zu einem Lieblingsereignis der Salzburger Kinder entwickelt hat, liegt nahe. Erwachsene sind aber ebenso angetan; und dass sich in Folge immer wieder neue Forschungskooperationen ergeben haben, unterstreicht den Erfolg des Konzepts. Mehr als 60 000 Salzburgerinnen und Salzburgern demonstriert uni:hautnah alljährlich, wie spannend und abwechslungsreich Forschung sein kann.

Fazit: Die Paris-Lodron Universität Salzburg hat in den letzten Jahren die richtigen Akzente gesetzt und in Salzburg einen Mikrokosmos für erfolgreiche europäische Forschungspolitik etabliert. Die Profilbildung bzw. die damit verbundenen Schwerpunktsetzungen sowie eine kontinuierliche, attraktive Darstellung von Forschungsthemen nach außen hin führten zu zahlreichen nationalen und internationalen Kooperationen. Ob vier Christian Doppler Labors in zwei Jahren, eine Steigerung der Drittmitteleinwerbungen um mehr als 70 Prozent in vier Jahren oder die bevorstehende Errichtung des Uniparks in Salzburg/Nonntal – der Paris-Lodron Universität Salzburg scheinen die Ideen nicht auszugehen. Das ist gut so, sowohl für den Wirtschaftsstandort als auch für den Wissenschaftsstandort Salzburg. ◀

pally at a broad public. Every year in November the Europark is transformed into a wonder world of scientific discovery and adventure for three days. Visitors to this the largest Salzburg shopping centre are given the opportunity to work on scientific experiments. The projects presented offer accessible science, so it comes as no surprise that this attraction has quickly progressed into one of the famous happenings among Salzburg's children. Adults are just as enthused, though, and the fact that new research cooperations have always resulted underscores the success of the concept. uni:hautnah demonstrates to more than 60,000 Salzburg citizens every year how exciting and varied research can be.

Summary: Paris-Lodron University of Salzburg has laid the right foundations in recent years and established a microcosm for successful European research politics in Salzburg. The profile that has been developed, the focuses that go with it, the continuous development and the attractive presentation of research topics to the public lead to numerous international cooperations. Whether it be the four Christian Doppler laboratories set up in the last two years, the more than 70% increase in outside funding in the last four years or the construction of the Unipark in Salzburg/Nonntal, Paris-Lodron University of Salzburg never seems to run out of ideas. And that is good, both for the commercial and for the scientific venue Salzburg. ◀

uni: hautnah – die Forschungsschau im Europark weckt alljährlich großes Interesse an den Forschungsleistungen der Universität Salzburg

uni: hautnah – The academic fair held in the Europark arouses great interest in the research done at Salzburg University every year

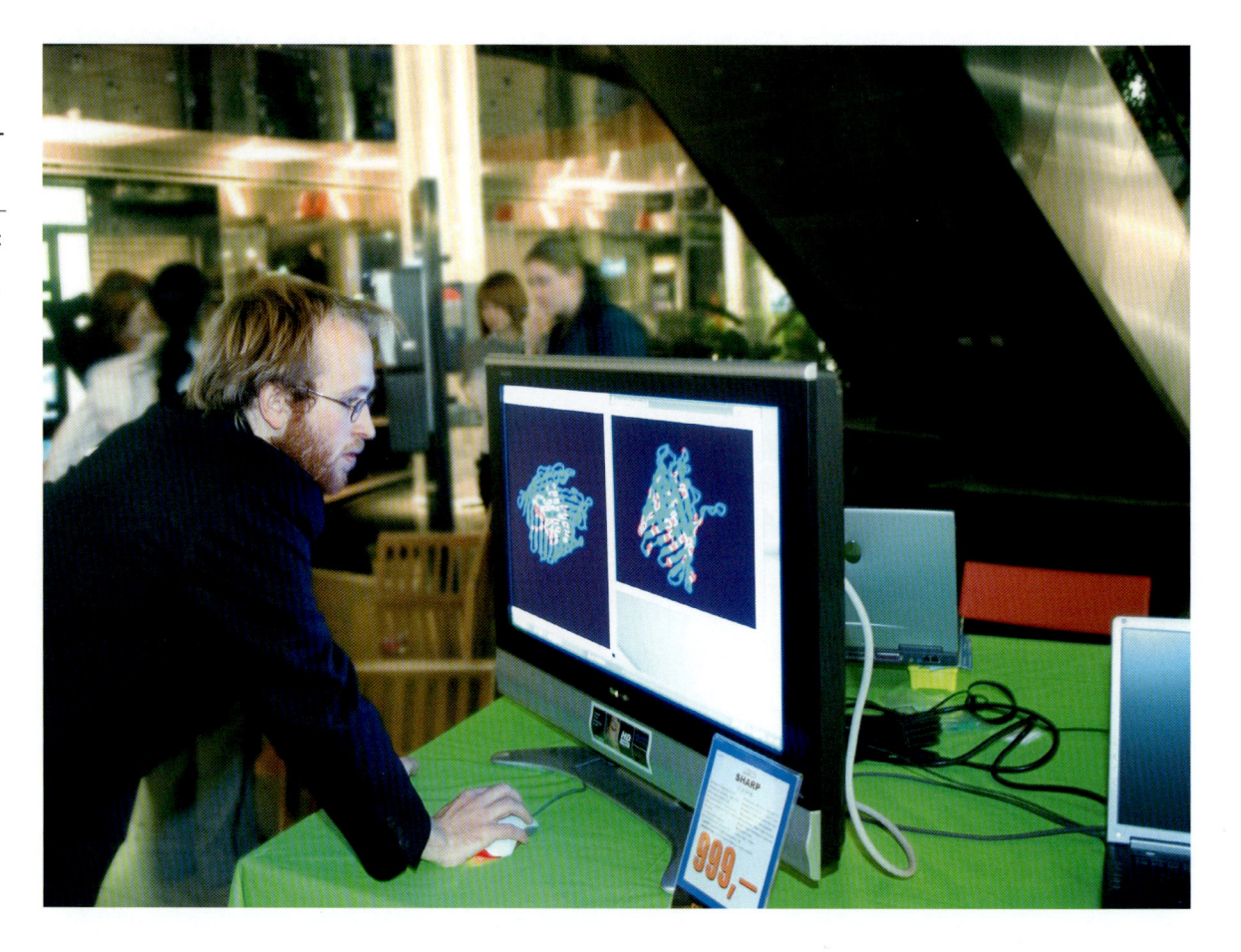

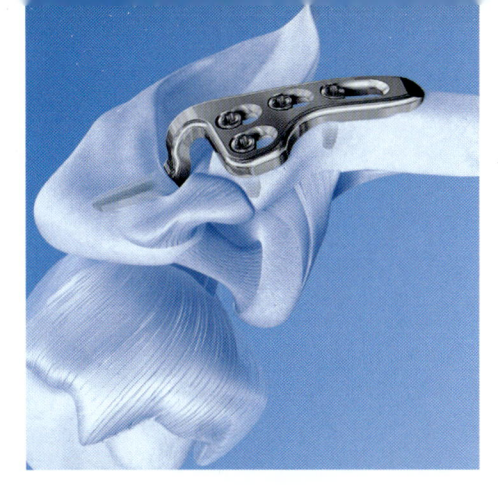

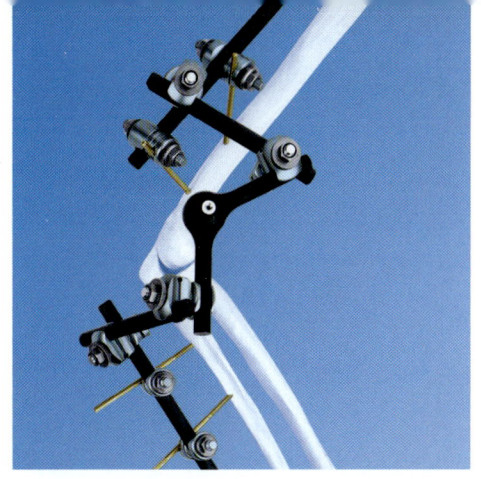

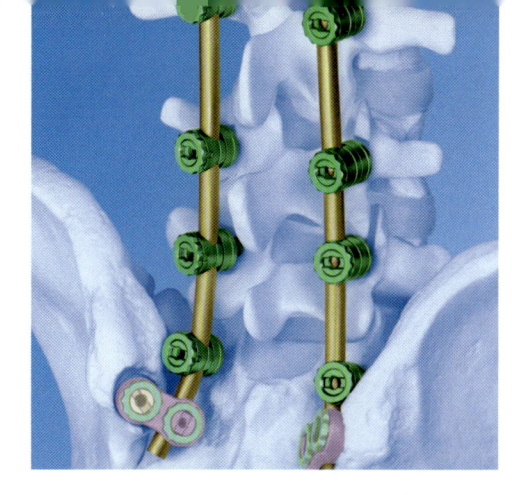

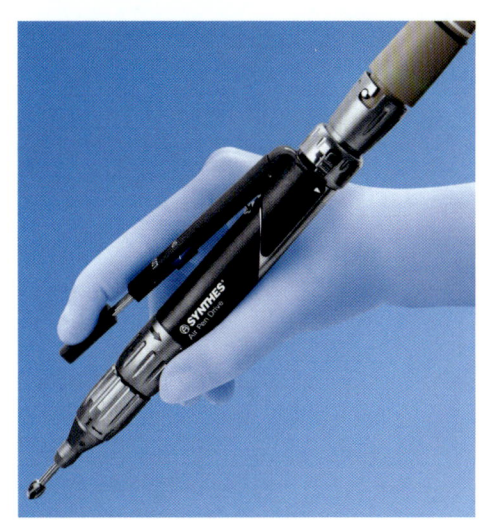

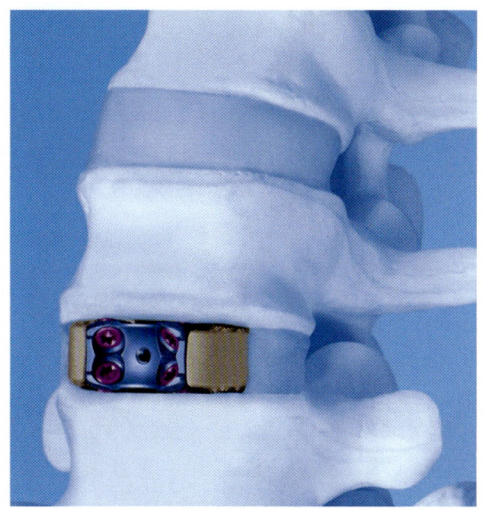

Synthes Österreich GmbH, Salzburg

wurde 1963 als Tochtergesellschaft der Mathys AG Bettlach, Schweiz, gegründet und ist seit 2004 ein Tochterunternehmen von Synthes Inc., einem der weltweit führenden Produzenten von Implantaten und Instrumenten für die Traumatologie.

Synthes Österreich mit Firmensitz in Salzburg ist der österreichische Repräsentant für Originalinstrumente und -implantate der AO/ASIF (Arbeitsgemeinschaft für Osteosynthesefragen) und beschäftigt zurzeit ca. 45 Personen in den Bereichen Verkauf, Marketing, Kundenservice und Administration. Zusätzlich produzieren etwa 55 hoch qualifizierte Mitarbeiter Implantate und Instrumente.

Synthes ist verbunden mit der AO/ASIF und unterstützt deren Trainingsprogramm durch Organisation und Bereitstellung von Kursmaterial.

Qualitativ hochwertige Implantate und Instrumente bilden die Basis für erfolgreiche Operationen! Synthes Österreich sieht seine Mission darin, die Anforderungen und Wünsche seiner Kunden dadurch zu erfüllen, Instrumente, Implantate und Maschinen für die Behandlung von Knochenfrakturen in den Bereichen Traumatologie, Wirbelsäulen-, Maxillofazial- und Neurochirurgie anzubieten. Die herausragende Qualität von Synthes Implantaten und Instrumenten ist ein wesentlicher Grund für den weltweiten Erfolg.

Synthes Austria GmbH, Salzburg

was founded in 1963 as a subsidiary of Mathys AG Bettlach, Switzerland and has been a subsidiary of Synthes Inc., one of the world's leading producers of implants and instruments in the field of traumatology since 2004.

Synthes Austria with its registered office in Salzburg is the official representative for original instruments and implants of the AO/ASIF (Association for the Study of Internal Fixation) in Austria and currently employs around 45 people in sales, marketing, customer service and administration. In addition, about 55 highly qualified employees produce implants and surgical instruments.

Synthes is associated with the AO/ASIF and supports its educational program by organizing events and supplying course material.

High-quality implants and instruments are the basis for successful operations! Synthes Austria sees its mission in fulfilling its customers' needs by providing them with implants, instruments and power tools for the treatment of bone fractures in the fields of traumatology, spine, cranio-maxillofacial and neuro surgery. The outstanding quality of Synthes implants and surgical instruments is one of the main reasons for the global success of this brand.

Verschiedene Synthes Produkte

Several Synthes products

www.synthes.com

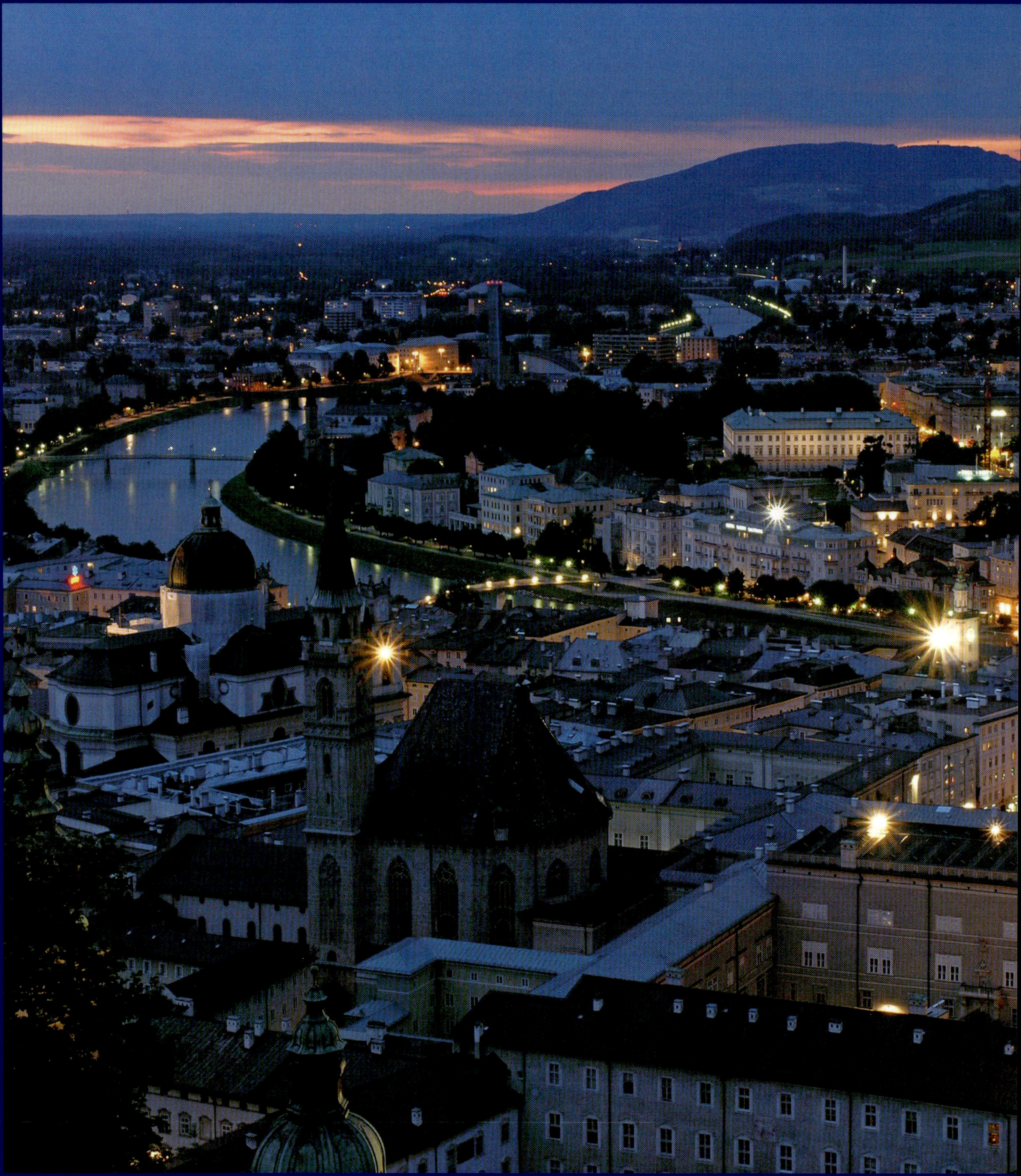

MMag. Herbert Brugger
Tourismus Salzburg GmbH

Salzburg – eine Stadt von Weltformat

Salzburg – a Cosmopolitan City

Selten findet man auf kleinem Raum ein dermaßen harmonisches Zusammenspiel zwischen Landschaft und Architektur, Kunst und Kultur, Tradition und Moderne, wie es Salzburg seinen Besuchern zu bieten vermag. Ein Spaziergang durch die von Mönchs-, Festungs- und Kapuzinerberg eingerahmte und den Fluss Salzach geteilte Stadt lässt Geschichte atmen und überrascht gleichzeitig mit spannenden Ausblicken auf Modernes. Die Fakten sind liebenswert und beeindruckend zugleich.

Salzburg zählt nur rund 150 000 Einwohner, jedoch mehr als 4 000 Kulturveranstaltungen jährlich und an die 20 barocke Kirchenbauten.

Salzburg war bereits zur Römerzeit eine bedeutende Verwaltungsstadt, an einer wichtigen Heerstraße und Nord-Süd-Verbindung gelegen. Gegründet gegen Ende des 7. Jahrhunderts, wurde die Stadt bis zu Beginn des 19. Jahrhunderts von unabhängigen katholischen Fürsterzbischöfen regiert, die auch die politische Macht inne hatten. Reichtum und Wohlstand sind auf den jahrhundertelangen Handel mit Salz zurückzuführen, dessen Einkünfte es den Landesherren ermöglichte, eine Stadt zu erbau-

Seldom can one find such a harmonious interaction of landscape and architecture, art and culture, tradition and modernity in such a small space as Salzburg offers its visitors. A stroll through this town; framed by the Mönchsberg, Festungsberg and Kapuzinerberg hills and bisected by the Salzach river, immerses you in history while at the same time surprising with enthralling glimpses of the present day and future. The facts are both endearing and impressive.

Salzburg has a population of only 150,000, but more than 4,000 cultural events a year and around 20 Baroque churches.

As long ago as during Roman rule, Salzburg was already a major administrative town situated on a key military road and north-south connection. Founded at the end of the 7th century, the town was governed by independent catholic Prince Archbishops until the early 19th century. Their prosperity was based on centuries of trade with salt, and the income this generated enabled the religious/political leaders to build a city that is often referred to as the "Rome of the North", due to its Italian flair. And the "white gold" salt even lent the city its name.

**Der barocke Salzburger Dom beherrscht das Bild der Altstadt. Sein Architekt Santino Salari stammte aus Italien und schuf den bedeutendsten Kirchenbau jener Zeit nördlich der Alpen.
Hoch über der Stadt auf dem Mönchsberg thront die mittelalterliche Festung Hohensalzburg**

**The Baroque Salzburg Cathedral dominates the cityscape of the Old Town. With it, the Italian architect Santino Salari created the greatest church structure of his time north of the Alps.
High above the city on the Mönchsberg stands the medieval fortress Hohensalzburg**

en, die mit ihrem italienischen Flair als das „Rom des Nordens" bezeichnet wird. Das „weiße Gold", das Salz, verlieh der Stadt ihren Namen.

Der berühmteste Sohn der Stadt verzaubert bis heute Musikliebhaber aus aller Welt. *Wolfgang Amadeus Mozart*, dessen Geburtshaus in der Getreidegasse zu den meistfotografierten Motiven zählt, wurde am 27. Januar 1756 in Salzburg geboren. Hier entstanden über 350 seiner schönsten Werke, und es wurde der Grundstock zu seiner einzigartigen Karriere gelegt, die Mozart zu dem machte, was er heute unumstritten ist: der Welt bedeutendster und meist gespielter Komponist, der mit seiner Musik ein neues Kapitel in der Musikgeschichte aufschlug.

Den internationalen Ruhm verdankt Salzburg dem unvergleichbaren Charme ihres Stadtbildes, das die *UNESCO* dazu veranlasste, die Salzburger Altstadt in die Liste der *Weltkulturerbe* als besonders schützenswert aufzunehmen.

„Die Atmosphäre von Salzburg ist durchdrungen von Schönheit, Spiel und Kunst…", meinte schon Max Reinhardt, Theaterregisseur und Hauptinitiator der Salzburger Festspiele. 1920, kurz nach dem Ersten Weltkrieg, realisierte Max Reinhardt

Salzburg's most famous son still today enchants music-lovers from all over the world. *Wolfgang Amadeus Mozart*, whose birthplace in the Getreidegasse lane is one of the most photographed buildings, was born in Salzburg on January 27, 1756. He composed more than 350 of his most beautiful works here, and they were to form the foundation of an unparalleled career that made Mozart what he is today indisputably recognised as being: the most important and most played composer the world has ever seen; a phenomenon who opened up a new chapter in music history.

Salzburg owes its international renown to the incomparable charm of its cityscape, which prompted *UNESCO* to add the old town to the list of *world cultural heritage sites* as worthy of special protection.

"The atmosphere of Salzburg is permeated by beauty, play and art…", was how Max Reinhardt put it; theatre director and main initiator of the Salzburg Festival. In 1920, shortly after the First World War, Max Reinhardt succeeded, together with other Salzburg-based artists and intellectuals, in realising his dream of transforming the entire city into a stage. The foundation of the *Salzburg Festival* gave

Der Name Salzburg

Geschichte

Salzburg hieß zur Römerzeit Iuvavum, ein Name, der wohl von den Kelten übernommen wurde, möglicherweise aber noch weiter zurückreicht. Eine sprachlich gesicherte Erklärung dieses Namens ist bis heute nicht gelungen. In den meisten Städten mit antiker Vergangenheit wurde der römische Name zur Grundlage für die mittelalterliche Bezeichnung (z. B. Lentia/Linz, Brigantium/Bregenz). In Salzburg hingegen erfolgte ein Bruch mit der römischen Vergangenheit, an die Stelle von Iuvavum trat der neue Name Salzburg. Erstmals ist das deutsche Wort „Salzburch" mit Bezug auf das Jahr 739 in der um 755 abgefassten Lebensbeschreibung des Hl. Bonifatius überliefert. Im neuen Namen Salzburg kam die politische und wirtschaftliche Funktion des frühmittelalterlichen Bischofssitzes an der Salzach deutlich zum Ausdruck.

Die Silbe „burg" nimmt auf die herzogliche Burg und zeitweilige Residenz der bayerischen Herzöge aus dem Geschlecht der Agilolfinger an diesem Ort Bezug. „Salz" weist auf Salzburg als Hauptumschlagplatz des Reichenhaller Salzes hin. Große Anteile der Salzproduktion in Reichenhall waren als Schenkungen der Bayernherzöge an die Salzburger Kirche gekommen. Das namengebende „Weiße Gold" war die wirtschaftliche Basis für den späteren Aufstieg Salzburgs.

The Name Salzburg

History

In the days of the Roman Empire, Salzburg was called Juvavum; a name that was probably taken over from the previous inhabitants, the Celts, and which may even go back further than that. To this day there is no linguistically uncontested explanation for this name. In most cities with a history that reaches back to antiquity, the Roman name became the basis for the medieval one (e.g. Lentia/Linz, Brigantium/Bregenz). In Salzburg, however, there was a break with the Roman history, with the name Salzburg replacing Juvavum. The German word "Salzburch" is first mentioned with regard to the year 739 in the life story of Saint Boniface, written in 755. The new name Salzburg clearly expressed the political and economical function of the medieval diocesan town on the Salzach. The "burg" syllable refers to the ducal castle and sporadic residence of the Bavarian dukes from the Agilolfinger dynasty here. "Salz" points to Salzburg as being the main trading centre for salt from Reichenhall. Much of the salt produced in Reichenhall came to the Salzburg church as a gift from the Bavarian dukes. And the "white gold" salt was also the commercial foundation for Salzburg's subsequent rise to prosperity.

---

gemeinsam mit anderen in Salzburg ansässigen Künstlern und Intellektuellen seinen Traum, die ganze Stadt in eine Bühne zu verwandeln. Mit der Gründung der *Salzburger Festspiele* erfuhr die Stadt Salzburg einen wesentlichen Impuls in Richtung Internationalisierung, der bis heute anhält. Der „Jedermann" – das erste Stück der Festspiele – ist bis heute unverzichtbarer Bestandteil eines der hochkarätigsten Musikfestivals Europas. Der weltberühmte Dirigent Herbert von Karajan, am 5. April 1908 in Salzburg geboren, gründete 1967 die Osterfestspiele und 1973 die Pfingstfestspiele, deren hohes Niveau Jahr für Jahr tausende Kunst- und Kulturliebhaber zu schätzen wissen.

Aber auch Hollywood hat seine Spuren in der Stadt hinterlassen. Einer von drei Japanern hat ihn gesehen, für drei Viertel aller Touristen aus den USA ist er der Grund für ihren Salzburg Besuch und seine Melodien sind mittlerweile international bekanntes Liedgut. Die Rede ist von dem mit fünf Oskars gekrönten Evergreen „The Sound of Music", der sich seit seinem Erscheinen vor vierzig Jahren ungebrochener Beliebtheit erfreut. Der Hollywoodfilm *„The Sound of Music"* wurde in der Stadt Salzburg und ihrer unmittelbaren Umgebung gedreht; noch heute können die Drehorte besucht werden.

the city of Salzburg an important impulse in the direction of internationalisation, the effects of which are still apparent today. "Jedermann" – the first oeuvre of the Festival – is to this day an indispensable part of one of Europe's highest quality music festivals. The world famous conductor Herbert von Karajan, born in Salzburg on April 5, 1908, founded the Easter Festival in 1967 and the Whitsun Festival in 1973, that thousands of art and culture fans hold in high esteem.

Hollywood has also left its mark on the city. One out of every three Japanese has seen it; for three-quarters of all tourists from the USA it is the reason why they visit Salzburg, and its melodies are known around the globe. It is, of course "The Sound of Music", winner of five Oscars and still just as hugely popular today as it was on its debut forty years ago. The Hollywood film *"The Sound of Music"* was filmed in the city and surrounds of Salzburg. And the film locations are still today the popular sites of tourist pilgrimages.

A City with many Facets

High above the city on the Festungsberg hill stands the majestic *Hohensalzburg Fortress*, past residence of the governing Prince Archbishops. A visit

Der Residenzplatz mit Residenz. Hier werden einmal im Jahr die Salzburger Festspiele eröffnet

Residenzplatz and the Residenz. This is where the Salzburg Festival is opened every year

Der repräsentative Residenzplatz entstand zwischen 1595 und 1605. In der Mitte befindet sich ein monumentaler Barockbrunnen, entstanden unter Erzbischof Guidobald Graf Thun

The magnificent Residenzplatz was built between 1595 and 1605. At its centre is a monumental Baroque fountain built under the auspices of Archbishop Guidobald Graf Thun

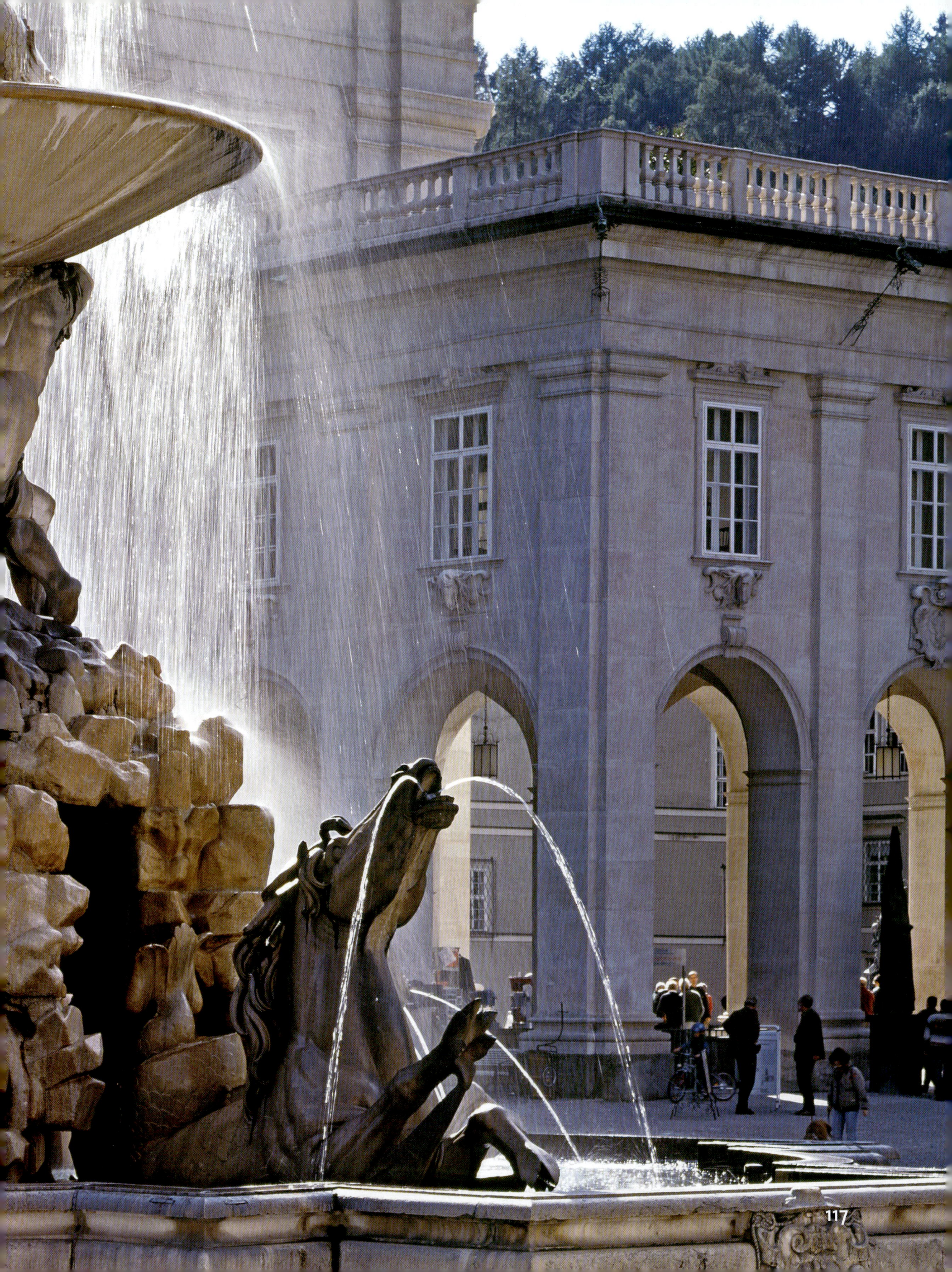

Die Salzburger Residenz mit ihren über 180 Prunkräumen zählt zu den historisch wertvollsten Bauwerken der Stadt. Sie wird heute noch für Repräsentationszwecke genutzt. Bereits Mozart musizierte hier für den damaligen Regenten

Salzburg's Residenz with its more than 180 superlative rooms is one of the city's most highly valued historical buildings. Mozart even played here for the regent of the time. Today it is only used for representative purposes

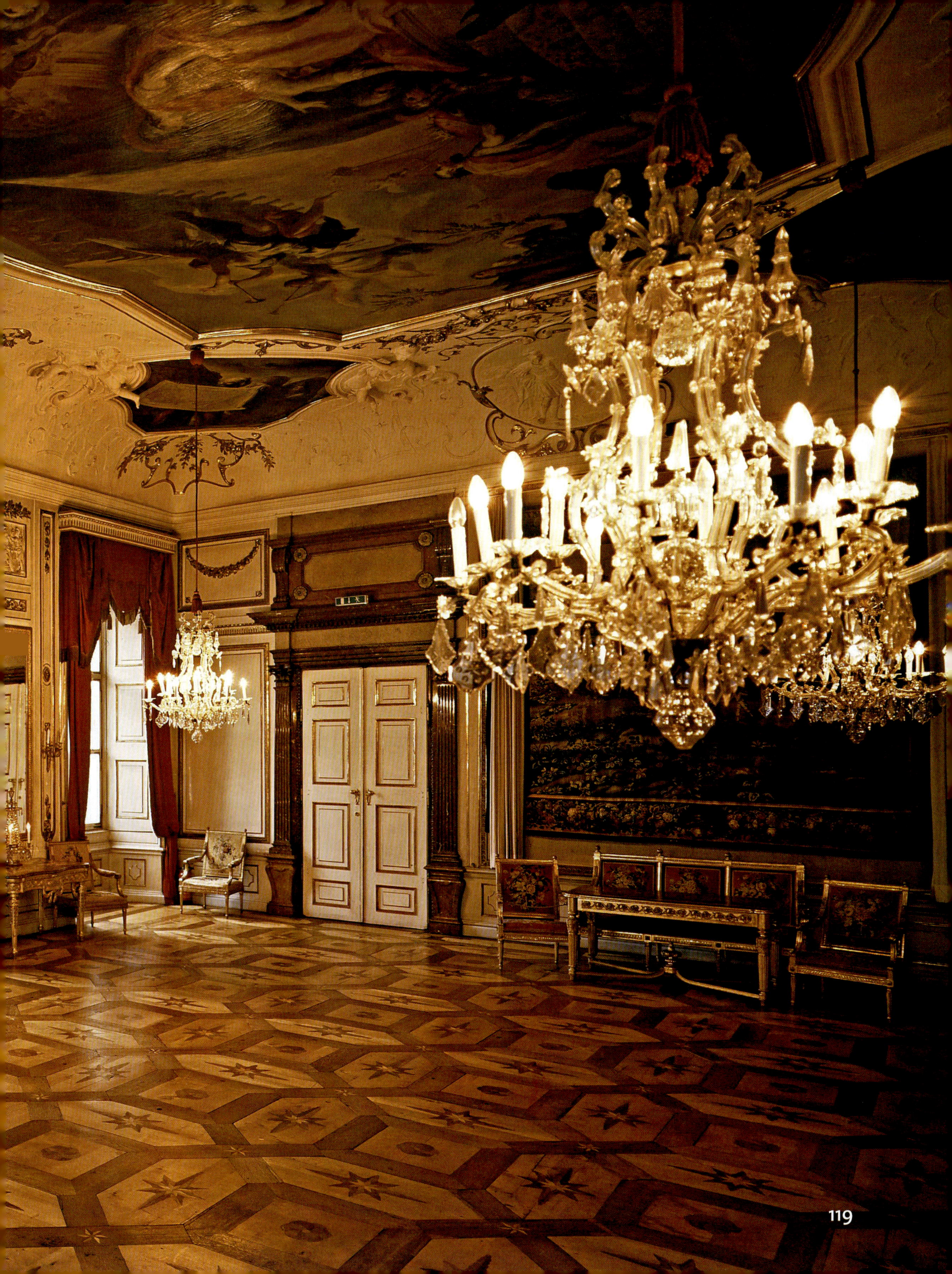

**Die mittelalterliche Altstadt:
Getreidegasse
Hafnergasse**

**The medieval Old Town:
Getreidegasse
Hafnergasse**

Eine Stadt mit vielen Facetten

Hoch über der Stadt auf dem Festungsberg thront die *Festung „Hohensalzburg"*, zeitweilige Residenz der Fürst-Erzbischöfe. Ein Besuch des Wahrzeichens der Stadt offenbart sechs Jahrhunderte an eindrucksvoller Baugeschichte und bietet Einblick in damalige Lebensverhältnisse. Lässt man den Blick dann rundum wandern, offenbaren sich die vielen Gesichter der Mozartstadt. Da ist zum einen der *Festspielbezirk* mit dem Großen Festspielhaus und dem Haus für Mozart. Da findet man das mittelalterliche Salzburg mit seinen Bürgerhäusern und engen Gassen, deren berühmteste wohl die *Getreidegasse* ist. Da blickt man in die Wiege der Stadt, to the city's landmark reveals six centuries of impressive architectural history and offers an insight into how life was back then. Looking around, the many faces of the Mozart city reveal themselves. There is the *Festival District* with its large Festspielhaus concert hall and the Haus für Mozart. This is where the Medieval Salzburg can be found, with its stately houses and narrow lanes, the most famous of which would have to be *Getreidegasse*. Here you catch a glimpse of the city's nursery, the *Klosterbezirk St. Peter* district, nuzzled up against the Festungsberg and holding one of the city's most beautiful cemeteries. And then there is the grandezza of the cathedral that impresses with its mighty dome and magnificent façade of Untersberg marble.

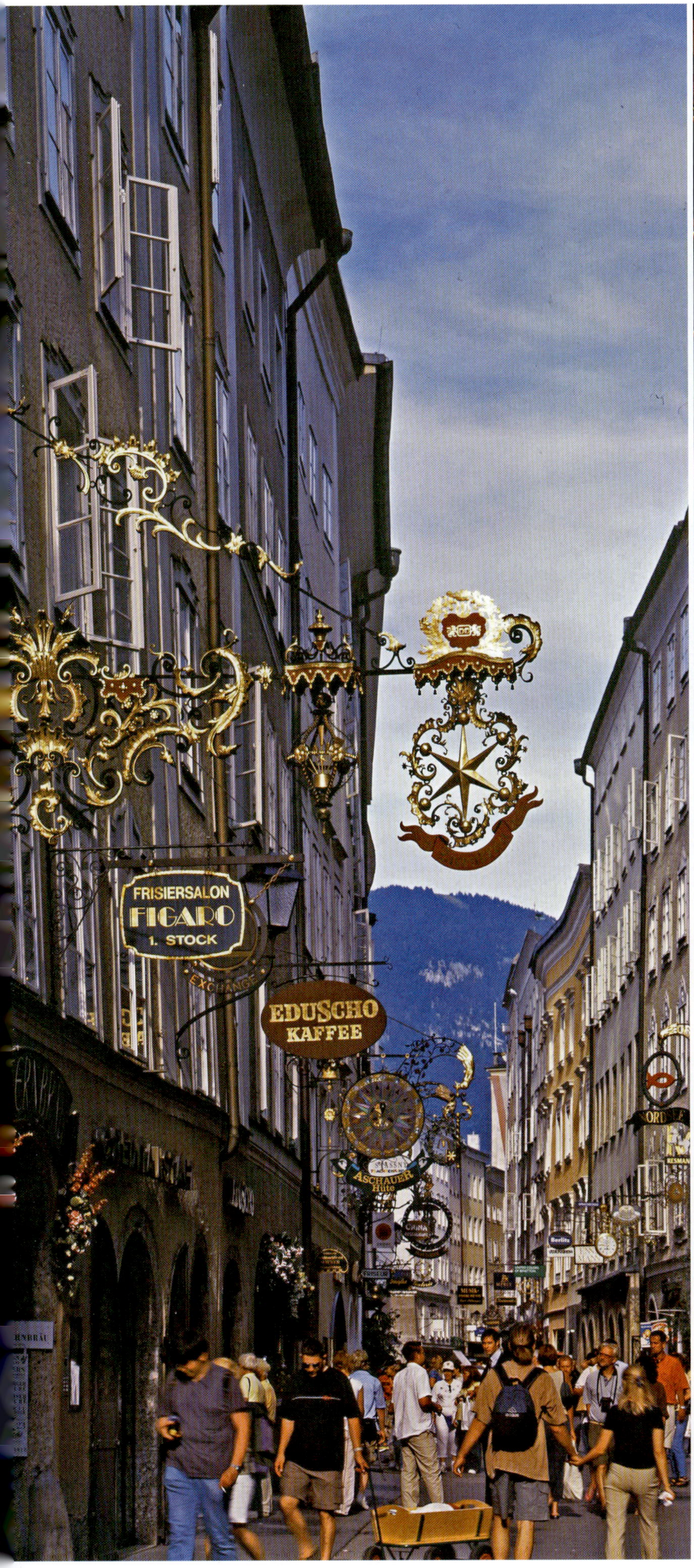
FRISIERSALON
FIGARO
1. STOCK
EDUSCHO
KAFFEE

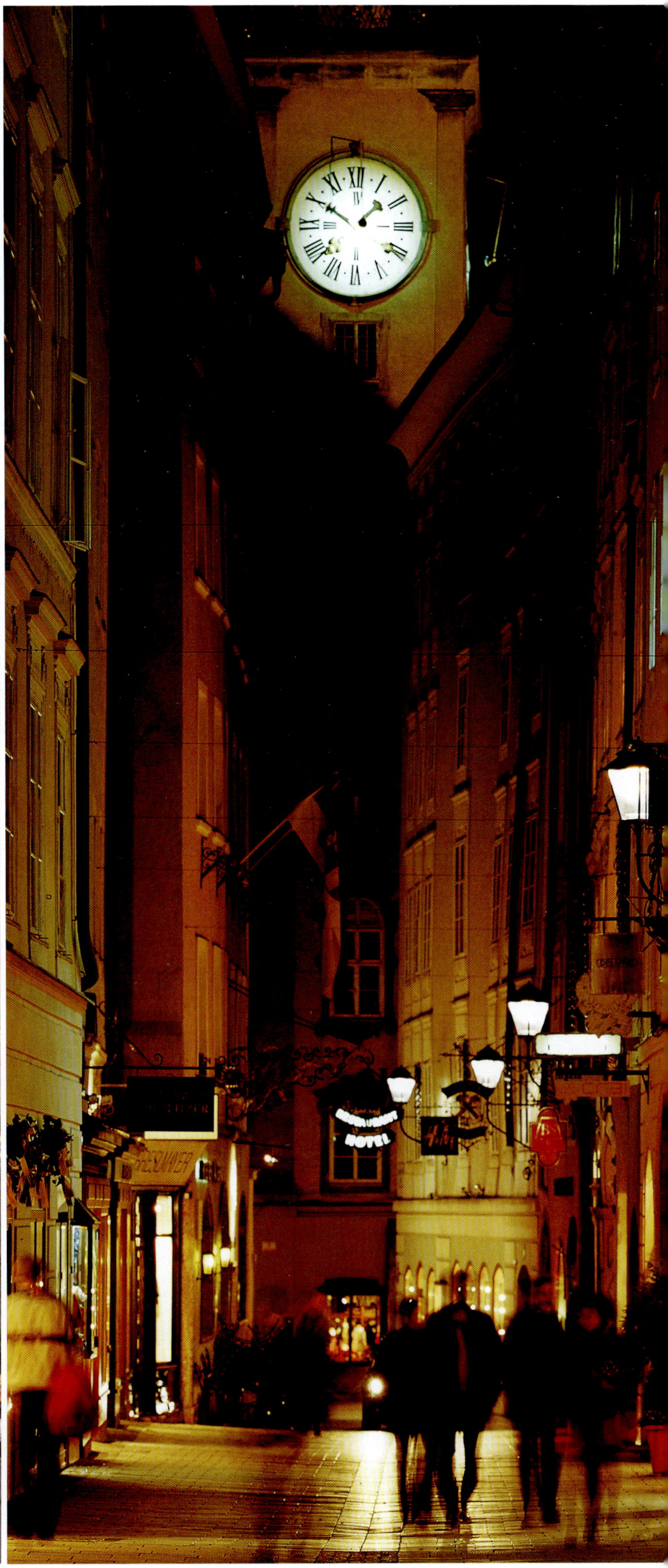

Einer der schönsten Friedhöfe der Stadt liegt im Klosterbezirk St. Peter, der sich eng an den Festungsbezirk schmiegt

One of the city's most beautiful cemeteries lies in the St. Peter's Archabbey quarter, nestled up against the fortress district

den *Klosterbezirk St. Peter*, der sich eng an den Festungsberg schmiegt und den wohl schönsten Friedhof der Stadt beherbergt. Und da besticht die Grandezza des Doms mit seiner mächtigen Kuppel und der prachtvollen Fassade aus Untersberger Marmor.

Rund um die sich mediterran öffnenden Plätze der Stadt tönt aus jeder Ecke Musik, da verlocken die Köstlichkeiten der typischen Kaffeehäuser, und im Winter laden die historisch gewachsenen *Christkindlmärkte* am Dom- und Residenzplatz zum romantischen Winterzauber ein.

Modern Art am Mönchsberg – Kunst an einem besonderen Ort

Puristisch, schlicht und beeindruckend bildet die großzügige Architektur des „Museum der Moderne", am Mönchsberg gelegen, ein reizvolles Gegenstück zur historischen Altstadt. Auf vier Ebenen werden thematische Ausstellungen der Kunst des 20. und 21. Jahrhunderts gezeigt. Atemberaubend der Blick von der Terrasse des vom internationalen Star-Architekten Matteo Thun ausgestatteten Restaurants „m32".

Rechts der Salzach befindet sich der nächste Berg, dominiert vom Kapuzinerkloster, dem er auch seinen Namen verdankt. Ein Besuch führt am ehe-

Music exudes from every corner, all around the Mediterranean-styled squares of the city, where the delicacies of the typical cafes entice. And in winter the sparkling *Christmas markets* on the Cathedral and Residence Squares invite you to enjoy their magical romance.

Modern art on the Mönchsberg hill – art in a special place

Puristic, chaste and imposing, the generous architecture of the "Museum der Moderne" on the Mönchsberg poses a delightful contrast to the historical old town. Thematic exhibitions of 20th and 21st century art are on display on four levels here. Breathtaking the view from the terrace of the "m32" restaurant, fitted by the international star architect Matteo Thun.

To the right of the Salzach is the next hill, this one dominated by the Capuchin Monastery, to which it also owes its name. A visit here takes one past the house of the world-renowned author Stefan Zweig. And if you are lucky, you might spy some of the chamois climbing around the steeps of the hill while you walk. A breathtaking backdrop, not only for bridal couples, is the *Mirabellgarten*, whose castle holds one of Europe's most beautiful wedding venues.

maligen Haus des weltberühmten Schriftstellers Stefan Zweig vorbei. Und hat man Glück, kann man während der restlichen Wanderung den am Berg beheimateten Gämsen bei ihren alpinen Kletterkunststücken zusehen. Atemberaubende Kulisse nicht nur für Brautpaare bietet der *Mirabellgarten*, dessen Schloss Europas schönsten Trauungssaal beherbergt.

Kultur und Natur gehören in Salzburg zusammen, und das bedeutet die Seele baumeln lassen an den Ufern der Salzach. Und wer es sportlich liebt und in kurzer Zeit möglichst viel von Stadt und Umgebung sehen will, der ist gut beraten, bei den zahlreich vorhandenen Fahrradverleihen einen Drahtesel anzumieten. Salzburg bietet ein hervorragend ausgebautes Radwegenetz, die Distanzen sind gering und neben der sportlichen Betätigung gelangt man in den Genuss, etwa das vor den Toren der Stadt an einem romantischen Weiher gelegene Schloss Leopoldskron zu sehen.

Salzburgs Altstadt lädt zum Bummeln und Flanieren ein

Kleine Läden und Manufakturen halten eine bisweilen uralte Tradition aufrecht. Bäckermeister und Kürschner, Likörerzeuger und Weber, Konditoren und Schneider und noch viele mehr beleben die schma-

Culture and nature go hand in hand in Salzburg, and that means relaxing on the banks of the Salzach. Or for those who like to take a more sporting approach and see as much of the city and surrounds as possible in a short period of time, hiring a bike from one of the many rental companies in town is a capital idea. Salzburg has an excellent array of bike paths. The distances are short and in addition to the sporting effect, one also has the opportunity to view Leopoldskron castle, nestled on a romantic lake outside the city gates.

Salzburg's old Town centre invites you to Stroll and Stray

Small shops and manufactures uphold a now ancient tradition. Master bakers and furriers, liqueur makers and weavers, confectioners and tailors and many more besides vivify the narrow lanes with their romantic inner courtyards. These so typical shopping addresses of Salzburg's old town range from the fascinating world of spirits at No. 39 Getreidegasse to the last protectorate of umbrella making, Kirchtag at 22 Getreidegasse, right through to the Eldorado for cheese gourmets. And you can also find finest leather and delicate lace in Salzburg's old town. Tradition and modernity are here not only in gastronomy and culture, but also in

Das Museum der Moderne umfasst zwei Häuser in exponierter Lage: das Rupertinum in der Salzburger Altstadt sowie das Museum auf dem Mönchsberg (Foto). Gezeigt werden neben der umfangreichen Sammlung auf ca. 3 000 qm auch Wechselausstellungen von internationalem Rang

The Museum of Modern Art can be found in two prominent buildings: the Rupertinum in the Old Town and the museum on the Mönchsberg (photo). Alongside the large permanent collection covering 3,000 m², internationally renowned guest exhibitions can also be viewed here

Die älteste noch bestehende Salzburger Apotheke ist die „Alte fürsterzbischöfliche Hofapotheke". Sie stammt aus dem Jahr 1591 und liegt gegenüber der Residenz am Alten Markt. Das barocke Kleinod ist ein touristischer Magnet

The oldest Salzburg pharmacy still in operation is the "Alte fürsterzbischöfliche Hofapotheke". It went into business in 1591 and is located opposite the Residenz at Alter Markt. This little Baroque jewel is a veritable tourist magnet

- Polychresttee -

Die Traditionellen Kaffeehäuser

Traditional Coffee Shops

1–2 Café Tomaselli am Alten Markt
3–5 Café Bazar am Salzachkai
6 Café Fürst am Alten Markt
7–8 Café Demel – das frühere Café Glockenspiel am Mozartplatz

1–2 Café Tomaselli on Alter Markt
3–5 Café Bazar at Salzachkai
6 Café Fürst on Alter Markt
7–8 Café Demel – the former Café Glockenspiel at Mozartplatz

Braukunst auf höchster Stufe –
Die Stieglbrauerei zu Salzburg

Wenn für Salzburgs Schüler das Jahr 1492 auf dem Unterrichtsplan steht, dann lernen sie wie überall auf der Welt, dass in diesem Jahr Christoph Kolumbus Amerika entdeckt hat.

Was kein Salzburger erst in der Schule lernen muss ist, dass 1492 auch die Stieglbrauerei zu Salzburg erstmals urkundlich erwähnt wurde. Damals führte vom alten Brauhaus, das mitten in der Stadt Salzburg stand, eine kleine Stiege zum Almkanal hinunter. Diese kleine Stiege gab der Braustätte den Namen „Prewhaus bey dem Stieglein". In den mehr als 500 Jahren hat sich zwar viel getan – das Unternehmen hat sich von einer kleinen Salzburger Braustätte zu Österreichs größter Privatbrauerei entwickelt – aber eines ist gleich geblieben: Die Stiege ist noch heute das Markenzeichen der Brauerei, die das Stadtbild Salzburgs wie kein anderes Unternehmen prägt.

„Braukunst auf höchster Stufe", so lautet das Qualitätsversprechen der in Privatbesitz befindlichen Brauerei. Deshalb wird in Österreichs größter Privatbrauerei auch streng nach dem Reinheitsgebot von 1516 ausschließlich mit Wasser, Hopfen und Malz am Standort Salzburg gebraut. Verwendet werden dafür ausschließlich hochwertige, Natur belassene Rohstoffe, die aus Österreich stammen.

Die sortenreiche Produktpalette des Unternehmens umfasst: Stiegl-Goldbräu, die 12-grädige Salzburger Bierspezialität, Stiegl-Pils, Stiegl-Weizengold und Stiegl-Gaudi-Radler u.v.a.

The fine art of brewing beer –
Stieglbrauerei in Salzburg

When kids in Salzburg's schools learn about the year 1492, they find out, just like all school pupils, that this was the year Christopher Columbus discovered America.

But what the real Salzburger doesn't have to wait until school to learn is that 1492 is also the year in which the brewery Stieglbrauerei in Salzburg first found written mention. Back then there was a little stairway that led from the old brewery in the middle of town down to the Almkanal. It was this little flight of stairs from which the brewery lent its name "Prewhaus bey dem Stieglein" (brewery by the little stairs). Over the last 500 years, a lot has happened at Stieglbrauerei – it has grown to become Austria's largest private brewing company. But one thing has never changed: the little stairway is still the trademark of the brewery that has left its mark on Salzburg's cityscape like no other enterprise.

"Braukunst auf höchster Stufe" (top-step brewing quality) is the promise this privately-owned company makes and keeps. Even today, as Austria's largest private brewery, it brews strictly according to the purity law of 1516, using only water, hops and malt to make its beers. Only the finest quality natural ingredients, most of which originating from Austria, find their way into a Stiegl beer.

Some of the company's many products include: Stiegl Goldbräu the 12% original wort Salzburg beer speciality, Stiegl-Pils, Stiegl-Weizengold and Stiegl-Gaudi-Radler.

Seit 1492 braut Stiegl in Salzburg das beliebteste Bier der Österreicher mit bestem Quellwasser vom nahen Untersberg

Stiegl has been brewing the Austrians' favourite beer in Salzburg since 1492, with the best spring water from nearby Untersberg

www.stiegl.at

Der Garten von Schloss Mirabell mit seinen Skulpturen, dem „Zwergerlgarten" und „Heckentheater" lässt jedes Besucherherz höher schlagen

The gardens of Mirabell Palace with its "Zwergerlgarten" (Dwarfs' Garden) and "Heckentheater" outdoor theatre capture the sight-seer's imagination

len Gassen mit ihren romantischen Innenhöfen. Die so typischen Einkaufsadressen von Salzburgs Altstadt reichen von der faszinierenden Welt der Spirituosen in der Getreidegasse Nr. 39 über die letzte Schirmherrschaft der Schirmmanufaktur Kirchtag in der Getreidegasse 22 bis hin zum Eldorado für Käse-Feinspitze. Aber auch feinstes Leder und zarte Spitze findet man in Salzburgs Altstadt. Tradition und Moderne finden sich in Salzburg nicht nur in Gastronomie und Kultur sowie Architektur wieder, sondern auch im Shoppingerlebnis der Stadt.

architecture and shopping. Alongside traditional and historical shops are beautiful, world-renowned modern luxury stores such as DONUM by Erika Swarovski and new international fashion trends at "Cobra Couture".

A SPECIAL TRADITIONAL AND CONTEMPORARY CULINARY TREAT

Salzburg has any number of excellent localities for every taste: from the bar high above the roofs of the

Neben traditionsreichen und historischen Geschäften präsentieren sich liebevoll namhafte moderne Luxusläden wie DONUM by Erika Swarovski oder neue Trends am internationalen Modehimmel „Cobra Couture".

KULINARISCH EIN TRADITIONELLER UND ZEITGENÖSSISCHER HOCHGENUSS

An Lokalen für jeden Geschmack hat Salzburg eine ganze Menge zu bieten, von der Bar hoch über den

Der Rupertikirtag ist ein Domkirchweihfest, abgehalten um den 24. September in Salzburg. Er ist eines der traditionellen Volksfeste Österreichs

Rupertikirtag is a cathedral festival held around 24 September in Salzburg. It is one of the traditional Austrian festivals

Dächern Salzburgs übers romantische Straßencafé bis zum Beisl oder Gourmettempel. Liebhaber gepflegter Gastronomie und Kulinarik auf höchstem Niveau finden in Salzburg ein wahres Eldorado. Nur wenige Orte in Österreich vermögen auf so geringer Fläche mit einer derart stattlichen Anzahl an haubenprämierten Gourmettempeln und international bekannten und ausgezeichneten Kochkünstlern zu überraschen.

Mit rund 12 000 Studenten ist Salzburg auch Hochschulstadt (Paris Lodron Universität, Universität Mozarteum) sowie Kur- und Kongressstadt. Das neue Kongresszentrum im Herzen der Mozartstadt entspricht mit 15 000 Quadratmetern Fläche den modernsten Anforderungen. Zeichen für den internationalen Stellenwert Salzburgs ist die Tatsache, dass Salzburg – nach der Bundeshauptstadt Wien – die Stadt mit den meisten konsularischen Vertretungsbehörden ist. Seitens der Politik werden intensive Kontakte zu den Konsulaten gepflegt, wobei die Zusammenarbeit die behördlichen Agenden ebenso wie die gegenseitige Unterstützung bei wissenschaftlichen, wirtschaftlichen und touristischen Aktivitäten umfasst.

Salzburg ist Sitz der Europäischen Akademie der Wissenschaften. Der berühmte Maler Oskar Ko-

city, to the romantic street café and on through to the cosy Austrian "Beisl" taverns and gourmet restaurants. Lovers of cultivated gastronomy and top quality culinary delicacies find a veritable Eldorado in Salzburg. There are few places in Austria that can boast such a stately number of gourmet temples and internationally renowned and award-winning chefs in such a small area.

Salzburg is also a university town, with around 12,000 students (Paris Lodron University, University Mozarteum), and a spa and congress venue to boot. The new congress centre in the heart of the Mozart town is 15,000 square metres of state-of-the-art exhibition space. One sign of the international significance of Salzburg is the fact that it is home to the most consular authorities after the federal capital Vienna. In the political sector, close relationships are cultivated to the consulates, with the collaboration encompassing not only administrative agendas, but also mutual support in the fields of science, commerce and tourism.

Salzburg is home to the European Academy of Sciences. And the famous artist Oskar Kokoschka founded the "Schule des Sehens" (School of Seeing) in Salzburg, which is today known as the "International Summer Academy".

koschka gründete in Salzburg die „Schule des Sehens", heute bekannt unter dem Namen „Internationale Sommerakademie".

4 000 Kulturelle Veranstaltungen jährlich

Das Jahr wird in Salzburg kulturell mit den international bekannten Mozartwochen eingeläutet. Ende Januar können sich Musikliebhaber auf Orchesterkonzerte mit der Camerata Salzburg und dem Mozarteum freuen. Gefolgt von den Oster- und Pfingstfestspielen erlebt man in Salzburg einen kulturellen Frühling von höchstem Niveau. Neben den Sommerfestspielen mit Promi-Charakter im Juli bietet die Stadt auch zahlreiche zeitgenössische Kulturgenüsse wie die Sommerszene im Juni und eine Vielzahl an Galerien und Ausstellungen. Wenn der kraftvolle Herbst seine Tore öffnet, lädt Salzburg zum Jazzherbst mit internationalen Musikern in die Altstadt ein. Die stillste Zeit im Jahr wird vom Salzburger Adventsingen im Großen Festspielhaus begleitet. Ganzjährig bieten das Salzburger Marionettentheater und die Salzburger Schlosskonzerte sowie Mozart Dinner Konzerte ein abwechslungsreiches Programm. ◀

4,000 Cultural Events per Year

In Salzburg the cultural year is heralded in with the internationally famed Mozart Weeks. At the end of January, music lovers flock to the orchestra concerts of the Camerata Salzburg and the Mozarteum. This is then followed by the Easter and Whitsun festivals, that ensure a cultural springtime of the highest quality. Alongside the Summer Festival with its celebrity character in July, the city also has numerous contemporary cultural events on offer, like the Summer Scene in June and many galleries and exhibitions. When the mighty autumn opens its gates, Salzburg invites the world to its old town centre for the "Jazzherbst" (Autumn Jazz Festival) with top international musicians. The contemplative time of the year is accompanied by the Salzburger Adventsingen in the Grosses Festspielhaus. The Salzburg Marionette Theatre, the Salzburg Castle Concerts and the Mozart Dinner concerts make sure that any gaps in the calendar are always filled with an ever-changing programme. ◀

Der Salzburger Christkindlmarkt. Hier stimmen Volkskunst, Glühwein und vieles mehr auf die Weihnachtszeit ein

The Salzburg Christmas Market. Here you can get into the Christmas Spirit with local handicrafts, mulled wine and much more besides

Information und Buchung:
Salzburg Information
Tel: +43/662/88987-0
e-mail: hotels@salzburg.info
www.salzburg.info

Kulinarisches

Culinary Delights

27 Haubenköche gibt es in Salzburg und Umgebung: drei mit drei Hauben, sieben mit zwei Hauben und 17 mit einer Haube

1. M32 im Museum der Moderne – www.m32.at
2. Ikarus im Hangar 7 am Flughafen – www.hangar-7.com
3–5. Riedenburg – www.riedenburg.at
6–8. Esszimmer – www.esszimmer.com
9–10. magazin – www.magazin.co.at
11. Sacher Salzburg – Zirbelzimmer – www.sacher.com

There are 27 chefs with the revered distinction of one or more "chef's hats" in Salzburg and surrounds: Three with three hats, seven with two, and 17 with on chef's hat

1. M32 in the Museum of Modern Art – www.m32.at
2. Ikarus in Hangar 7 at the airport – www.hangar-7.com
3–5. Riedenburg – www.riedenburg.at
6–8. Esszimmer – www.esszimmer.com
9–10. magazin – www.magazin.co.at
11. Salzburg Sacher – Zirbelzimmer – www.sacher.com

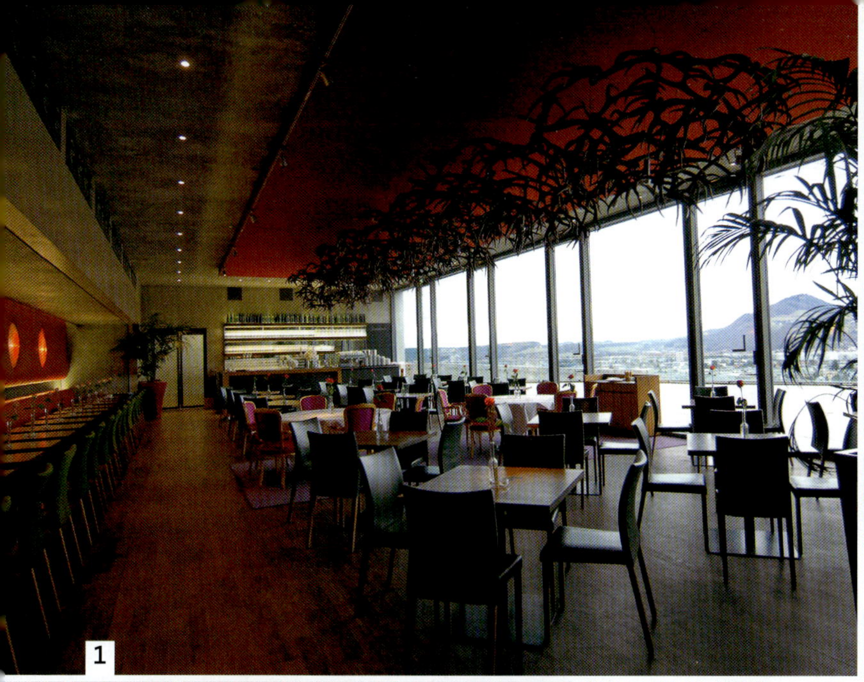
1

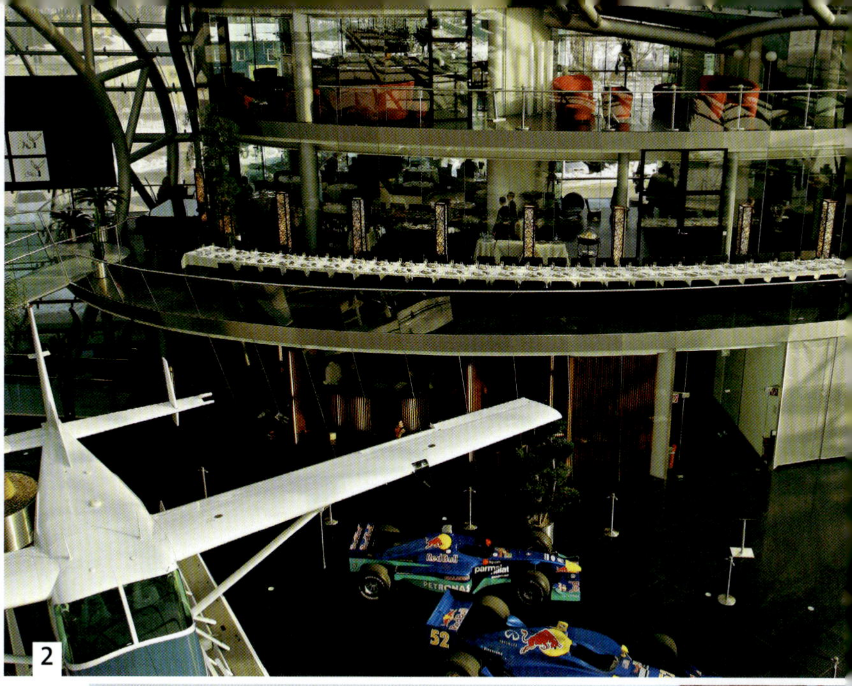
2

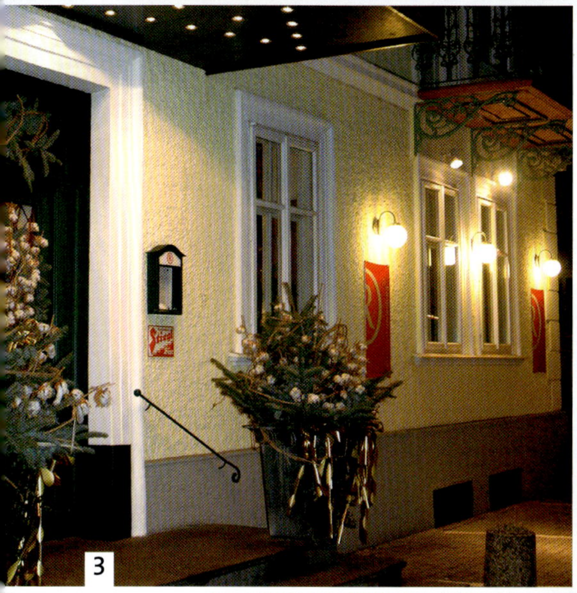
3

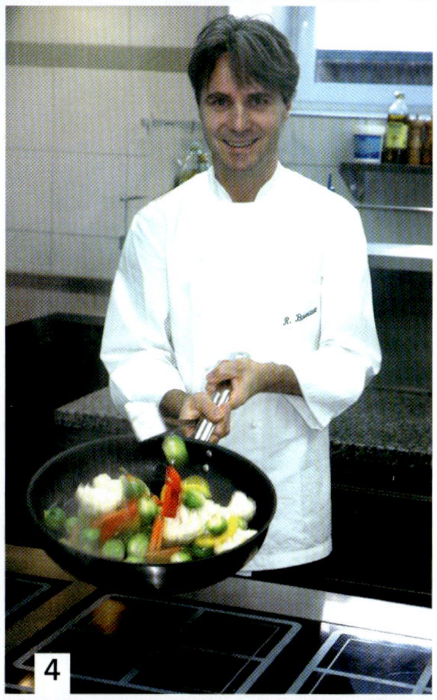
4

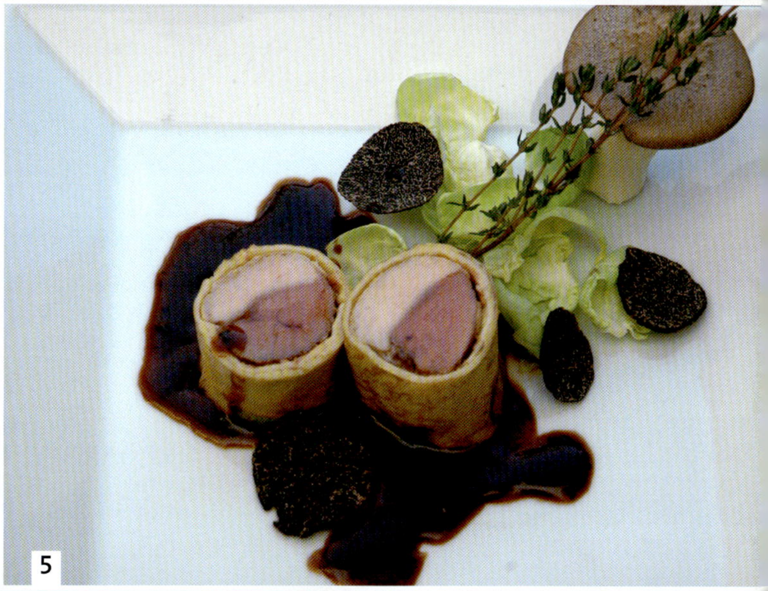
5

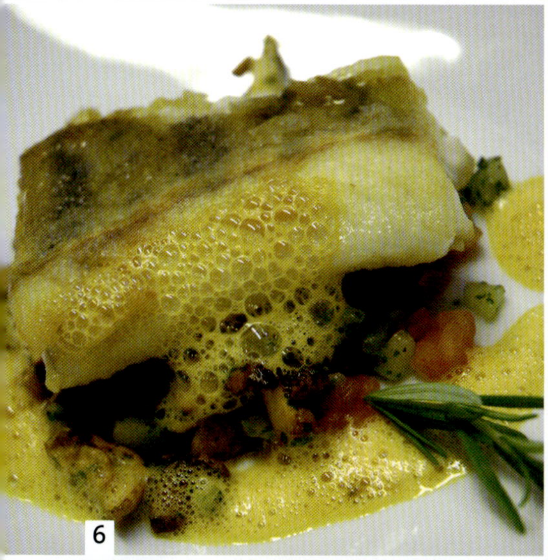
6

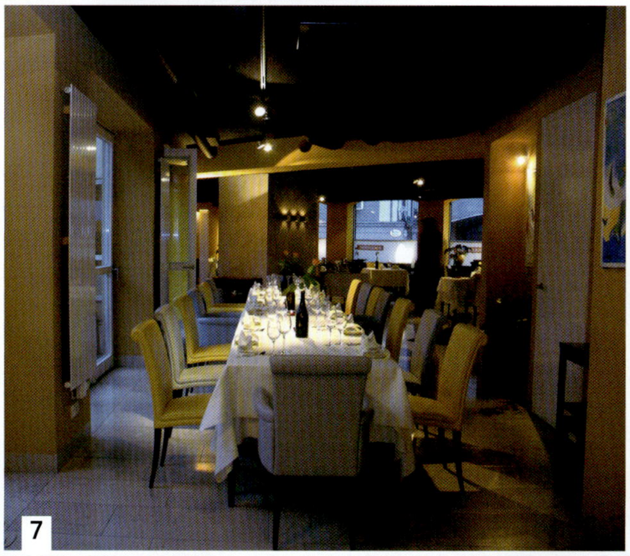
7

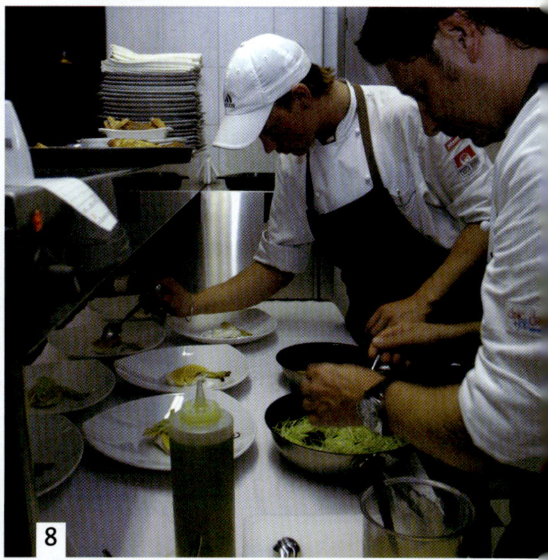
8

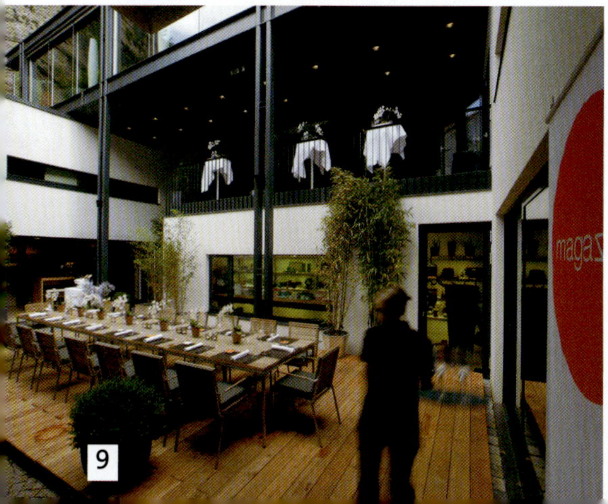
9

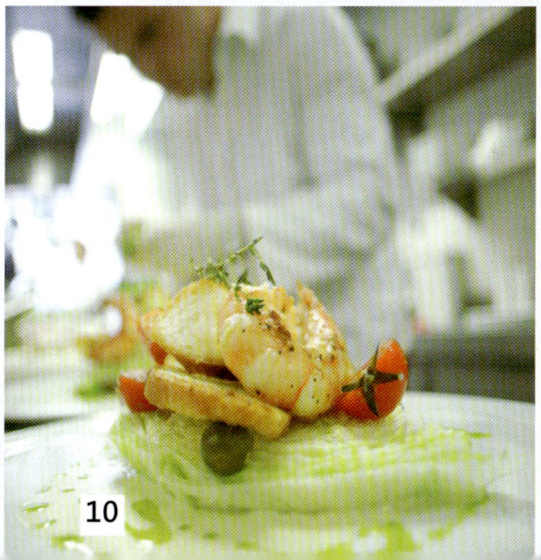
10

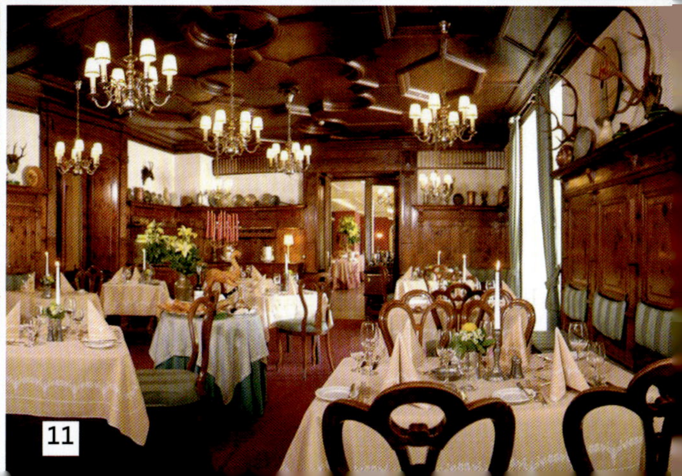
11

1. Blick in den Innenhof des Stiftes St. Peter und zum Eingang des Restaurants Stiftskeller St. Peter
2. Im heutigen Michael Haydn-Zimmer erhielt 1763 Johann Michael Haydn, Bruder des berühmten Joseph Haydn, in den alten Klostermauern Quartier
3. Arkadenhof & Willibaldhöhle – im Sommer schattiger Garten und im Winter romantischer Winterwald mit Glühweinstand und traditionellen Bläsern

1. The courtyard of St. Peter monastery and the entrance to the Stiftskeller St. Peter restaurant
2. In 1763, Johann Michael Haydn, brother of the famous Joseph Haydn, lodged within the old monastery walls in what is today known as the Michael Haydn Room
3. Arkadenhof & Willibaldhöhle – in summer a shady garden and in winter a romantic winter forest with mulled wine stand and traditional brass music

Stiftskeller St. Peter, Salzburg

Der Anno 803 erstmals urkundlich erwähnte Stiftskeller St. Peter liegt malerisch im Herzen der Salzburger Altstadt. Seinen Ursprung hat der Stiftskeller St. Peter in einer Regula des Heiligen Severins, der schon vor 1 600 Jahren verfügte, dass es jedem Mönch erlaubt sein möge, täglich eine „Hemina" Wein zu trinken. Der Überschuss des in eigenen Weinbergen angebauten Rebensaftes wurde schon damals von den Mönchen verkauft.

Als älteste Gaststätte Europas wurde der Stiftskeller St. Peter bereits von dem Gelehrten Alkuin, einem Gefolgsmann Kaiser Karl des Großen, im Jahre 803 urkundlich erwähnt. Im Spätmittelalter erfuhr der Stiftskeller St. Peter eine literaturgeschichtliche Beschreibung durch den „Mönch von Salzburg", einem Dichter und Komponisten.

1720 wandelte sich der Stiftskeller – Adel, Bürgerturm und Klerus kehrten ein – Michael Haydn fand um 1760 unter Abt Beda Seebauer Unterkunft im Obergeschoss des Stiftskellers. Der Salzburger Haydn komponierte ein Lied zum Lobe des „Peterweines", des heutigen Prälatenweines.

Weder verheerende Brände, noch die nach der um 1786 vom Stiftskeller neu erworbenen „Biergerechtigkeit" aufkeimenden Aufstände der Salzburger Wirte konnten den erfolgreichen Weg des Stiftskellers aufhalten. Durch das engagierte Geschick des damaligen Erzabtes konnten sogar Plünderungen und Enteignungen im 2. Weltkrieg verhindert werden und der Peterbezirk blieb vor großen Schäden verschont.

Im März 1992 übernahm die Haslauer Gastronomie, zu der auch die Ch. Event Gastronomie im Mode-Event Center Bergheim gehört, den Stiftskeller St. Peter.

Stiftskeller St. Peter, Salzburg

First mentioned in official documents in 803, the Stiftskeller St. Peter is located in a picturesque spot in the heart of the historical old town of Salzburg. The Stiftskeller St. Peter has its origins in a regula issued by St. Severin more than 1,600 years ago, stating that every monk may have the right to drink one "hemina" of wine a day (just less than half a litre). Indeed, he already sold the excess wine from his own vineyard to the monks.

The oldest public house in Europe, the Stiftskeller St. Peter first finds mention in official documents in 803, by the scholar Alkuin, a liege of Charlemagne. In the late Middle Ages, the Stiftskeller St. Peter was described in the historical-literary writing of the "Monk of Salzburg" – a poet and composer.

In 1720 the Stiftskeller changed – nobility, bourgeoisie and clergy began to frequent it – Michael Haydn found lodgings on the upper floor around 1760 under abbot Beda Seebauer. The Salzburger Haydn even composed a piece of music singing the praises of the "Peter wine", known today as the Prelate's wine.

Neither devastating fires nor the uprising of Salzburg's publicans after the so-called "Beer Justice" in 1786 could stop the Stiftskeller on its path to legendary status. The deftness of the arch abbot even prevented it being plundered or disappropriated during World War 2, and even the Peter's quarter was spared from major damage.

In March 1992, the company Haslauer Gastronomie took over the management of the Stiftskeller St. Peter. It also owns the Ch. Event Gastronomie in the Bergheim Fashion Event Center.

1996 wurde das Mozart-Dinner-Konzert im historischen Barocksaal uraufgeführt und erfreut sich seither größter Beliebtheit.

Bis zu 800 Gästen in 12 verschiedenen Räumen bietet der Stiftskeller St. Peter Platz – ob in privater Atmosphäre im Refugium oder dem festlichen Ambiente des Barocksaales mit seinen prunkvollen Deckenmalereien – erleben Sie die Stadt Salzburg an einem historisch wertvollen Ort.

In den 1 200 Jahren entstanden: 14 unterschiedliche Räume, die bis heute erhalten sind, ein uriges Kellergewölbe, gemütliche, holzvertäfelte und stilvolle Stuben sowie prunkvolle Räume wie der Barocksaal und das Haydnzimmer die Ihrer Veranstaltung den passenden Rahmen geben.

- Genießen Sie unvergessliche Stunden bei kulinarischen Schmankerln oder heimischen Spezialitäten. Erlesene à la carte Karte, traumhafte Menüs, exquisite Buffets. Lassen Sie sich von unserem Küchenchef beraten.
- Durch seine hervorragende Lage, Größe und Ausstattung bietet das Haus erstklassige Bedingungen für ein gelungenes Incentive- bzw. Rahmenprogramm. Nennen Sie uns Ihre Wünsche, wir werden sie für Sie umsetzen. Gerne sind wir Ihnen bei der Ausarbeitung eines Rahmenprogrammes für Ihre Veranstaltung behilflich.
- Einer der glanzvollsten Höhepunkte des Jahres im Stiftskeller St. Peter ist der Advent. In liebevoller Arbeit wird das gesamte Haus sehr aufwendig und „himmlisch" dekoriert. Der Arkadenhof und die Willibaldhöhle werden in einen romantischen Winterwald verwandelt.
- Genießen Sie den Advent bei Glühwein oder Punsch zu Klängen traditioneller Musik.

The Mozart Dinner concert premiered in the historical baroque hall in 1996 and has remained enormously popular to this day.

The Stiftskeller St. Peter offers space for up to 800 guests in 12 different rooms – from the private atmosphere in the Refugium to the festive feeling of the baroque hall with its magnificent frescos – experience the city of Salzburg in a historically unparalleled setting.

Built in the 1 200s: 14 different rooms that are still preserved to this day in their original splendour, a rustic cellar, cosy, stylish wooden parlours and fabulous halls like the baroque and Haydn halls mean that you can always find the right venue for your event.

- Enjoy unforgettable hours with culinary delights or local specialities, exquisite à la carte, fantastic menus, delicious buffets. Our chef will be happy to give you his recommendation.
- With its top location, ample size and fine fittings, the Stiftskeller offers the best framework for an incentive or other thematic programme. Tell us what you need and we will turn it into something special for you, even helping plan your entertainment.
- One of the highlights of the year in the Stiftskeller St. Peter is Advent. The entire building is decorated with great Christmas care and dedication. The Arcade Court and the Willibald Cavern are transformed into a romantic winter forest.
- Savour the pre-Christmas spirit of Advent with a mulled wine or punch to the beautiful background of traditional music.

4 Das Refugium mit einer kunstvollen Kassettendecke und dem alten Kachelofen mit Kacheln der einzelnen Erzäbte aus dem Stift St. Peter

5 Der Barocksaal mit seinen prunkvollen Stuckaturen und prachtvollen Deckenmalereien gibt einer Hochzeitsfeier oder exklusiven Veranstaltung einen unvergleichlichen Rahmen

4 The Refugium with its artistic coffered ceiling and the old tiled stove with tiles from each of the arch-abbots of the Stift St. Peter monastery

5 The Baroque Hall with its magnificent stuccos and frescos is an unforgettable venue for an exclusive event or wedding celebration

www.haslauer.at

Die große Orgel auf der Westempore des Salzburger Doms. Sie hat 58 Register und wurde im Jahr 1988 von der Schweizer Firma Metzler erbaut

The organ on the West Gallery of Salzburg Cathedral. It has 58 stops and was built in 1988 by the Swiss company Metzler

137

Die Franziskanerkirche in Salzburg ist eine der ältesten Kirchen der Stadt. Ihre Ursprünge gehen auf das 8. Jahrhundert zurück. Nach zahlreichen Veränderungen im Laufe der Jahrhunderte erhielt die Kirche ihr heutiges Aussehen. Der Hochaltar stammt von Michael Pacher und in seiner jetzigen Form von Johann Fischer von Erlach. 1983 wurde das Gotteshaus saniert und renoviert

---

The Franciscan church is one of the oldest churches in the city of Salzburg. Its origins go as far back as the 8th century AD. Numerous modifications throughout the centuries have lent the church its appearance. The high altar was originally built by Michael Pacher, and in its current form by Johann Fischer von Erlach. The church was renovated and redeveloped in 1983

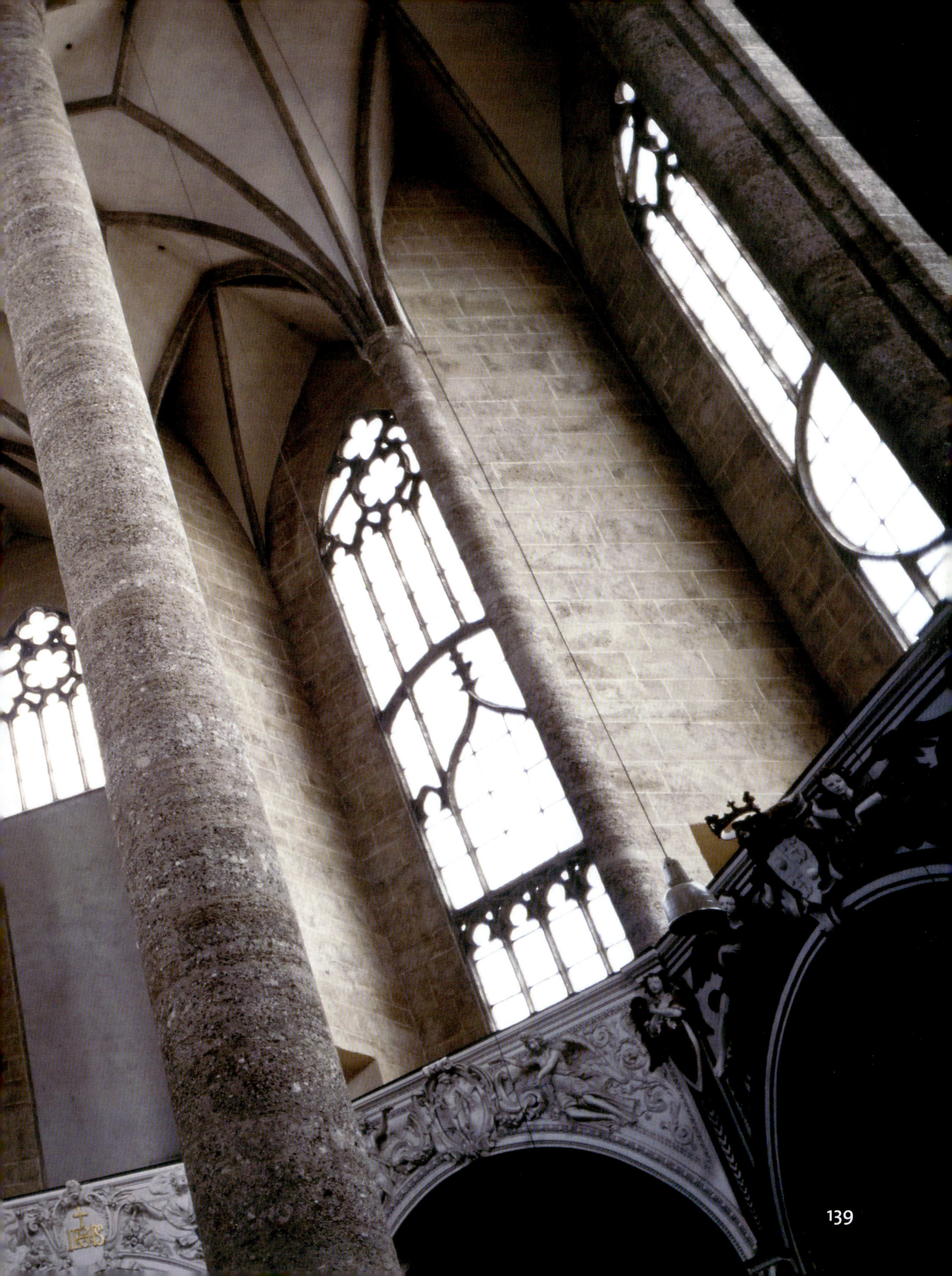

Die Stiftskirche St. Peter. Hier wurde am 26. Oktober 1783 Mozarts c-Moll-Messe uraufgeführt. St. Peter ist das älteste, seit seiner Gründung bewohnte Benediktinerkloster im deutschsprachigen Raum. Der heutige Bau geht auf eine romanische Basilika zurück und erhielt im 17. und 18. Jahrhundert seine barocke Ausstattung

The St. Peter collegiate church. Mozart's Mass in C-Minor was played for the first time here on 26 October 1783. St. Peter is the oldest Benedictine monastery in the German-speaking world that has been inhabited since its founding. Today's building is based on a Romanic basilica and was given its Baroque fittings in the 17th and 18th centuries

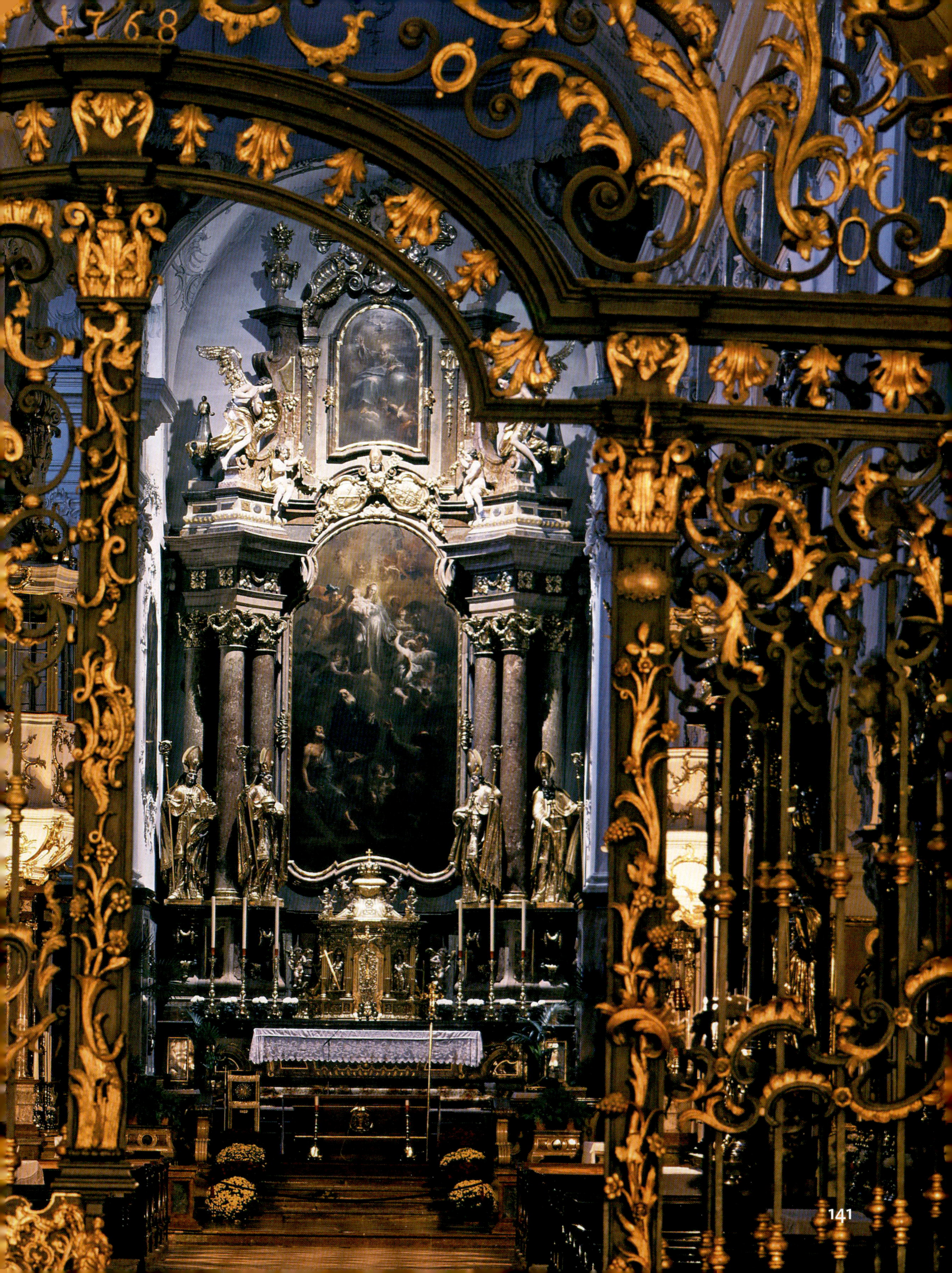

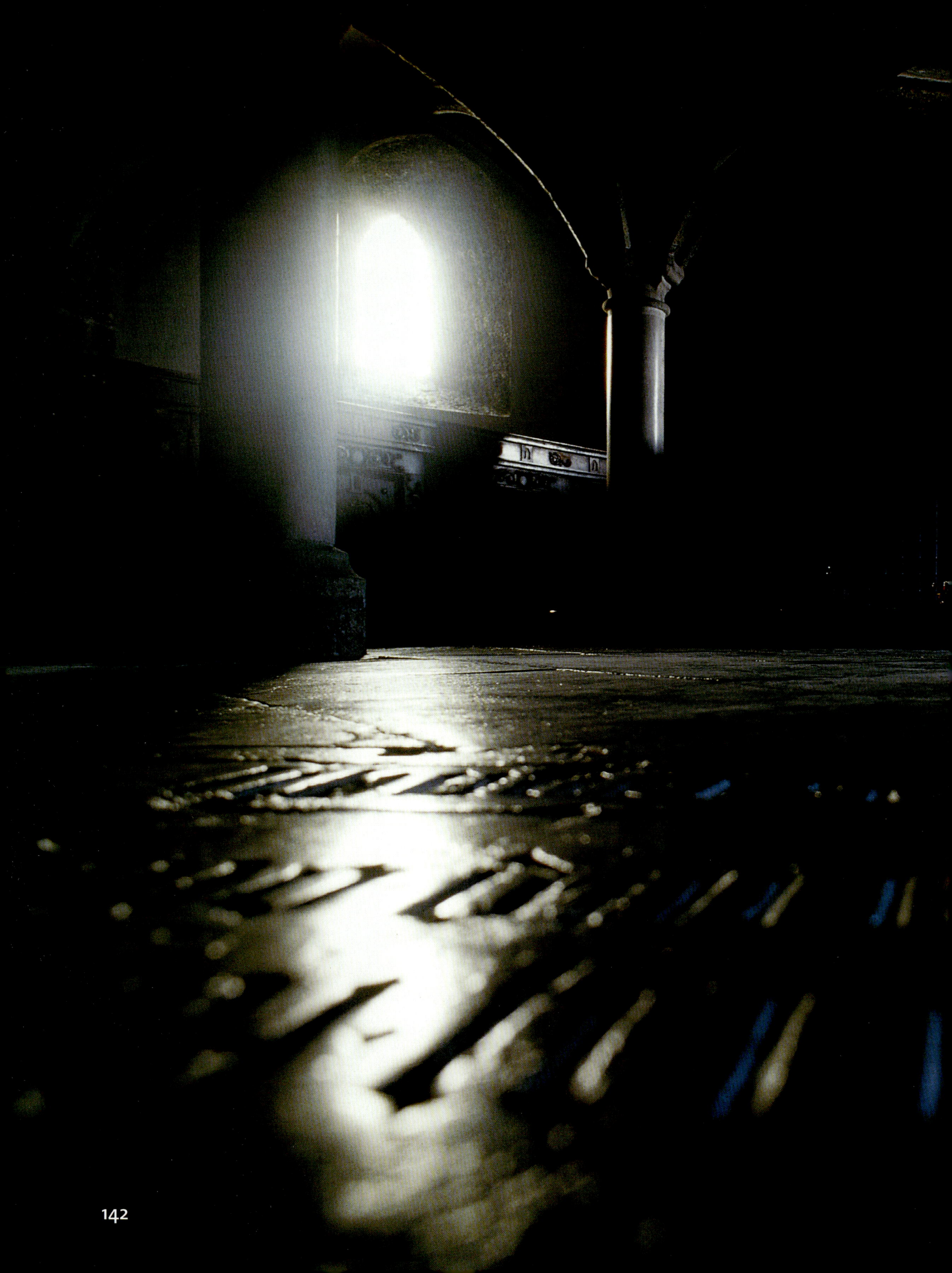

Die gotische Krypta (1463) des Benediktinerinnenstifts Nonnberg. Berühmt wurde das Stift durch den Film „The Sound of Music" – die Geschichte der Trapp-Familie, denn hier war die spätere Baronin Trapp Novizin, bevor sie als Kindermädchen zur Familie Trapp kam

The Gothic crypt (1463) of the Nonnberg Benedictine abbey. The abbey was made world famous by the film "The Sound of Music", as it was here that the future Baroness von Trapp was a novice before being given the position of governess of the Trapp family children

Die Kollegienkirche ist das Meisterwerk des Barockarchitekten Johann Fischer von Erlach (1656 – 1723). Als Universitätskirche erbaut, wurde sie im Jahr 1707 eingeweiht. Der Innenraum zeichnet sich durch seine besondere Klarheit aus. Auf diese Weise wollte Fischer nicht von der architektonischen Wirkung ablenken

The Kollegienkirche is a masterpiece by Baroque architect Johann Fischer von Erlach (1656 – 1723). Built as a university chapel, it was consecrated in 1707. The interior is characterised by its special clarity, which Fischer designed in this way so as not to distract attention from the overall architectural effect

Seit gut 350 Jahren kommen die Pilger zum Wallfahrtsort Maria Plein, auf einem Hügel über der Stadt Salzburg gelegen. Ihr Ziel ist das Gnadenbild „Maria Trost", das im Inneren der Basilika aufbewahrt wird. Schon Mozart soll nach Maria Plein gekommen sein

People have undertaken pilgrimages to Maria Plein located on a hill above the city of Salzburg for more than 350 years. They come to see the "Maria Trost" image that is kept in the basilica there. Even Mozart is said to have visited Maria Plein

Marcus Sitticus ließ im 17. Jahrhundert von Antonio Solari „zu seinem und seiner Nachfolger Vergnügen" Schloss Hellbrunn errichten. Er schuf das erste Gartentheater Europas. Auch das Menü wurde im Freien eingenommen. Das Foto zeigt das „Freiluftesszimmer". Die Rinne in der Tischmitte war mit Wasser gefüllt und diente als Kühlschrank

Marcus Sitticus had Antonio Solari build Hellbrunn Castle in the 17th century "for the amusement of himself and his successors". He created the first garden theatre in Europe here. Even the menu was consumed open-air. The photograph shows the "open-air dining room". The groove in the middle of the table was filled with water and served as a refrigerator

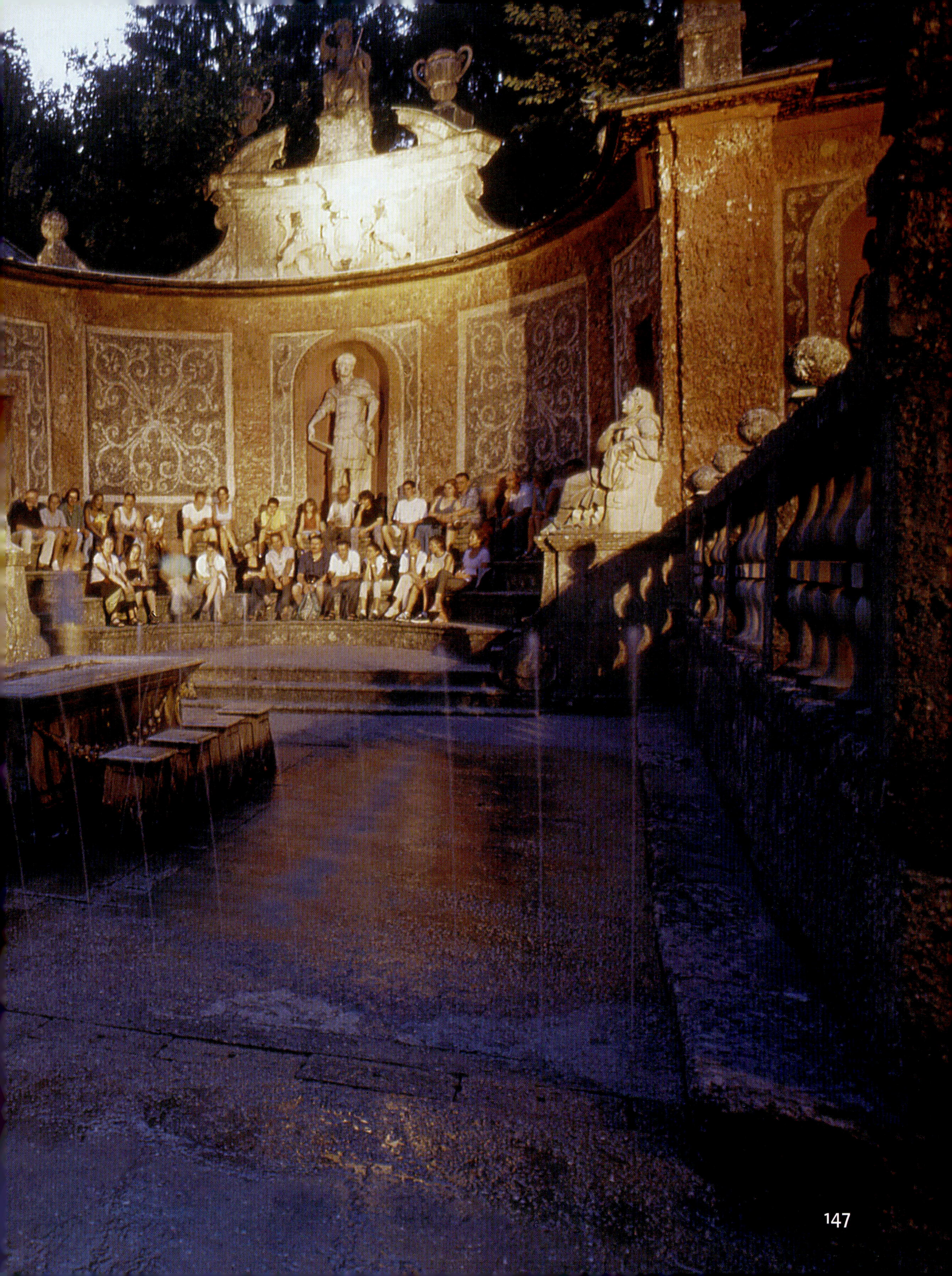

Gewiss im Sinne von Marcus Sitticus wird heute die Anlage von Schloss Hellbrunn „theatralisch" beleuchtet. Im Hintergrund erstrahlt das Monatsschlösschen

The gardens of Hellbrunn are today illuminated "theatrically", which would almost certainly have appealed to Marcus Sitticus. In the background you can see the Monatsschlösschen or "one-month palace"

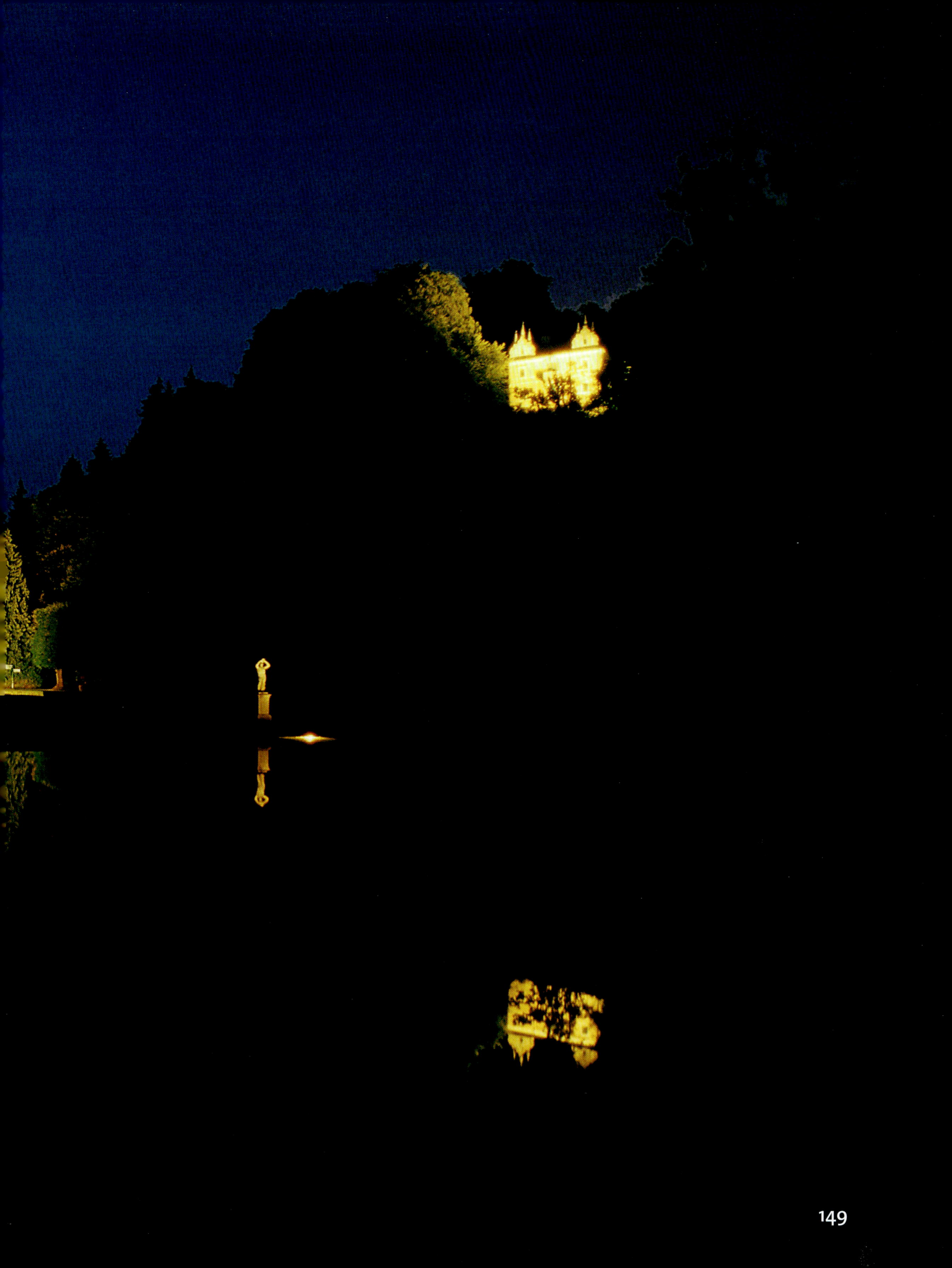

Schloss Leopoldskron wurde als „Lustgebäude" und Familiensitz von Fürsterzbischof Leopold Anton Freiherr von Firmian Leopoldskron von 1736 bis 1744 erbaut. Max Reinhardt machte das heruntergekommene Haus, den Park und die Insel im See zur Bühne. Zur Festspielzeit traf sich hier alljährlich Europas Kulturprominenz

---

Leopoldskron Palace was built from 1736 to 1744 as a summer residence and family home of prince bishop Leopold Anton Freiherr von Firmian. Max Reinhardt made the run-down building, the park and the island in the lake to his stage. Europe's cultural elite meets here every year for the Salzburg Festival

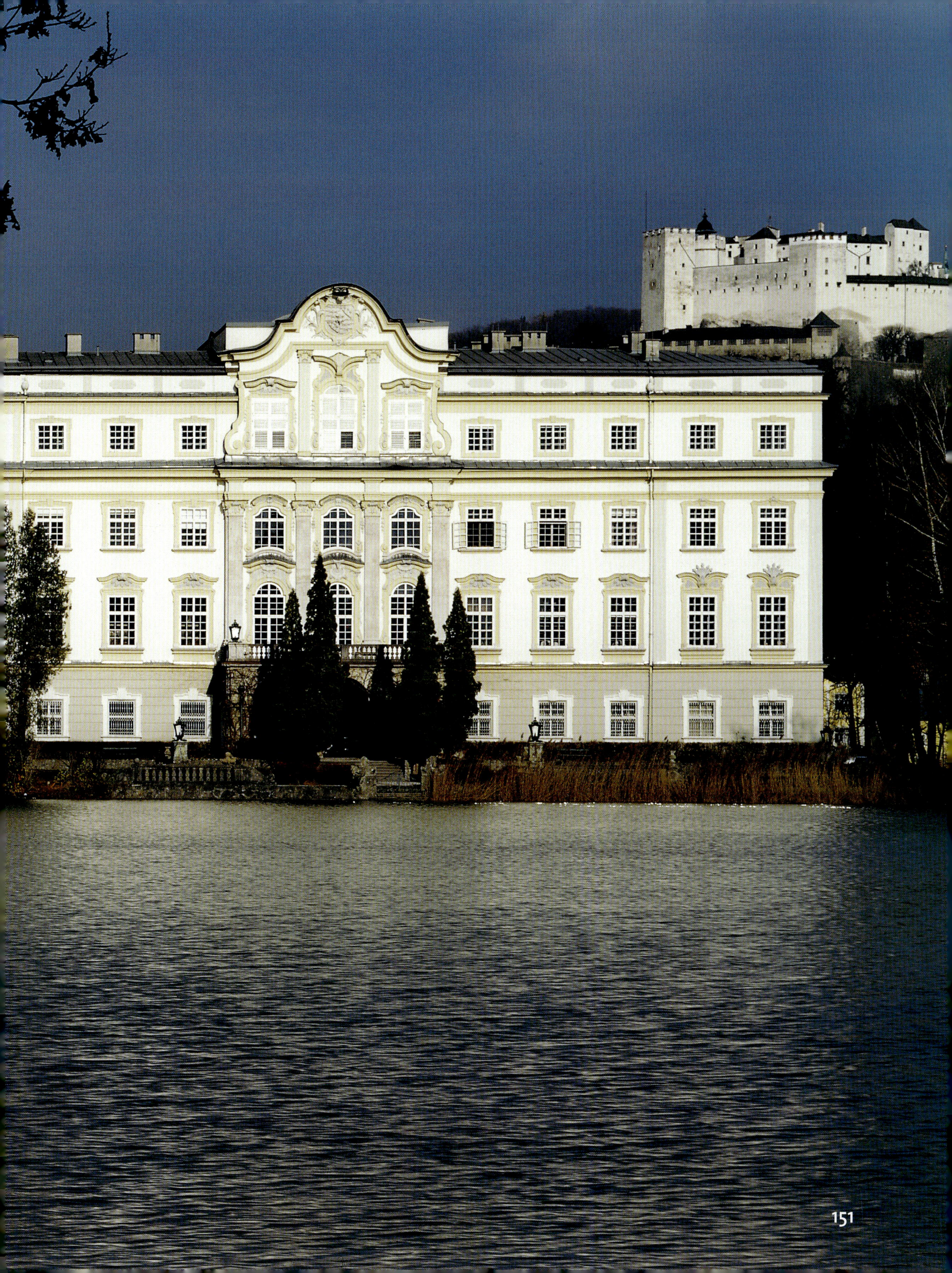

Der Marmorsaal von Schloss Leopoldskron. Hier fanden zu Max Reinhardts Zeiten Feiern und Lesungen statt. Das Anwesen war 1851 Ausweichdomizil für König Ludwig I. wegen seiner Affäre mit Lola Montez. Heutiger Besitzer des Schlosses ist die NGO Salzburg Seminar

The Marble Room of Leopoldskron Palace. This is where parties and readings were held during the Max Reinhardt era. In 1851 the property was a hideaway for King Ludwig the First because of his love affair with Lola Montez. The NGO Salzburg Seminar is today the palace's owner

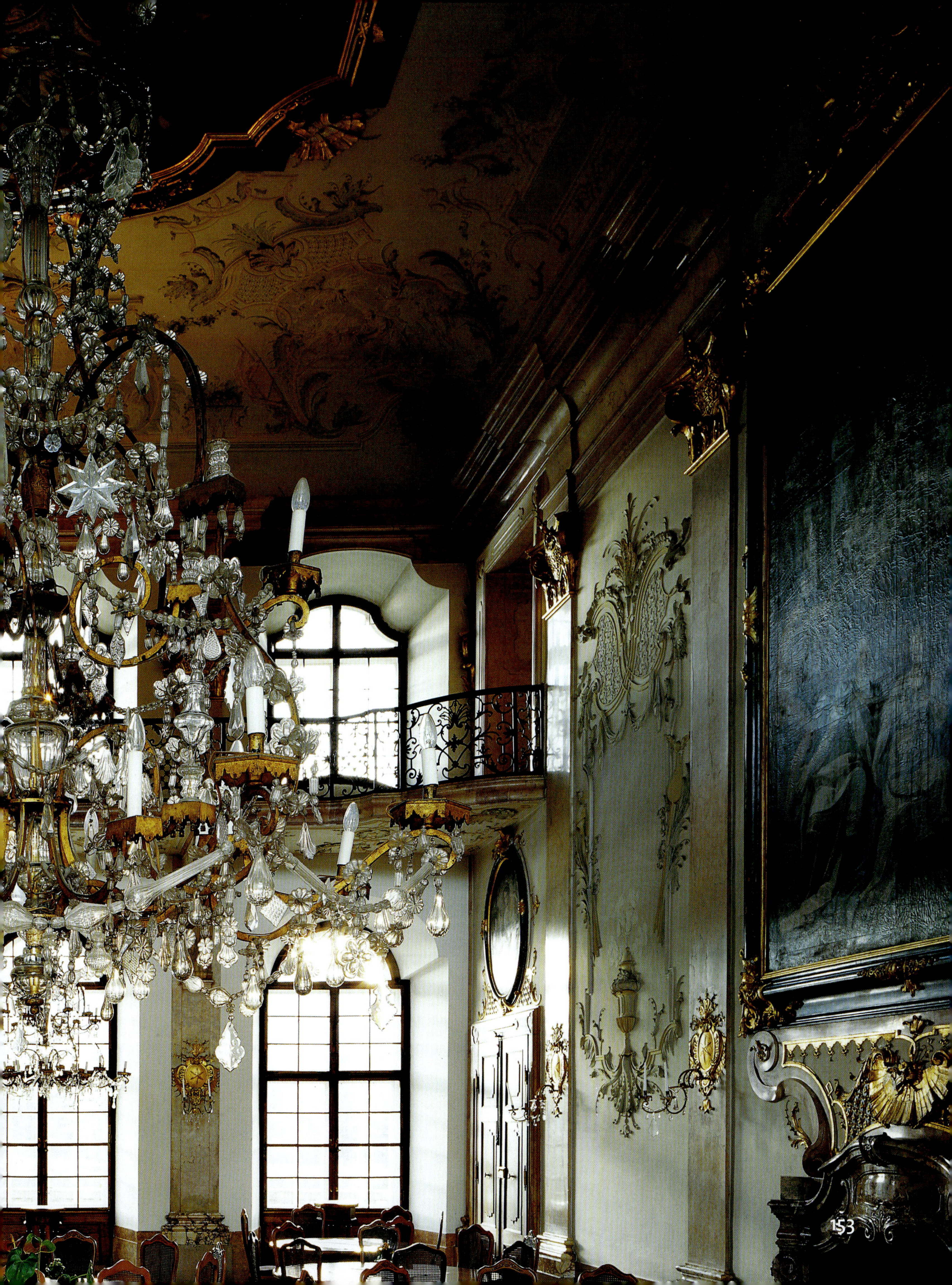

Festspiele/Festivals

21.6. – 14.7.2007
SommerSzene/Summer Scene

Internationales Avantgarde – Festival
Thema „China & Indien"
Szene Salzburg
Tel. +43/662/843448
www.sommerszene.net

27.7. – 31.8.2007
Salzburger Festspiele/Salzburg Festival

Oper: Armida, Eugen Onegin, Der Freischütz, Le nozze di Figaro u.a.
Schauspiel: Ein Fest für Boris, Jedermann, Molière, Eine Passion, Ein Sommernachtstraum
Konzerte: Orchesterkonzerte, Kammerkonzerte, Mozart-Matinéen, Solistenkonzerte u.a.
Salzburger Festspiele
Tel. +43/662/8045-500
www.salzburgfestival.at

12.10. – 28.10.2007
Salzburger Kulturtage/Culture Days Salzburg

Oper: Der Barbier von Sevilla, Hänsel und Gretel
Ballett: St. Petersburger Ballett-Theater
Orchesterkonzerte: Mozarteum Orchester Salzburg, Nordwestdeutsche Philharmonie, Junge Philharmonie u.a.
Kammerkonzerte: Mozart Quartett Salzburg u.a.
Schauspiel: Nestroy
Kirchenmusik: Domkonzert
Salzburger Kulturvereinigung
Tel. +43/662/845346
www.kulturvereinigung.com

25.10. – 4.11.2007
Salzburger Jazz Herbst 2007/Autumn Jazz Festival 2007

Golden Striker Trio, Rebecca Carrington, Carla Bley Band, Esbjörn Svensson Trio, Vienna Art Orchestra, Dee Dee Bridgewater, Paco de Lucia Group u.v.m.
Vienna Entertainment
Tel. +43/1/5048500
www.viennaentertainment.com

Theater und Konzerte/Theatres and Concerts

Mitte September bis Mitte Juni
Salzburger Landestheater/City Theatre

Musiktheater/Oper, Operette, Musical/Ballett, Schauspiel
Premieren: Der Talismann, Hänsel und Gretel, Die Scott Joplin Story, Der Vogelhändler, Leutnant Gustl, Bernarda Albas Haus u.a.
Salzburger Landestheater
Tel. +43/662/871512-222
www.salzburger-landestheater.at

Ganzjährig
Salzburger Marionettentheater/Salzburg Marionette Theatre

Opern: von W.A. Mozart, G. Rossini, E. Humperdinck
Operette: von J. Strauß
Ballett: von P.I. Tschaikowskij
Salzburger Marionettentheater
Tel. +43/662/872406-0
www.marionetten.at

Salzburger Schlosskonzerte/Salzburg Palace Concerts

Im Marmorsaal des Schlosses Mirabell spielen österr. und internationale Solisten und Ensembles Werke von Mozart u.a.
Konzertdirektion der Salzburger Schlosskonzerte
Tel. +43/662/848586
www.salzburger-schlosskonzerte.at

Salzburger Festungskonzerte/Salzburg Fortress Concerts

Werke der großen Meister, insbesondere Mozart
Kammerkonzerte im Fürstenzimmer und Wappensaal der Festung Hohensalzburg
Konzertdirektion der Salzburger Festungskonzerte
Tel. +43/662/825858
www.mozartfestival.at

Mozart Dinner Concert/Mozart Dinner Concert

Im historischen Barocksaal des Stiftskellers St. Peter spielt das Amadeus Consort in Kostümen aus Mozarts Zeit die berühmtesten Arien und Duette – 3-gängiges Mozart Dinner nach Rezepten der Mozart Zeit
Salzburger Konzertgesellschaft
Tel. +43/662/8286950
www.salzburg-concerts.com

April bis Oktober 2007
Mozart Lunch Concert/Mozart Lunch Concert

Ensemble AmaDuo Salzburg in historischen Kostümen. Lieder, Arien und Klaviersonaten von W.A. Mozart im historischen Haydnsaal des Stiftskellers St. Peter
Salzburger Konzertgesellschaft
Tel. +43/662/8286950
www.salzburg-concerts.com

Mai bis September 2007
Salzburger Lunch-Concerts/Salzburg Lunch Concerts

jeden Freitag:
Im Gotischen Saal, St. Blasius
Konzertdirektion Nerat
Tel. +43/662/436870
www.lunchconcerts.at

Ganzjährig
Mozart Klaviersonaten/Mozart piano sonatas

jeden Freitag und Samstag:
Klavierkonzerte im Romanischen Saal der Erzabtei St. Peter
Salzburger Veranstaltungsagentur ORPHEUS
Tel. +43/662/875161
www.agenturorpheus.at

August 2007
Nachmittagskonzerte/Concerts in the afternoon

in der Schlosskirche Mirabell:
Eine klassische Konzertstunde mit Werken von W.A. Mozart, Schubert, Chopin, Mendelssohn u.a.
Gesellschaft Musica sacra Salzburg
Tel. +43/662/823788
www.nachmittagskonzerte.at

1.7. – 24.9.2007
Fünf-Uhr-Konzerte/Concerts at Five

Kammermusik aus der großen Tradition Salzburgs
im Michael-Haydn-Museum
Täglich außer Mittwoch
Johann-Michael-Haydn-Gesellschaft
Tel. +43/662/844576-19, +43/3612/26080
www.5-Uhr-Konzerte.com

20.7. – 31.8.2007
Internationale Salzburger Orgelkonzerte
International Salzburg Organ Concerts

In der Franziskanerkirche
www.kirchen.net/franziskanerkirche

14.4. – 29.9.2007
Mozart Requiem/Mozart Requiem

jeden Samstag:
In der Kollegienkirche mit dem Chor und Orchester der Salzburger Konzertgesellschaft
Salzburger Konzertgesellschaft
Tel. +43/662/8286950
www.salzburg-concerts.com

28.7. – 19.8.2007
Siemens Festspielnächte/Siemens Festival Nights

täglich Vorführungen
von Festspielproduktionen auf einer Großbildleinwand am Kapitelplatz
www.festspielnaechte.at

Mitte Mai bis Mitte Oktober 2007
Sound of Salzburg Dinner & Show
Sound of Salzburg Dinner & Show

täglich:
Salzburger Volksmusik, Salzburger Operette und Werke von W.A. Mozart sowie „Sound of Music" Melodien
The Sound of Austria Veranstaltungs GmbH
Tel. +43/662/826617
www.soundofsalzburgshow.com

DIVERSES/MISCELLANEOUS

28.7. – 4.8.2007
Salzburg World Fine Art Fair/Salzburg World Fine Art Fair

Kunst-, Juwelen- und Antiquitäten-Messe in der Residenz
ArtCultureStudio
Tel. +41/22/9061520
www.salzburg-faf.com

20.9. – 24.9.2007
Rupertikirtag/St. Rupert's Day Fair

Kirchweihfest auf den Plätzen rund um den Dom
Altstadt Marketing
Tel. +43/662/845453
www.salzburg-altstadt.at

30.11. – 31.12.2007
7. Winterfest im Volksgarten/ Winter Festival in Volksgarten

Internationale Varietékunst im Circuszelt.
Festival im Volksgarten GmbH
Tel. +43/662/887580
www.winterfest.at

ADVENTS- UND WEIHNACHTSVERANSTALTUNGEN
ADVENT AND CHRISTMAS EVENTS

22.11. – 24.12.2007
Salzburger Christkindlmarkt/Salzburg Christkindl Market

täglich am Dom- und Residenzplatz,
in der Altstadt von Salzburg
Traditioneller Christkindlmarkt mit handwerklichen Produkten, traditionellen Schmankerln, umfangreichem Veranstaltungsprogramm vor dem Dom u.v.m, Turmblasen jeden Sams-tag am Residenzplatz, Krippenausstellung im Residenzhof
www.christkindlmarkt.co.at

22.11. – 24.12.2007
Hellbrunner Adventzauber/Hellbrunn Advent Market

jeweils Mittwoch bis Sonntag sowie am Feiertag 8.12.
Romantischer Adventmarkt und umfangreiches Rahmenprogramm im Schlosshof und Schloss Hellbrunn
www.adventzauber.tv

22.11. – 24.12.2007
Weihnachtsmarkt am Mirabellplatz
Christmas Market on Mirabell Square

täglich geöffnet
Kunstvoll dekorierte Hütten mit traditionellem Charme, kulinarischen Köstlichkeiten, u.v.m. Musikalisches Rahmenprogramm vor dem Schloss Mirabell jeweils Mittwoch, Samstag und Sonntag
www.weihnachtsmarkt-salzburg.at

22.11. – 23.12.2007
Stern Advent Markt/Stern Advent Market

täglich geöffnet
Kunst & Handwerk im Sterngarten
Originelle Ideen, eigenwillige Formen, lebendiges Handwerk, Traditionelles und völlig Neues
www.sternadvent.at

ab 1.12. sowie am 8.12.2007
Stimmungsvoller Adventmarkt/Romantic Advent Market

im Burghof der Festung Hohensalzburg
jeweils Samstag und Sonntag im Advent
Mit heimischem Kunst- und Handwerk, originellen Geschenkideen, weihnachtlichen Köstlichkeiten und Rahmenprogramm
www.salzburg-burgen.com

30.11. – 16.12.2007
Salzburger Adventsingen/Salzburg Advent Singing

Da hat vor dem Stall der Äpfibam bliaht
Musikalisch-szenisches Gesamtwerk von Tobias Reiser jun.
Salzburger Heimatwerk
Tel. +43/662/843182
www.salzburgeradventsingen.at

1.12. – 16.12.2007
Salzburger Advent®/Salzburg Advent

Adventsingen mit echter Volksmusik,
festlicher Barockmusik, Adventlyrik und Prosa,
sowie Theaterstück in der Stadtpfarrkirche St. Andrä
Salzburger Advent®
Tel. +43/662/629192
www.salzburgeradvent.at

30.11. – 8.12.2007
Tobi Reiser Adventsingen/Tobi Reiser Advent Singing

mit dem Ensemble Tobias Reiser, Salzburger Dreigesang,
Bertl Göttl, Salzburger Hiatabuam u.a.
in der Großen Universitätsaula
Vorverkauf: Kartenbüro Polzer
Tel. +43/662/8969
www.polzer.com

8.12. – 16.12.2007
A b'sondere Zeit
"A special time of the year" – Traditional Advent songs

Adventsingen mit besinnlichen Texten, heimatlichen alpenländischen Volksweisen und Hirtenspiel im Mozarteum
Kartenbüro Polzer
Tel. +43/662/8969
www.salzburg.gv.at/landeshilfe/landeshilfe_veranstaltungen.htm

30.11. – 23.12.2007
Adventserenaden/Advent Serenades

im Gotischen Saal/St. Blasius (Ende Getreidegasse)
Volksmusik und Klassik, Advents- und Weihnachtslieder,
Lesung bei Kerzenlicht
Konzertdirektion Nerat
Tel. +43/662/436870
www.adventserenaden.at

Sonderausstellungen/Exhibitions

11.5. – 28.10.2007
Dommuseum zu Salzburg/Cathedral Museum

Ewald Mataré in Salzburg
Domplatz 1a, Eingang Domvorhalle
Tel. +43/662/844189
www.kirchen.net/dommuseum

Mai – Oktober 2007
Haus der Natur/Museum of Natural History

Schatzkammer Tropen – vergänglicher Reichtum
Museumplatz 5
Tel. +43/662/842653
www.hausdernatur.at

1.5. – 26.10.2007
Michael Haydn Museum/Michael Haydn Museum

Johann Michael Haydn (1737-1806)
Erzabtei St. Peter
Tel. +43/662/844576-19, +43/3612/26080
www.5-Uhr-Konzerte.com

28.7. – 28.10.2007
Museum der Moderne Salzburg Rupertinum
Museum of Modern Art Salzburg Rupertinum

Jan Fabre. Die verliehene Zeit
Wiener-Philharmoniker-Gasse 9
Tel. +43/662/842220
www.museumdermoderne.at

21.7. – 11.11.2007
Museum der Moderne Salzburg Mönchsberg
Museum of Modern Art Salzburg Mönchsberg

Mahjong Chinesische Gegenwartskunst aus der Sammlung Sigg
Mönchsberg 32
Tel. +43/662/842220
www.museumdermoderne.at

14.7. – 4.11.2007
Residenzgalerie Salzburg/Residenz Gallery Salzburg

Die Schöne und das Ungeheuer
Geschichten ungewöhnlicher Liebespaare

17.11. – 3.2.2008

Der Glanz der Dinge
Stilllebenmalerei aus vier Jahrhunderten
Residenzplatz 1
Tel. +43/662/840451
www.residenzgalerie.at

15.6. – 9.9.2007
Salzburger Barockmuseum/Salzburg Baroque Museum

Versailles – Der Garten des Sonnenkönigs
Orangerie des Mirabellgartens
Tel. +43/662/877432
www.barockmuseum.at

ab Juni 2007
Salzburg Museum Neue Residenz
Salzburg Museum New Residence

Der Mythos Salzburg – spannende Einblicke in die Salzburger Geschichte, Kunst und Kultur/ „Salzburg persönlich" – Salzburger Persönlichkeiten wie Künstler, Literaten, Wissenschaftler usw. / Sonderausstellungsbereiche wie z.B. keltische Funde u.v.m.
Mozartplatz 1
Tel. +43/662/620808-700
www.salzburgmuseum.at

23.3. – 23.9.2007
Salzburg Museum – Spielzeug Museum
Salzburg Museum – Toy Collection

Spielzeug von A bis Z – Die Welt im Alphabet
Bürgerspitalgasse 2
Tel. +43/662/620808-300
www.salzburgmuseum.at

1.5. – 31.10.2007
Salzburg Museum – Volkskunde Museum
Salzburg Museum – Folklore Museum

Gold und Silber in Andacht, Schmuck und Tracht
Monatsschlößl Hellbrunn
Tel. +43/662/620808-500
www.salzburgmuseum.at

FESTSPIELE / FESTIVALS   2008

25.1. – 3.2.2008
Mozartwoche / Mozart Week

Geistliche Werke – von Mozart bis zur Gegenwart
Singspiel konzertant: „Die Schuldigkeit des Ersten Gebots" KV 35
Konzertprogramm: Orchesterkonzerte mit u.a. Camerata Salzburg, Cappella Andrea Barca, Mozarteum Orchester Salzburg, Wiener Philharmoniker sowie Kammerkonzerte, Nachtkonzert, Solistenkonzert
Internationale Stiftung Mozarteum
Tel. +43/662/873154
www.mozarteum.at

15.3. – 24.3.2008
Osterfestspiele / Easter Festival

Oper: „Die Walküre" von R. Wagner
Orchesterkonzerte: Berliner Philharmoniker (Beethoven, Schostakowitsch, Haydn, Busoni, Brahms, Dvorák)
Konzertreihe „Kontrapunkte"
Osterfestspiele Salzburg
Tel. +43/662/8045-361
www.osterfestspiele-salzburg.at

9.5. – 12.5.2008
Salzburger Festspiele Pfingsten
Salzburg Whitsuntide Festival

Oper & Konzerte
Salzburger Festspiele Pfingsten
Tel. +43/662/8045-500
www.salzburgfestival.at

27.7. – 31.8.2008
Salzburger Festspiele / Salzburg Festival

(Beginn kann sich noch auf 26.7. ändern)
Oper, Schauspiel, Young Directors Project, Orchesterkonzerte, Kammerkonzerte, Mozart-Matinéen, Solistenkonzerte u.a.
Salzburger Festspiele
Tel. +43/662/8045-500
www.salzburgfestival.at

4.10. – 20.10.2008
Bachfest 2008 / Bach Festival 2008

Themenkreise:
Bach und Neue Musik,
Bach und Jazz,
Bach und Salzburg, Bach und Caldara
Tel. +43/662/4353710
www.salzburger-bachgesellschaft.at

SPORT / SPORTS

7.6. – 29.6.2008
UEFA EURO 2008™

Drei spannende Gruppenspiele in Salzburg:
10.6., 14.6. und 18.6.2008
Beginn: jeweils 20.45 Uhr
www.salzburg.info/euro2008

DIVERSES / MISCELLANEOUS

15.3. – 24.3.2008
Messe für Kunst & Antiquitäten
Int. Trade Fair for Art & Antiques

In den Prunkräumen der Residenz
MAC – Hoffmann & Co GmbH
Tel. +43/1/5871293
www.mac-hoffmann.com

10.5. – 19.5.2008
Salzburger Dult / "Salzburger Dult" – traditional fair

Das traditionelle Salzburger Volksfest am Messegelände
Messezentrum Salzburg
Tel. +43/662/240450
www.dult.at

19.9. – 24.9.2008
Rupertikirtag / St. Rupert's Day Fair

Kirchweihfest auf den Plätzen rund um den Dom
Altstadt Marketing
Tel. +43/662/845453
www.salzburg-altstadt.at

Für Detailinformationen wenden Sie sich bitte an:
For further information please contact:
TOURISMUS SALZBURG GMBH
Salzburg Information
Auerspergstraße 6, A-5020 Salzburg
Tel. +43/662/88987-0
Fax: +43/662/88987-32
E-mail: tourist@salzburg.info
http://www.salzburg.info

Alle Angaben ohne Gewähr, bzw. allfällige Änderungen möglich
All information subject to alteration
Stand/Status: April 2007

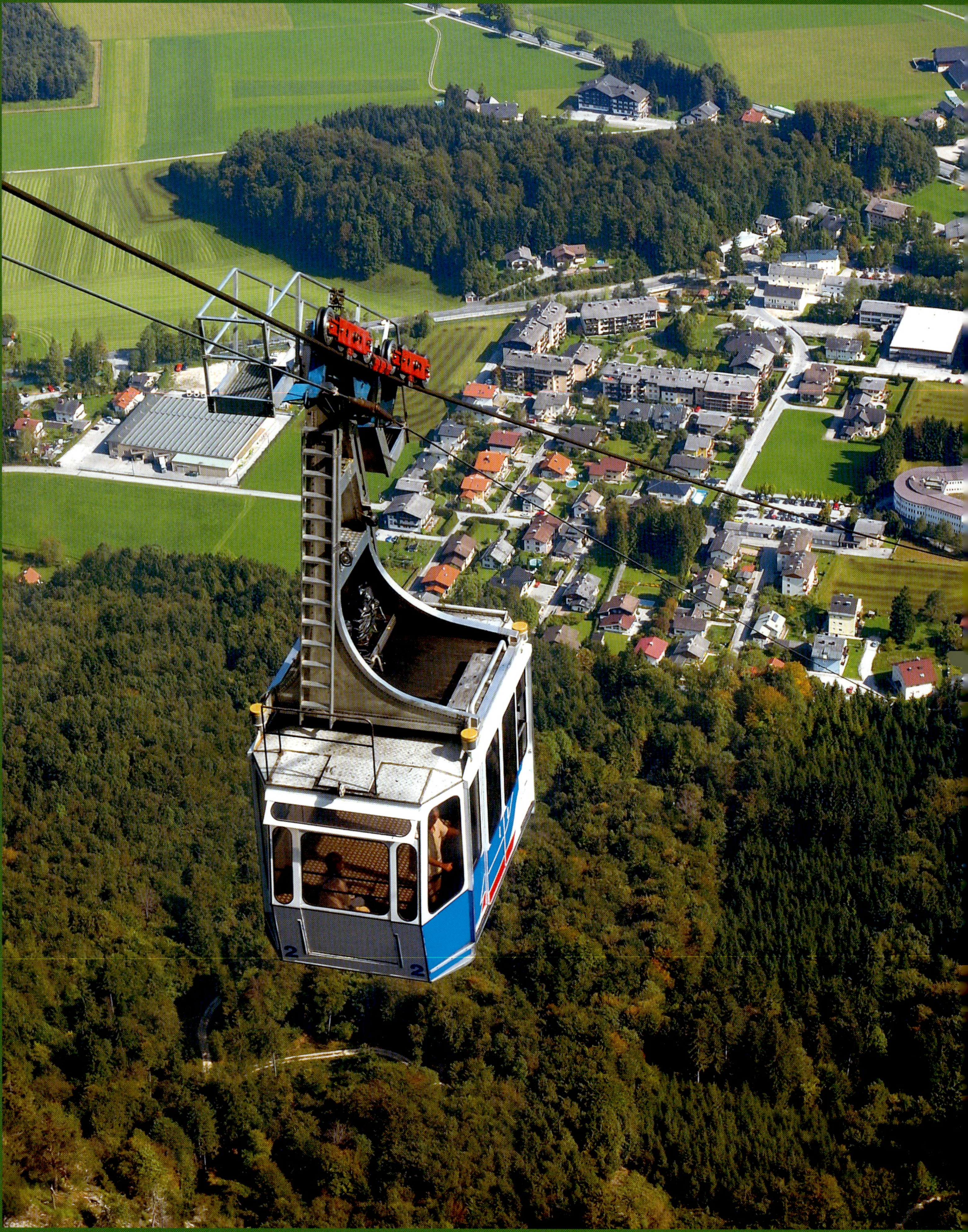

*Leo Bauernberger
Geschäftsführer der SalzburgerLand
Tourismus Gesellschaft*

Tourismus –
Freizeit und Erholung
im SalzburgerLand

Tourism –
fun and relaxation
in SalzburgerLand

Das SalzburgerLand blickt auf 200 Jahre touristische Erschließung zurück und zählt damit zu den ältesten Tourismusregionen Europas. Die „Entdeckung" des Berglandes setzte unter dem Einfluss der salzburgerischen Spätaufklärung gegen Ende des 18. Jahrhunderts ein. Durchdrungen von der ästhetischen Naturwahrnehmung der Frühromantik durchwanderten die Gelehrten das Land und brachten einem breiten Lesekreis das SalzburgerLand näher. Zu Beginn des 19. Jahrhunderts folgten Scharen von Künstlern, die Stadt und Land in ihren Gemälden verewigten.

Verkehrsgeografisch befanden sich die Gebirgsgaue um die Mitte des 19. Jahrhunderts in einer Abseitslage. Während zur Sommerzeit alljährlich die Touristen in die Stadt strömten, reisten wenig Fremde in das Gebirge. Mit dem Bau der „Salzburg-Tiro-

SalzburgerLand looks back on a 200-year history of tourism, which makes it one of the oldest tourist regions in Europe. The "discovery" of this mountain paradise began under the influence of Salzburg's late Enlightenment period at the end of the 18th century. Permeated by the aesthetic perception of early Romanticism, scholars travelled the country introducing SalzburgerLand to a large group of readers. By the beginning of the 19th century, artists were flocking to the city and state of Salzburg to eternalise it in their works.

The mountain districts were off the beaten track in the mid 19th century. While tourists came to the city in droves during the summer months, very few of them ventured into the mountains. The construction of the "Salzburg-Tyrol railway" and the Seltzthalbahn line in 1875 marked the creation of

**kleines Bild:
Die Schmittenhöhe ist ein äußerst beliebtes Skigebiet. Im Hintergrund das Kitzsteinhorn**

Das grandiose Großglockner-Alpenpanorama

**small picture:
Schmittenhöhe is a very popular ski field. Here you can see the Kitzsteinhorn in the background**

The magnificent Grossglockner alpine panorama

ler-Bahn" und der Seltzthalbahn 1875 wurden die infrastrukturellen Voraussetzungen für den touristischen Aufschwung in den Gebirgsregionen geschaffen. Lokal- und Kleinbahnen erschlossen Ende des 19. Jahrhunderts abgelegene und wirtschaftlich benachteiligte Landesteile, und Zahnradbahnen brachten erstmals ein touristisches Massenpublikum in hochalpine Regionen. Der Erste Weltkrieg beendete die Ära des Bahnbaus. Neben der Verschlechterung der wirtschaftlichen Verhältnisse zeichnete sich bereits der Aufstieg des Automobils als Verkehrsmittel der Zukunft ab.

Nach Ende des Ersten Weltkrieges setzte der Skitourismus mit Beginn der 20er Jahre neue touristische Impulse. Die am 31.12.1927 in Betrieb genommene Schmittenbahn blieb jedoch für 2 Jahrzehnte die einzige mechanische Hilfe für Winter-

the infrastructural prerequisites for a boom in tourism in the mountain regions. Local and narrow-gauge railways opened up distant and economically disadvantaged districts at the end of the 19th century, and rack-and-pinion railways brought mass tourism to the high alpine regions for the first time. The First World War ended the era of railway construction. Along with the worsening economic situation, the rise of the automobile as the vehicle of the future put an end to rail's reign as the number one mode of land transport.

After the end of WWI, the beginning of the 20th century brought new impulses with it in the form of ski tourism. However, the Schmittenbahn remained the only mechanical aid for winter sports in the state for the two decades following its commissioning on 1927-12-31. Summer tourism, too, was

Auf dem Pinzgauer „Arnoweg" die Bergwelt entdecken – ein ganz besonderes Vergnügen für Naturliebhaber

Discover the world of the Alps on the Pinzgau "Arnoweg" track – a very special treat for nature lovers

sportzwecke im Lande. Auch der „Sommerfrischler-Tourismus" beschränkte sich in erster Linie auf punktuell erschlossene Touristenzentren. Der Bau der Gaisbergstraße 1929 und vor allem der Glocknerstraße 1935 entsprach den Bedürfnissen des sich entfaltenden automobilen Tourismus, zog jedoch aufgrund der tristen internationalen Wirtschaftslage vorerst keine Besuchermassen ins Land.

Nach dem Zweiten Weltkrieg verzeichneten die Alpen als Erholungsraum einen beträchtlichen Bedeutungsgewinn. Neben dem Aufschwung des Tourismus erfuhr der alpine Raum eine Aufwertung als Wirtschaftsstandort. Sowohl im gesamteuropäischen als auch im nationalen Vergleich erfuhr das SalzburgerLand einen ökonomischen und demografischen Aufschwung. Optimale landschaftliche Voraussetzungen für den Sommer- und Winterfremdenverkehr wie auch die Möglichkeit zur autonomen Wirtschaftsgestaltung auf föderaler Grundlage boten auf regionaler Salzburger Ebene außergewöhnlich günstige Bedingungen für eine dynamische Tourismusentwicklung.

Auch wenn die alpine Landschaft in ihrem Erscheinungsbild vielfach durch die touristische Infrastruktur geprägt war, waren Gemeinden mit touristischer Monofunktion eine große Ausnahme. Die immense Bedeutung insbesondere des Wintertourismus für die wirtschaftliche Aufwertung des Gebirgslandes stand dennoch außer Frage. Eindrucksvoll spiegelt sich die Dynamik der massentouristischen Erschließung im Aufstieg von Saalbach zu einer ganz großen Wintersportdestination der Alpen: Um die Jahrhundertwende noch ein abgelegenes Dorf fern aller Verkehrsverbindungen, übertrafen die Nächtigungszahlen von 1981 bereits jene des gesamten Bundeslandes im Tourismusjahr 1929/30 – dem erfolgreichsten der gesamten Zwischenkriegszeit. Im Winter 2005/06 konnte die kaum 3 000 Einwohner zählende Gemeinde rund 1,5 Millionen Nächtigungen verzeichnen und liegt damit österreichweit an zweiter Stelle der Nächtigungsstatistik.

Gründung der SalzburgerLand Tourismus Gesellschaft

Im Jahr 1986 wurde das Salzburger Tourismusgesetz verabschiedet und gleichzeitig die SalzburgerLand Tourismus Gesellschaft gegründet. Damit war die Basis für den weiteren Erfolg des Salzburger Tourismus geschaffen. Das SalzburgerLand war das erste Bundesland Österreichs, das die Tourismusagenden aus der Landeshoheit in die eigene Gesellschaft ausgegliedert hat.

Und die Zahlen sprechen für sich: Mit 13,54 Millionen Nächtigungen und einem Plus von über 2% im Winter 2005/06 wurde das beste Wintersai-

largely restricted to selected tourist centres. The construction of the Gaisbergstraße road in 1929, and even more importantly the Glocknerstraße road in 1935 answered to the needs of the developing automobile tourism. However, due to the troubled international economic situation, they didn't initially draw the masses into the state that had been hoped for.

After the Second World War the Alps gained considerably in significance as a leisure area. Alongside the tourism boom, the alpine region also grew in commercial importance. SalzburgerLand thrived economically and demographically, both in comparison to Europe as a whole and to other Austrian regions. Perfect scenic conditions for summer and winter tourism, and the possibility to structure the economy autonomously on a federal basis meant that the Salzburg region had an outstanding foundation on which to build a dynamic tourism boom.

Districts relying completely on tourism remained the exception, even if the alpine landscape was often shaped by tourist infrastructures. And there was no question of the immense importance of in particular winter tourism for the economic upswing in the mountain areas. The dynamism of mass tourism is reflected in Saalbach's rise to one of the major winter sports destinations in the Alps: no more than an isolated village far from any roads or other means of transport at the turn of the century, the number of overnight stays here in 1981 exceeded those of the entire state in the 1929/30 tourism year – the most successful of all the years between the World Wars. In the winter of 2005/06 this community of hardly 3,000 people reported around 1.5 million overnight stays, which placed it second in Austria's accommodation statistic.

The foundation of the SalzburgerLand Tourism Company

The Salzburg Tourism Act was passed in 1986, and with it the SalzburgerLand Tourism Company was founded. This formed the basis for the continued success of Salzburg's tourism. SalzburgerLand was the first state in Austria to spin off the responsibility for tourism from the state government into an independent company.

And the figures show that this was a good move: the best winter season on record was achieved in the winter of 2005/06 with 13.54 million overnight stays and a plus of more than 2 percent. Arrivals even increased by more than 4 percent. Summer accommodation also rose in 2006 up to more than 9.6 million overnight stays. The total number of stays in the tourism year 2005/06 thus amounted to 23.2 million, which meant that the goal of breaking the 23 million limit was clearly achieved.

Immer mehr Sportbegeisterte haben für sich den Skilanglauf entdeckt

More and more fitness fans are discovering cross country skiing

Abseits der Pisten ist das Tiefschneefahren für Geübte ein unvergessliches Erlebnis

The off-piste powder is an unforgettable experience for practiced skiers

sonergebnis aller Zeiten erzielt. Bei den Ankünften gab es sogar einen Zuwachs von mehr als 4%. Auch die Sommernächtigungen 2006 sind gestiegen: Es konnte ein Zuwachs auf mehr als 9,6 Millionen Nächtigungen verzeichnet werden. Die Gesamtnächtigungen im Tourismusjahr 2005/06 lagen bei 23,2 Millionen, womit das angepeilte Ziel, die 23 Millionen-Grenze zu überschreiten, klar erreicht wurde.

Die SalzburgerLand Tourismus Gesellschaft als Entwicklungsagentur für touristische Angebote hat in ihrem zwanzigjährigen Bestehen eine Vielzahl an

As a development agency for tourism, the SalzburgerLand Tourism Company has produced numerous new products in the twenty years since its inception. Among these are the Wanderbare Almsommer walking tracks and the Salzburger Bauernherbst pastoral activity calendar that goes into its twelfth year in 2007. It is also responsible for everything from the signs to the marketing for the network of cycle paths, with its ever popular Mozart and Tauern cycle tracks, the Golf Alpin group and the card products such as the Salzburg Super Ski Card and the SalzburgerLand Card.

kleines Bild:
Auch bei einer Pferdeschlittenfahrt kann man die zauberhafte Winterlandschaft genießen

Artistischer „Höhenflug" eines Snowboard-Profis

small picture:
A carriage ride is a magical way to enjoy the winter landscape

An artistic flight of a professional snowboarder

neuen Produkten hervorgebracht. Dazu zählen der Wanderbare Almsommer und der Salzburger Bauernherbst, der 2007 bereits ins zwölfte Jahr geht. Weiters das Radwegnetz mit dem beliebten Mozart-Radweg oder dem Tauernradweg, den die SLTG von der Beschilderung bis zum Marketing umgesetzt hat sowie die Angebotsgruppe Golf Alpin und die Card-Produkte mit der Salzburg Super Ski Card und der SalzburgerLand Card.

Die Themenräume der SLTG

Die Sehnsucht nach Ruhe, Ausgeglichenheit, Schönheit und genussvollen Augenblicken ist aktueller denn je. Der Gast im SalzburgerLand kann sich seinen Wunschurlaub selbst komponieren, und zwar aus den Erlebniswelten „alles bewegen", dem Überbegriff für Sport und Abenteuer, „himmlisch wohl fühlen", das für Natur und Wellness steht und „kunstvoll genießen" als Synonym für Kultur und Genuss. Diese typischen Urlaubsmotive und damit das Angebot für die touristischen Märkte spiegeln sich in den Leitthemen und den konkreten Angeboten für die verschiedensten Zielgruppen wider: Ob Wandern, Radfahren, Golf oder Wellness im Sommer, Nordic Sports und Skilauf im Winter oder Brauchtum, Kultur und Kulinarik als Ganzjahresprogramm – das SalzburgerLand bietet ein facettenreiches und breites Angebotsspektrum für alle Interessensgebiete.

„Alles bewegen" steht für Sport und Spaß im Winter und im Sommer und bietet dem Urlaubsgast alles was das Sportlerherz begehrt.

Im Wintertourismus ist das SalzburgerLand unbestritten eine Fixgröße im internationalen Wintertourismus. Über 1 700 Pistenkilometer, 2 200 Kilometer Loipen und 580 Liftanlagen. Jahr für Jahr vertrauen sich 160 000 Gäste den bestens ausgebildeten Ski- und Snowboardlehrern an. Auch den Einkehrschwung perfektioniert man im SalzburgerLand: In 380 Hütten und Restaurants werden die Wintersportler nach allen Regeln der Gastfreundschaft und Kochkunst bewirtet.

Ob Nordic Skiing, Nordic Walking oder Nordic Cruising – auch die etwas andere Form des Wintersports ist im SalzburgerLand kein Fremdwort. Nicht nur Konditionsfans und Leistungssportler, sondern auch Naturliebhaber finden daran Gefallen und kommen bei den nordischen Sportarten voll auf ihre Kosten.

Neben Skifahrern, Snowboardern und Nordischen bietet sich auch den Abenteurern und sportlich Ambitionierten so einiges: Ein absolutes Muss für Adrenalin-Junkies ist zum Beispiel das Snowkiten, bei dem es nicht bergab, sondern bergauf geht. Reichlich rasant ist auch das Snow-Tubing, wo man in einem großen Gummireifen sitzend den

The SalzburgerLand Tourism Company special motifs

The longing for peace and quiet, balance, beauty and moments of indulgence is stronger than ever among people today. Visitors to SalzburgerLand can put together their very own holiday package, drawing from the adventure worlds *"alles bewegen"* (move everything), covering sports and adventure, *"himmlisch wohl fühlen"* (heavenly relaxation), for nature and spa, and *"kunstvoll genießen"* (artistic pleasures) as a synonym for culture and indulgence. These typical holiday motifs, and thus the range of offers for the tourist markets, are reflected in the guiding themes and actual products for the various target groups. Be it hiking, cycling, golf or wellness in summer, Nordic sports and skiing in winter or tradition, culture and dining all year round – SalzburgerLand has a multi-faceted and broad range of options for the entire spectrum of interests.

"Alles bewegen" stands for sports and fun in winter and summer and offers the holidaymaker everything the sporting heart desires.

SalzburgerLand is without doubt a major player in international winter tourism. It boasts more than 1,700 kilometres of ski runs, 2,200 kilometres of cross country skiing runs and 580 ski lifts. Year for year, 160,000 skiers place themselves in the hands of the excellent ski and snowboard instructors here. And SalzburgerLand is perfect for nailing that last turn into the après ski establishments too: 380 lodges and restaurants treat winter sports fans to top hospitality and cuisine.

Whether it be Nordic Skiing, Nordic Walking or Nordic Cruising – winter sports with a difference are also at home in SalzburgerLand. Not only fitness fans and professional sportspeople love to train here, nature lovers are also in their element with the Nordic sports.

Alongside skiing, snowboarding and the Nordics, adventurers and those looking for a sporting challenge also have a great deal to choose from here: for example snow-kiting is an absolute must for adrenaline junkies. Snow-Tubing is also a rush, hurtling down the mountain sitting in a rubber tube. Less hectic, but all the longer are the many toboggan runs, like the 14 km downhill track in Bramberg am Wildkogel.

Summer brings with it a varied programme of sporting opportunities for the holidaying guest. The SalzburgerLand Tourism Company focuses here on the *"Wanderbarer Almsommer"*: SalzburgerLand is Austria's leader in the field of mountain hiking, with more than 1,800 alpine meadows and 550 properties. The Wanderbarer Almsommer combines hiking with the world of adventure and culinary pleasures

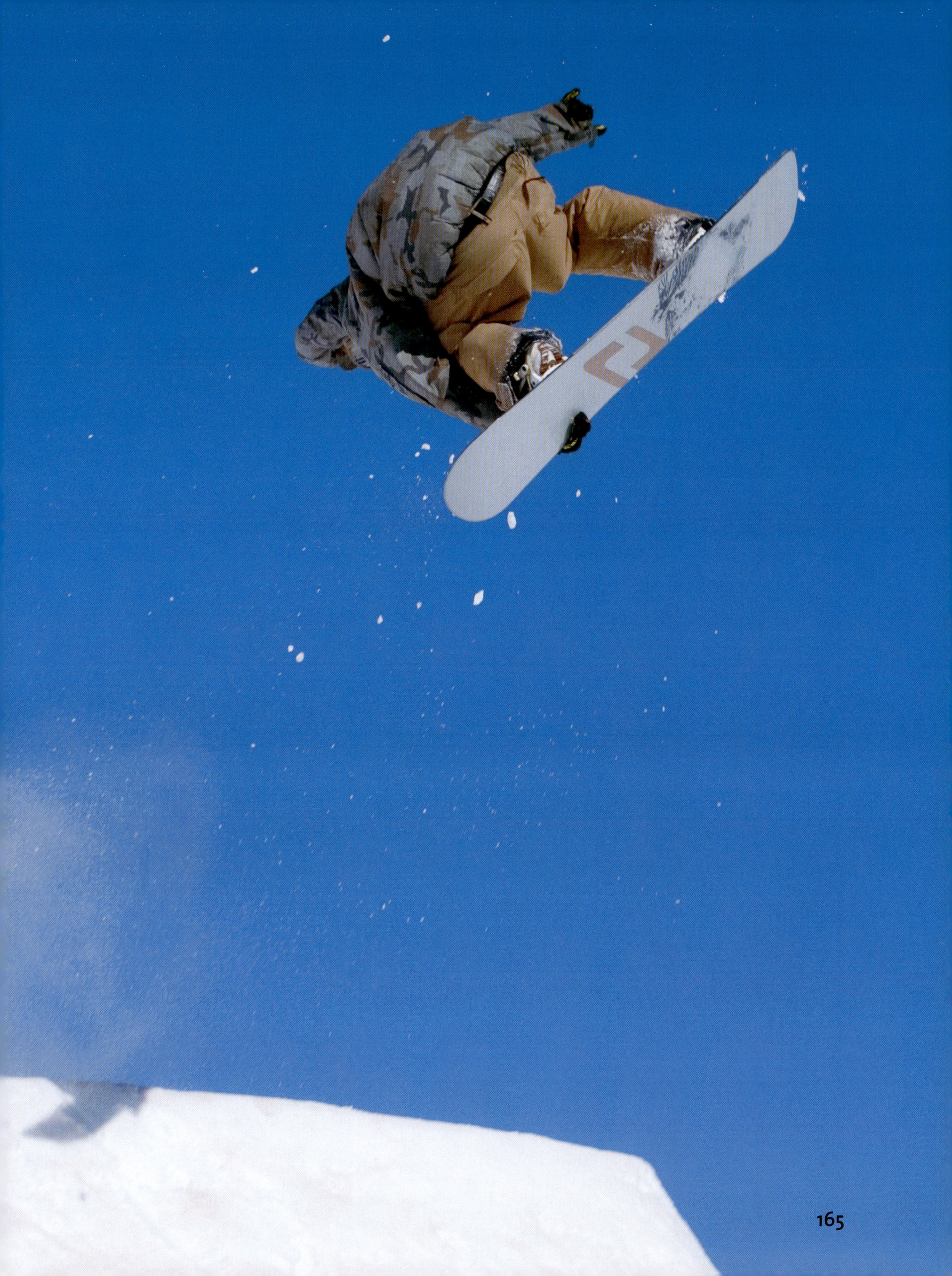

1 Fliegen im Paraglider, Golfen, Wandern oder Rad fahren – es gibt kaum eine Sportart, die im Salzburger Land nicht ausgeübt werden kann

2 Im Golfclub Lungau

3 Auf dem Salzburger Almenweg

4 Der Tauernradweg, im Hintergrund die Burg Werfen

1 Paragliding, golf, hiking and biking – there are opportunities to try out almost every sport there is in Salzburger Land

2 At Lungau golf club

3 On the Salzburger Almenweg track

4 The Tauern cycle path with Werfen castle in the background

rechte Seite von oben nach unten:
Almwirtschaft im Nationalpark Hohe Tauern

Auf dem Bauernherbst wird fröhlich gefeiert: mit Musik und kulinarischen Spezialitäten

right page
from top to bottom:
Alpine restaurant in Hohe Tauern national park

Music and culinary specialities at the autumnal Bauernherbst celebration

166

Berg hinab rutscht. Weniger schnell, dafür umso länger, geht es bei den vielen Rodelbahnen, wie der 14 km langen Bahn in Bramberg am Wildkogel, hinunter.

Im Sommer findet der Urlaubsgast ein vielfältiges Programm an unterschiedlichen Sportmöglichkeiten. Schwerpunktmäßig setzt die SalzburgerLand Tourismus Gesellschaft dabei vor allem auf den „Wanderbaren Almsommer": Mit über 1 800 Almen und 550 bewirtschafteten Hütten ist das SalzburgerLand das almenreichste Land Österreichs. Der Wanderbare Almsommer verbindet das Wandern mit der Erlebnis- und Genusswelt der Almen, die sich an den attraktivsten Plätzen zwischen Talboden und Gipfelwelt befinden. Die SLTG hat sich mit diesem Leitthema für den Sommer zum Ziel gesetzt, das Thema Wandern mit neuen Inhalten zu füllen und spezielle Angebote zu entwickeln, die den Bedürfnissen der Gäste entsprechen. Eines dieser neuen Angebote ist der „Salzburger Almenweg": Mit über 350 Kilometern, die an 120 bewirtschafteten Almen vorbeiführen, verläuft er durch die Pongauer Bergwelt. Gekennzeichnet ist der Weg mit dem Symbol des Enzians. Wichtig ist auch die Qualität des Angebots: Vor Beginn der Almsommer-Saison wurden die Salzburger Almsommer-Hütten zertifiziert. Sie erfüllen definierte Kriterien und entsprechen so dem Anspruch des Gastes auf geprüfte Qualität. So müssen die Hütten zum Beispiel einen typischen Almcharakter aufweisen und die Bewirtschaftung bzw. das Angebot regionaler und selbst erzeugter Produkte muss gegeben sein. Die zertifizierten Hütten werden mit dem Almsommer-Qualitätslogo ausgezeichnet und in den Hüttenführern als solche ausgewiesen.

Der Trend zum Wandern hält an: Laut der aktuellen Deutschen Reiseanalyse 2006 planen 38% der deutschen Bevölkerung über 14 Jahre, in den nächsten drei Jahren einen Naturlaub zu verbringen.

Unter dem Themenbereich „Himmlisch wohlfühlen" bietet die SalzburgerLand Tourismus Gesellschaft ein breites Spektrum hinsichtlich Wellness und Natur an. Um sich auch im Wellnesstourismus als Top-Destination positionieren zu können, setzt die SLTG zusammen mit den Bundesländern Kärnten, Tirol und Vorarlberg auf die Tourismusmarke „Alpine Wellness".

Die Alpine Wellness-Hotels sind Wohlfühl-Oasen der Extra-Klasse inmitten der Bergwelt des SalzburgerLandes. Durch die Verwendung alpiner Materialien in der Architektur und bei der Einrichtung der Zimmer begibt man sich von der ersten Urlaubsminute an in eine andere Welt. In allen Alpinen Wellness Häusern ist das Jahrhunderte alte Wissen um alpine Heilmittel die Basis für ein ganz spezielles Gesundheits- & Wellness-Angebot. Wo

that the alpine meadows have to offer, at the most beautiful locations between the bottom of the valley and the mountain summits. With this theme, the Tourism Company has set itself the goal of injecting new ideas into hiking and developing special offers to answer to the guests' needs. One of these new offers is the "Salzburger Almenweg" (Salzburg alpine meadow track), which passes through the Pongau mountain area with more than 350 kilometres of track that pass by 120 alpine farms. This track is marked with the symbol of the gentian flower, and the quality of the offering is guaranteed: before the summer season begins, the Salzburger Almsommer mountain lodges are tested according to defined criteria and certified, so that guests calling in for replenishment after a long walk can rely on top quality service and culinary products. For example, the mountain restaurants have to be of a typical alpine meadow character and offer products from the region and of their own production. The certified lodges are awarded the Almsommer seal of quality and acknowledged as such in the restaurant guides.

The hiking trend is showing no signs of abating. According to the latest German vacation analysis in 2006, 38% of the German population of 14 years and above plan to take a holiday in the countryside in the next three years.

Under the heading "Himmlisch wohlfühlen", the SalzburgerLand Tourism Company offers a large range of spa and nature services. With the goal of establishing Salzburg as a top spa tourism destination, the SLTC has joined forces with the states of Kärnten, Tyrol and Vorarlberg in forming the tourism brand "Alpine Wellness".

The Alpine Wellness hotels are top-class spa oases in the midst of the mountain world of SalzburgerLand. The alpine materials used in the architecture and fittings of the hotel rooms means guests are transported into a whole new world from the moment they arrive in these spa hotels. All the Alpine Wellness hotels are based on the centuries-old knowledge of alpine remedies that ensure a special and unique health-spa experience. Where else can you relax in a bath of hay mixed with flowers from the alpine meadow, or sweat out your stress in a typical Kraxenofen sauna? When hiking or biking you pass by mountain lakes on your way to the mountaintops, where you can then sit down to a cosy snack to regain your strength for the descent. The altitude and healthy mountain climate are a key fitness factor here, especially for those suffering from allergies or asthma.

Alongside down-to-home Salzburg delicacies made predominantly from local raw products, the Alpine Wellness hotels also serve light and whole foods and vegetarian dishes. And it is just this bal-

Im Weissen Rössl am Wolfgangsee – das österreichische Hotel mit Tradition & modernem Lifestyle

In the Weisses Rössl at Lake Wolfgang – the Austrian hotel with the long tradition & modern lifestyle

ROMANTIKHOTEL IM WEISSEN RÖSSL

Ein gutes Stück Österreich

Wer kennt es nicht, das Weisse Rössl am Wolfgangsee, die Operette, den Film? Wer kennt es wirklich?

Das Weisse Rössl pflegt seine Traditionen, ohne darin zu verharren und reichert das Angebot für seine Gäste beständig mit zeitgemäßen Impulsen an.

Was allgegenwärtig im Weissen Rössl bleibt, ist der Wolfgangsee – ob vom Spa im See, von den Zimmerbalkonen oder den Restaurants aus. Der See mit seiner glatten, beruhigenden Fläche, eingerahmt von Wiesen und Bergketten, bildet ein energetisches alpines Panorama, an dem man sich nicht satt sehen mag.

Nicht nur Angebot und Ausstattung sind es, die dem Weissen Rössl das gewisse Etwas verleihen. Unsere gut geschulten Mitarbeiter verstehen es, unsere Gäste in einer sehr persönlichen, warmherzigen Atmosphäre zu umsorgen und zu verwöhnen.

Familie Trutmann-Peter hat eine Legende neu definiert, ein gutes Stück Österreich erhalten und ein Hotel geschaffen, um das zu tun, was im Leben wirklich zählt!

SPA im See
Atmen Sie tief durch und tanken Sie Energie.

Schwimmen im klaren Trinkwasser des Wolfgangsees, die reine Luft einatmen und die unberührte Natur der umliegenden Bergwelt bewusst genießen, Zeit für sich, Zeit für den anderen, Zeit für die Familie – Zeit für das, was im Leben wirklich zählt – das ist wohl der wertvollste Gewinn Ihrer Tage im Weissen Rössl!

ROMANTIC HOTEL IM WEISSEN RÖSSL

A good piece of Austria

Most of us know it: the Weisse Rössl hotel on the banks of Lake Wolfgang, the operatta, the film? But who of us really knows it?

The Weisse Rössl celebrates its traditions without clinging to them, always on the lookout for new, contemporary impulses to enrich its offering for its guests.

What is and remains omnipresent in the Weisse Rössl hotel is Lake Wolfgang – whether you are in the Spa in the Lake, on your room's balcony or in one of the restaurants. The lake, with its smooth, calming surface, beautifully framed by meadows and mountain ranges, is an energizing alpine panorama that one simply cannot get enough of.

It is not only the products, services and other features that give the Weisse Rössl that little something special though. Our highly trained staff know how to spoil and treat our guests to a very special experience in a personal, warm atmosphere.

The Trutmann-Peter family has redefined a legend here, preserving a good piece of Austria and creating a hotel where you can do what really counts in life!

SPA in the lake
Take a deep breath and fill up with energy.

Swim in the crystal clear drinking-quality water of Lake Wolfgang. Breathe in the pure clean air and take the time to really enjoy the untouched nature of the surrounding mountain landscape; time for yourself, time for others, time for the family; time for

In unserem 1 200 m² großen „SPA im See" erwarten Sie ein ganzjährig geheiztes Seebad 30°C, ein Erlebnishallenbad mit Granderwasser, eine Sauna mit Seeblick, Dampfbäder, Wärmeliegen und eine Infrarotkabine. Im Ruheraum oder Fitnessraum mit Panoramablick wird Sie die atemberaubende Kulisse des Wolfgangsees verzaubern.

Vergessen Sie den Alltag in unserem **REVIDERM SPA!** Bringen Sie Ihren Körper mit Seele und Geist in Einklang! REVIDERM verbindet wirksame Anti-Age Methoden der Kosmetik-Wissenschaft mit einem Wellness-Angebot auf höchstem Niveau.

Keller, Kunst und Küche
Ein gutes Essen hält Herz und Seele zusammen!

Tagsüber freuen wir uns auf Ihren Besuch im „Seerestaurant" – dem schönsten Platz am See – mit traditionellen, österreichischen Gerichten, – Süßwasserfischen aus den Salzkammergutseen sowie Schmankerln aus der österreichischen Mehlspeisküche!

Abends verwöhnt Sie unser Restaurant-Team im à la carte Romantikrestaurant „Kaiserterrasse" mit einer exquisiten Auswahl an österreichischen Weinen aus unserem traditionellen Felsenkeller sowie mit kulinarischen Köstlichkeiten.

Wir freuen uns auf Ihren Besuch!

the things in life that really count. That is the most precious gift that the Weisse Rössl can give you!

In our 1,200 m² "SPA in the lake" you will find the lake swimming pool heated to 30°C, an indoor theme pool with Grander water, a sauna with a view over the lake, steam rooms, heated loungers and an infrared sauna. Do your thing, relaxing in the resting room or working out in the fitness centre, both with enchanting panoramic views across the lake.

Forget the daily grind in our **REVIDERM SPA!** Let your body and mind be at ease! REVIDERM combines scientific anti-aging cosmetics with a top-level range of wellness products and services.

Cellar, art and cuisine
A good meal keeps heart and soul together!

We look forward to seeing you during the day in our "Lake Restaurant" – the most beautiful spot on the lake – where we serve traditional Austrian cuisine, fresh water fish from the Salzkammergut lakes and delicious specialities from the Austrian pastry kitchen!

In the evening our restaurant team in the à la carte romantic restaurant "Kaiserterrasse" treats you to an exquisite selection of Austrian wines from our traditional wine cavern and culinary treats.

We look forward to your visit!

Bild oben:
Seebad – ganzjährig 30°C geheizt

Zeit zu Zweit in der romantischen Kaiserwanne mit Seeblick

Picture above:
The lake pool – heated to 30°C all year round

Together alone in the romantic Emperor's Bath with mountain views

www.weissesroessl.at

Drei Orte gehören zum Gasteiner Tal: Bad Gastein, Bad Hofgastein und Dorfgastein. Das ganze Jahr über spielt der Tourismus hier eine herausragende Rolle

There are three districts in Gastein valley: Bad Gastein, Bad Hofgastein and Dorfgastein. Tourism is the focus here all year round

sonst kann man heute noch im duftenden Almblumen-Heubad relaxen oder eine Schwitzkur im Kraxenofen genießen? Bei Wanderungen oder gemütlichen Bike-Touren geht's vorbei an Bergseen hinauf auf den Gipfel, wo man bei einer gemütlichen Jause schnell die Anstrengungen des Aufstiegs vergisst. Die alpine Höhenlage und das gesunde Klima in den Bergen, in dem auch Allergiker unbeschwert aufatmen können, sind dabei ein wesentlicher Fitnessfaktor.

Neben bodenständigen Salzburger Schmankerln, vorwiegend aus heimischen Produkten zubereitet, kommen in allen Alpine Wellness Hotels auch leichte Schon- und Vollwertkost sowie vegetarische Speisen auf den Tisch. Und genau dieser ausgewogene Mix aus Entspannung in alpiner Umgebung, vitalisierender Kulinarik und sanfter körperlicher Betätigung ist es, der Körper und Seele erholen lässt.

Aber nicht nur Wellnessurlauber, sondern auch Familien finden im SalzburgerLand ausgewählte Angebote. In 26 ausgewählten Family SalzburgerLand Betrieben wird man den großen Ansprüchen der kleinen Gäste vollends gerecht. Denn hier dreht sich alles um die Kids! Spezielle Kinder-Programme und Angebote wie Kinderwandertage mit Lamatrekking oder unvergessliche Stunden am Lagerfeuer lassen nicht nur Kinderherzen höher schlagen. Alle Familyhotels sind mit geräumigen und fami-

anced mix of relaxation in alpine surroundings, vitalising cuisine and gentle physical activity that helps body and soul recover from the pressures of everyday life.

But not only spa lovers find everything their hearts desire in Salzburg; there is also choice aplenty for families. 26 selected family SalzburgerLand hotels answer to the needs of the little holidaymakers. Because here it is all about the kids! Special children's programmes including activities such as children's hikes with llamas and unforgettable evenings by the campfire are not only great for the little ones; the bigger children among us also find the perfect excuse to rekindle memories of our own childhood. All the family hotels have spacious, family-friendly rooms and there are fun playrooms for days when the weather doesn't allow outings. Many of these hotels also offer generous spa areas, swimming pools with paddling pools and permanent babyphones.

Innumerable leisure-time activities and fascinating sights are available to tourists and locals with just one All-Inclusive Card. The SalzburgerLand Card offers free entry to more than 190 special attractions throughout the entire SalzburgerLand region. Whether you go to Rauris to pan for gold, take a ride in the steam train on the Taurach line in Lungau or visit the rocks or thermal alpine spa in

liengerechten Zimmern ausgestattet, und es gibt freundliche Kinderspielzimmer für weniger sonnige Tage. Viele Betriebe verfügen außerdem über einen großzügigen Wellnessbereich, Schwimmbäder mit Kinderplanschbereich oder permanent installierte Babyphones.

Umfangreiche Freizeitaktivitäten und attraktive Sehenswürdigkeiten mit nur einer All-Inclusive Card stehen dem Urlaubsgast sowie Einheimischen zur Verfügung. Die SalzburgerLand Card bietet freien Eintritt zu über 190 Sehenswürdigkeiten und Attraktionen im ganzen SalzburgerLand. Ob zum Goldwaschen nach Rauris, eine Dampfzugfahrt mit der Tauracbahn im Lungau oder ein Besuch in der Felsen- oder Alpentherme im Gasteinertal – dem vielfältigen Angebot sind kaum Grenzen gesetzt.

„Kunstvoll genießen" – darunter fallen Schlemmeradressen von Haubenlokalen, Schmankerl aus den Regionen sowie kulturelle Veranstaltungen. Der „Salzburger Bauernherbst" gehört dabei seit zwölf Jahren zum Fixpunkt der SalzburgerLand Tourismus Gesellschaft. Jährlich sind zwischen Ende August und Ende Oktober in den Bauernherbst-Festwochen sämtliche Dörfer auf den Beinen und feiern mit ihren Gästen die ertragreiche Ernte. Ob am Dorfplatz oder in den Bauernhöfen: Wirte, Bauern, traditionelle Vereine sowie Handwerker und Kunsthandwerker machen den Salzburger Bauernherbst zu einem Erlebnis für Jung und Alt. So nahmen im Jahr 2006 unter dem Motto „Salzburger Gwand und Trachten" über 365 000 Besucher an den Feierlichkeiten teil und verkosteten die regionalen Spezialitäten. Die traditionellen Salzburger Trachten standen dabei im Mittelpunkt. Bei vielen Bauernherbstfesten gibt es Trachtenmodenschauen, Trachten zum „selber Nähen" sowie zeitgemäße Kreationen junger Salzburger Modeschöpfer zu bewundern.

Das SalzburgerLand kann mit besonders hoher kulinarischer Qualität und Vielfalt für Gäste und Einheimische aufwarten. Wiesen, Wälder, Flüsse und Seen liefern die besten Zutaten dazu. Bioprodukte sind hier schon lange logisch, daher gibt es im SalzburgerLand auch den höchsten Anteil an Biobauern innerhalb der EU. Insgesamt sind es 3 400 Betriebe, die neben gesundheitlichen und tierschützerischen Motiven die Vermeidung von Schadstoffen als ihre oberste Maxime gesetzt haben. Nicht nur in der Landwirtschaft, auch in der Gastronomie wird immer mehr auf biologische Lebensmittel gesetzt. Ob im urigen Wirtshaus oder im gehobenen Restaurant: Nirgendwo sonst in Österreich kochen so viele haubengekrönte Häupter mit regionalen Produkten! Insgesamt sind es über 60 Haubenköche, die das SalzburgerLand zu einer Destination für Genießer und Feinschmecker werden lassen. Neben Johanna Meier, der ersten vier-Hauben-Köchin der Welt, sind es unter anderem Karl und Rudi Obauer,

Gasteinertal – there are virtually no limits to the options.

"Kunstvoll genießen" stands for culinary delights in fine restaurants, feasting on regional specialities and visiting cultural events. The "Salzburger Bauernherbst" with its rustic alpine farm traditions that accompany the end of the summer has been a focal point of the SalzburgerLand Tourism Company for over 12 years now. During the Bauernherbst festival weeks between the end of August and the end of October, all the villages in the area join together to celebrate the harvest with their guests. In the village squares and in the farmyards themselves, restaurateurs, farmers, traditional clubs, craftsmen and artisans make the Salzburg's autumn a time to remember. In 2006, for example, more than 365,000 people joined in the celebrations entitled "Salzburger Gwand und Trachten", enjoying the regional delicacies while feasting their eyes on the traditional Salzburg costumes. Many of the autumn farmer festivals held traditional costume fashion shows with sew-it-yourself traditional outfits and contemporary creations by young Salzburg fashion designers.

SalzburgerLand boasts exceptional culinary quality and variety for guests and locals. Meadows, forests, rivers and lakes provide the best ingredients. Organic products have been a matter of course here for a long time already, which is also why SalzburgerLand has the largest share of organic farmers of any region in the EU. In all there are 3,400 such farms, which, in addition to upholding the health and welfare of their animals, also avoid using pollutants. Both the agricultural and gastronomy sectors are placing ever more emphasis on organic foods. Whether in earthy taverns or high-class restaurants: nowhere else in Austria are there so many decorated chefs who use ingredients from the region! There are more than 60 chefs in SalzburgerLand that have been awarded coveted "chef's hats" that equate to stars outside Austria, and they make this state a prime destination for connoisseurs of fine food. Some of these worth mentioning are Johanna Meier, the first female

Gesundheit aus den Tiefen der Tauern: Im Gasteiner Heilstollen mit seiner radonhaltigen Luft werden die unterschiedlichsten Krankheiten erfolgreich behandelt

Wellbeing from the depths of the Tauern mountains: all manner of maladies are treated in the Gastein underground spa with its radon enriched air

Jörg Wörther, Gerhard Gugg, Andreas Döllerer und Karl Fleischhacker, die in der Gastronomieszene für kulinarische Höhenflüge sorgen. Höhenflüge der anderen Art gibt es auch im Ikarus im Hangar 7, wo unter der Patronanz des „Jahrhundertkochs" Eckart Witzigmann jeden Monat ein anderer internationaler Koch die Gaumen der Gäste verwöhnt.

Das wohl berühmteste kulturelle Ereignis im SalzburgerLand sind die Salzburger Festspiele von Mitte Juli bis Ende August. Am Programm stehen jedes Jahr ca. 180 Veranstaltungen, darunter Opern, Konzerte, Abende mit Schauspiel und Lesungen. Ganz im Zeichen von Mozarts 250. Geburtstag wurden im Jahr 2006 alle 22 Mozartopern bei den Salzburger Festspielen aufgeführt. Neben den Salzburger Festspielen als größte kulturelle Veranstaltung im Land Salzburg gibt es noch eine Reihe weiterer Festivitäten und Ereignisse: das Aspekte Festival der internationalen zeitgenössischen Musik im Februar, die Oster- und Pfingstfestspiele, die SommerSzene – Salzburgs Festival für zeitgenössische Tanz- und Performancekunst Mitte Juni bis Mitte Juli, der Diabelli Sommer in Mattsee, die Salzburger Kulturtage im Oktober und der Salzburger Jazzherbst Ende Oktober, Anfang September sind nur Auszüge aus dem breiten Spektrum kultureller Veranstaltungen.

Touristische Schwerpunkte und Ausblicke

Als neuer Schwerpunkt wird zukünftig vermehrt auf den *Jugendtourismus* gesetzt. Ohne Zweifel lockt das umfangreiche Sport- und Kulturprogramm jedes Jahr eine Vielzahl an Urlaubern in das SalzburgerLand. Dennoch gilt es, gerade die Jugendlichen in Zukunft noch stärker davon zu überzeugen, dass das SalzburgerLand alles bieten kann, was zu einem spannenden und abwechslungsreichen Urlaub gehört. Die SLTG arbeitet zur Zeit intensiv am Aufbau einer eigenen Jugendmarke, um das SalzburgerLand als Reisedestination abenteuerlustiger Jugendlicher zu verankern.

Auch die erfolgreiche Durchführung von sportlichen und kulturellen Großveranstaltungen wie die UCI Straßen Rad WM oder das Mozartjahr 2006 wird in Zukunft weiterbestehen. Mit der UCI Straßen Rad WM konnte aus touristischer Sicht eine nachhaltige Positionierung des SalzburgerLandes als Radurlaubs- und Sportdestination erreicht werden. Ein Nächtigungsplus von 22,6% in der Stadt und 14% in der Region Flachgau im September 2006 gegenüber dem Vorjahr machen diesen touristischen Erfolg auch messbar. In Punkto Rad- und Sportveranstaltungen finden 2007 gleich zwei weitere große Events wie die *Journalisten Rad-WM* und die *Eddy Merckx Classic* 2007 statt. Auch Events im

"four chef's hat" chef in the world, Karl and Rudi Obauer, Jörg Wörther, Gerhard Gugg, Andreas Döllerer and Karl Fleischhacker; all of whom provide for culinary highlights in the restaurant scene. And highlights of a different kind await in Ikarus im Hangar 7, where a different international chef spoils the guests' pallets every month under the auspices of the chef extraordinaire Eckart Witzigmann.

Perhaps the most famous cultural event in SalzburgerLand is the Salzburg Festival, which takes place from mid July to the end of August. Around 180 events including operas, concerts, theatre and readings gild the programme every year. For Mozart's 250th birthday in 2006, all 22 of Mozart's operas were performed at the Salzburg Festival. And next to this largest of the cultural events, there are also a number of other festivities and happenings all year round in the state of Salzburg: the Aspekte Festival of international contemporary music in February, the Easter and Whitsun Festivals, the SommerSzene – Salzburg's festival for contemporary dance and artistic performance from mid June to mid July, the Diabelli Summer in Mattsee, the Salzburg Culture Days in October and the Salzburg Jazz Autumn at the end of October are just a few examples from the broad range of cultural events on offer.

Tourist focuses and outlook

A new focus that more attention is to be paid to in the future is *youth tourism*. While it is true that the extensive range of sporting and cultural offerings attracts numerous holidaymakers to SalzburgerLand every year we want to convince young people even more that SalzburgerLand has everything that makes a holiday exciting and varied. The SLTC is currently working overtime on creating its own youth brand, in order to raise the profile of SalzburgerLand as a destination for adventure-seeking young holidaymakers.

We will also continue to hold major sporting and cultural events such as the UCI Road Cycling World Championships and the Mozart Year 2006. The UCI Road Cycling Worlds helped us consolidate SalzburgerLand in the minds of cycling fans as an ideal destination for cycling and sporting vacations. This success was even immediately quantifiable in the 22.6% rise in overnight stays in the city and the 14% increase in the Flachgau region in September 2006 compared to the previous year. And 2007 will also be a big year for cycling and sports with the *Journalists' Cycling World Championship* and the *Eddy Merckx Classic 2007* events being held here. We will also be helping organise events on the German market again in 2007, such as the Cross Country Ski-

Gleich zwei Radsportveranstaltungen finden 2007 in Salzburg statt: die Journalisten Rad-WM sowie die Eddy Merckx Classic 2007. Das Bild zeigt Teilnehmer der UCI Straßen Rad-WM 2006

There are two professional cycling events in Salzburg in 2007: the Journalists Cycling World Championships and the Eddy Merckx Classic. Here you can see competitors from the 2006 UCI Road Cycling World Championship

deutschen Markt, wie die Beteiligung am Langlauf Weltcup in Düsseldorf oder die Organisation der Winterwelt am Potsdamer Platz, werden im Jahr 2007 wieder durchgeführt. Mit Blick auf die *Euro 2008* möchte sich das SalzburgerLand im internationalen Sporteventbereich positionieren.

Darüber hinaus setzt die SLTG weiter auf bewährte Konzepte wie den „*Wanderbaren Almsommer*" und den „*Salzburger Bauernherbst*", die sich thematisch durch das Jahr 2007 ziehen werden.

Freizeit und Erholung werden im SalzburgerLand groß geschrieben. Alpine Wohlfühl-Oasen, die Ruhe verheißen. Und einladende Ziele für Menschen, die die Bergwelt mit ihren eindrucksvollen Stimmungen aus nächster Nähe erleben möchten. ◄

Nähere Informationen und Auskünfte:
SalzburgerLand,
Postfach 1
A -5300 Hallwang bei Salzburg
Tel.: +43(0)662 66 88 44
Fax: +43(0)662 66 88 66
info@salzburgerland.com
http://www.salzburgerland.com

ing World Cup in Düsseldorf and the Winterwelt am Potsdamer Platz in Berlin. SalzburgerLand also wants to use the *Euro 2008* European Soccer Championships to raise its profile even further in the field of international sporting events.

But we will also continue to concentrate on our perennial and proven concepts in 2007, such as the *"Wanderbarer Almsommer"* and the *"Salzburger Bauernherbst"* that spread across the entire year.

Leisure and relaxation are a key in SalzburgerLand. Alpine spas and inviting destinations entice people into our mountain paradise who want to experience the wonderful things we have to offer here at first hand. ◄

For more information contact:
SalzburgerLand,
PO box 1,
A -5300 Hallwang bei Salzburg
Tel.: +43(0)662 66 88 44,
Fax: +43(0)662 66 88 66
info@salzburgerland.com
http://www.salzburgerland.com

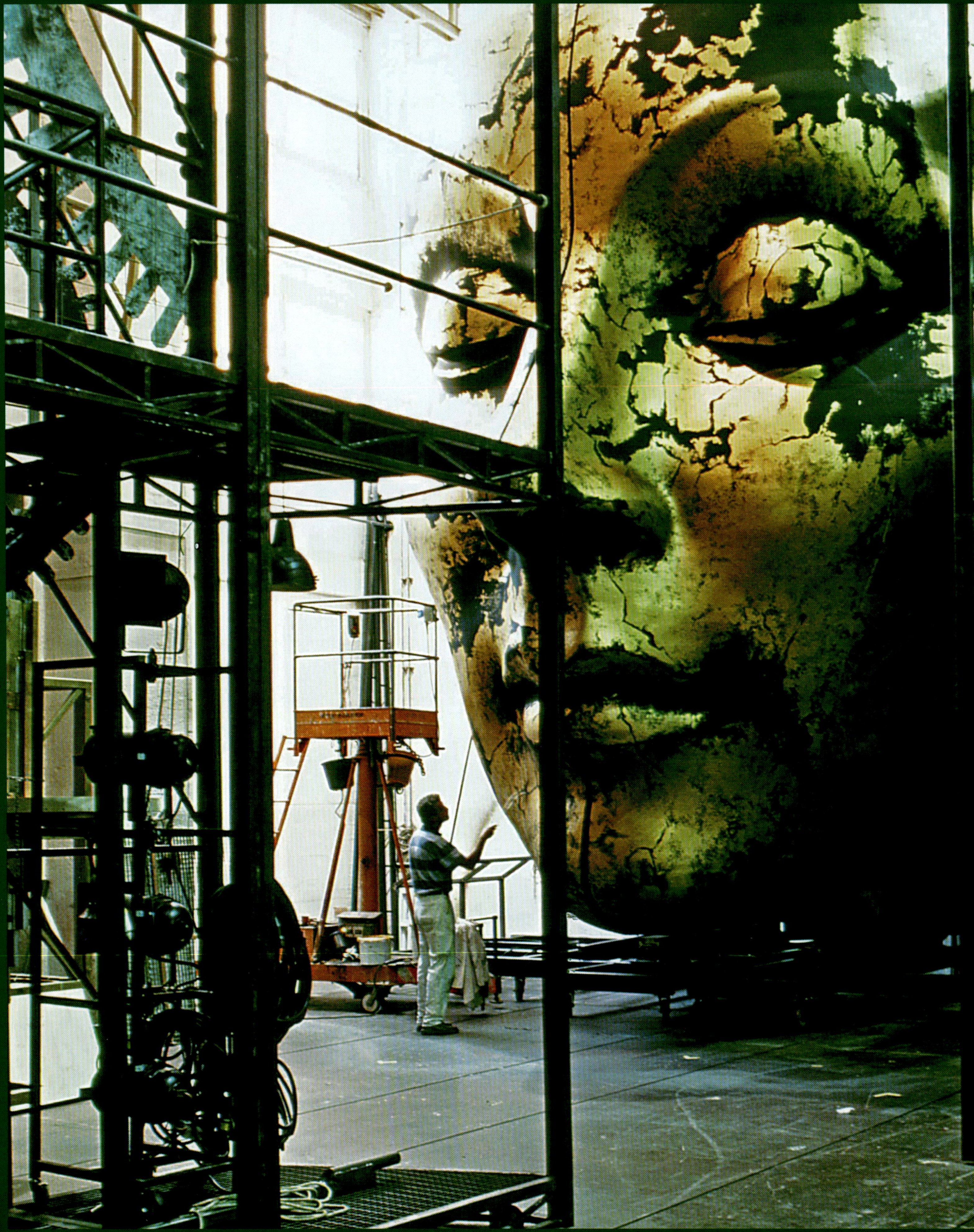

Mag. Ingrid Tröger-Gordon
Stadt Salzburg – Magistrat
Abteilungsleiterin der Kultur- und Schulverwaltung

Das Salzburger Kulturleben – Innovation und Kulturerbe

Cultural life in Salzburg – Innovation and cultural heritage

Böllerschützen eröffnen auf dem Kapuzinerberg alljährlich die Salzburger Festspiele

The pistolmen shoot off the starting gun to the Salzburg Festival every year on the Kapuzinerberg

Die internationale Strahlkraft der Kulturstadt Salzburg begründet sich in der gelungenen Mischung aus weltweit wahrgenommenen Festivals – allen voran die Salzburger Festspiele –, einem reichen kulturellen Erbe sowie einer einzigartigen Architektur und Einbettung in die einmalige Landschaft zwischen Gebirge und Flachland. Die Musik Mozarts und die konsequente Mozartpflege in Verbindung mit den Salzburger Festspielen und deren Ambitionen, alljährlich den internationalen Größen aus Kunst und Kultur in Salzburg „die" Bühne zu geben, haben Salzburg zu der Kulturmetropole gemacht, die sie heute ist.

Trotz der Konzentration des kulturellen Angebots in der Stadt Salzburg besticht auch das Land Salzburg durch äußerst vielfältige und innovative Kulturinitiativen.

Das städtische Kulturleben ist geprägt von den im Jahreskreis positionierten „Festivals" und einer überaus starken lokalen Kulturszene, die sich durch Spartenvielfalt, eine enorme Veranstaltungsdichte und eine hohe Qualität in der Umsetzung künstlerischer Projekte auszeichnet. Dass die Salzburger ihr Kulturangebot zu schätzen wissen, beweist ein um zehn Prozent über dem österreichischen Durchschnittswert liegendes Publikumsinteresse.

Stadt der Festspiele und Festivals – kulturelle Glanzlichter im Jahreskreis

Rund um den Geburtstag von Wolfgang Amadeus Mozart veranstaltet die Internationale Stiftung Mozarteum alljährlich im Jänner mit der **Mozartwoche** ein einzigartiges Musikfest, das auf eine über fünfzigjährige Tradition zurückblicken kann. Im Zentrum dieses Festivals steht die Beschäftigung mit dem Werk Mozarts mit dem Ziel, künstlerische Maßstäbe für die Interpretation und Bearbeitung des Werkes zu setzen. Neue Akzente wie beispielsweise die Verknüpfung mit zeitgenössischen Werken und die kontinuierliche Einbindung internationaler Musikgrößen sind Garanten für das weltweite Publikumsinteresse.

Das 1967 von Herbert von Karajan gegründete Festival **Osterfestspiele Salzburg** zählte von Anbeginn an zu den exklusivsten Musikfestivals der Welt. Durch die jahrelange Zusammenarbeit Herbert von Karajans als Dirigent und Regisseur mit den Berliner Philharmonikern und dem Salzburger Bühnenbildner Günther Schneider-Siemssen wurde eine eigene ästhetisch-musikalische Tradition geschaffen, die sich großen internationalen Zuspruchs erfreute. Heute werden die Osterfestspiele durch ihren charismatischen künstlerischen Leiter, Sir Simon Rattle geprägt.

The international radiance of the cultural city of Salzburg is founded on the successful mix of world-renowned festivals – most predominantly the Salzburg Festival – a rich cultural heritage, magnificent and unique architecture and its beautiful natural surroundings with breathtaking mountains and plains. The music of Mozart and the care taken in preserving his memory, the Salzburg Festival and its ambitious goal of providing a stage for the international greats of art and culture in Salzburg every year have helped make Salzburg the cultural metropolis it is today.

Despite the fact that the cultural offering is largely concentrated in the city of Salzburg, the state or Land of Salzburg also captivates the imagination with a broad range of often highly innovative cultural initiatives.

The city's cultural life is punctuated by the festivals held at different times throughout the year and a busy local cultural scene characterised by its diversity, intensity and artistic quality. And the Salzburg population appreciates the cultural opportunities its city offers, with local interest ten percent greater than the average in Austria.

City of festivals – the cultural highlights throughout the year

To celebrate Wolfgang Amadeus Mozart's birthday every year, the International Mozarteum Foundation holds a unique musical festival in January known as the **Mozart Week**. This tradition already looks back on a more than fifty-year tradition. It focuses on Mozart's oeuvre with the goal of setting artistic standards for its interpretation and production. New emphases such as the combining of Mozart's compositions with contemporary works and the continuous integration of major international stars guarantee that the festival always attracts great public interest from all over the globe.

The **Salzburg Easter Festival**, which Herbert von Karajan founded in 1967, has always been one of the world's most exclusive opera festivals, from its very first year on. The long-standing collaboration with Herbert von Karajan as conductor and director of the Berlin Philharmonics and the Salzburg stage designer Günther Schneider-Siemssen an aesthetic-musical tradition has been created that attracts great acclaim on the international stage. Today it is the charismatic Sir Simon Rattle who has put his mark on the Easter Festival.

The art of Baroque music is the focus in Salzburg during the Whitsunday holidays. It is practiced at its highest level at the Whitsun and Baroque Festival.

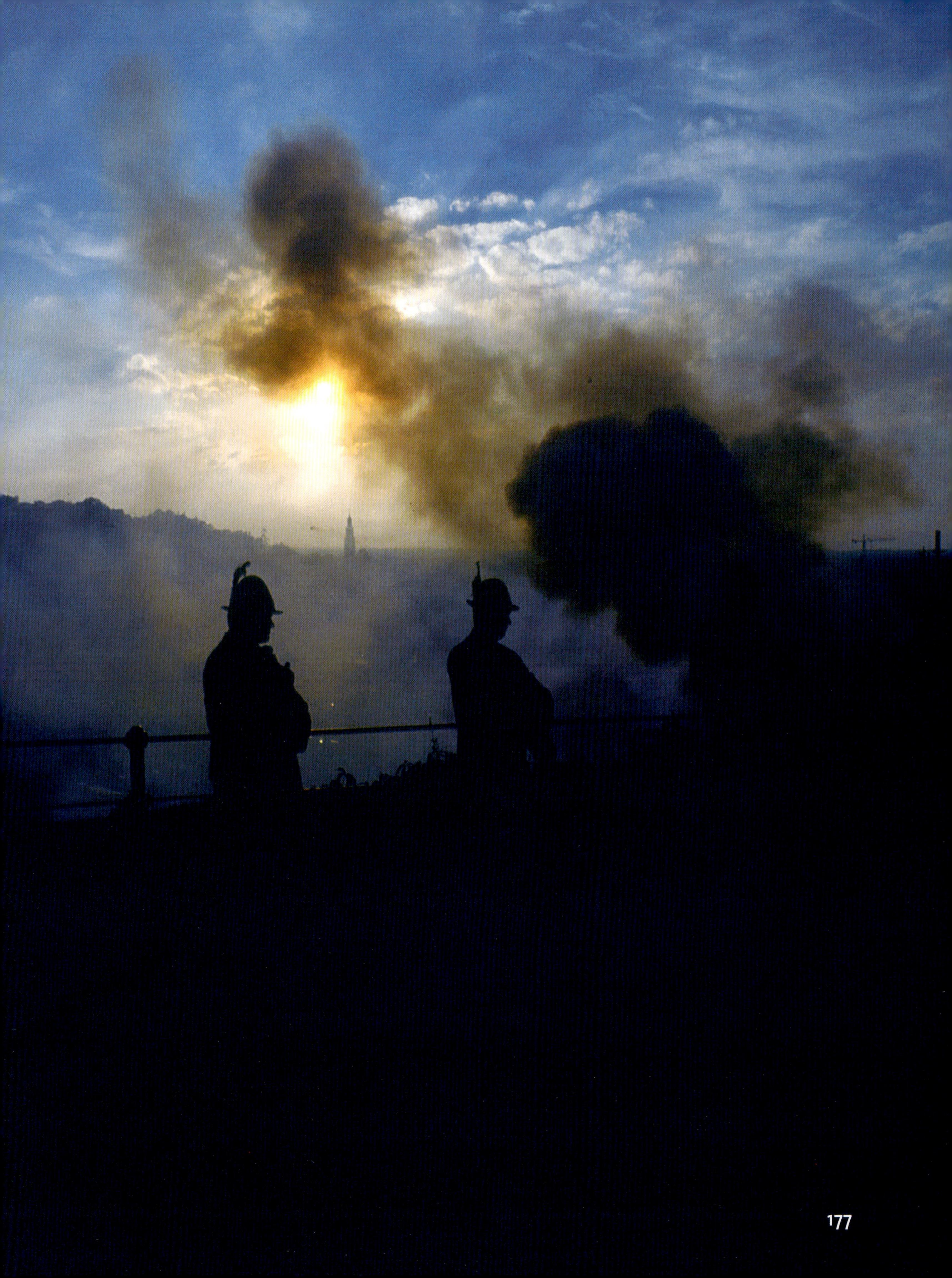

Feuerwerk auf dem Residenzplatz! Mit diesem Spektakel werden jedes Jahr die Salzburger Festspiele eröffnet. Der Platz wurde zwischen 1595 und 1605 von Erzbischof Wolf Dietrich von Raitenau umgestaltet. Für dieses großartige Projekt mussten 55 Bürgerhäuser niedergerissen werden

---

Fireworks on Residenzplatz. This is how the Festival is opened every year in Salzburg. The place was remodelled between 1595 and 1605 by Archbishop Wolf Dietrich von Raitenau. 55 houses had to be demolished for this magnificent project

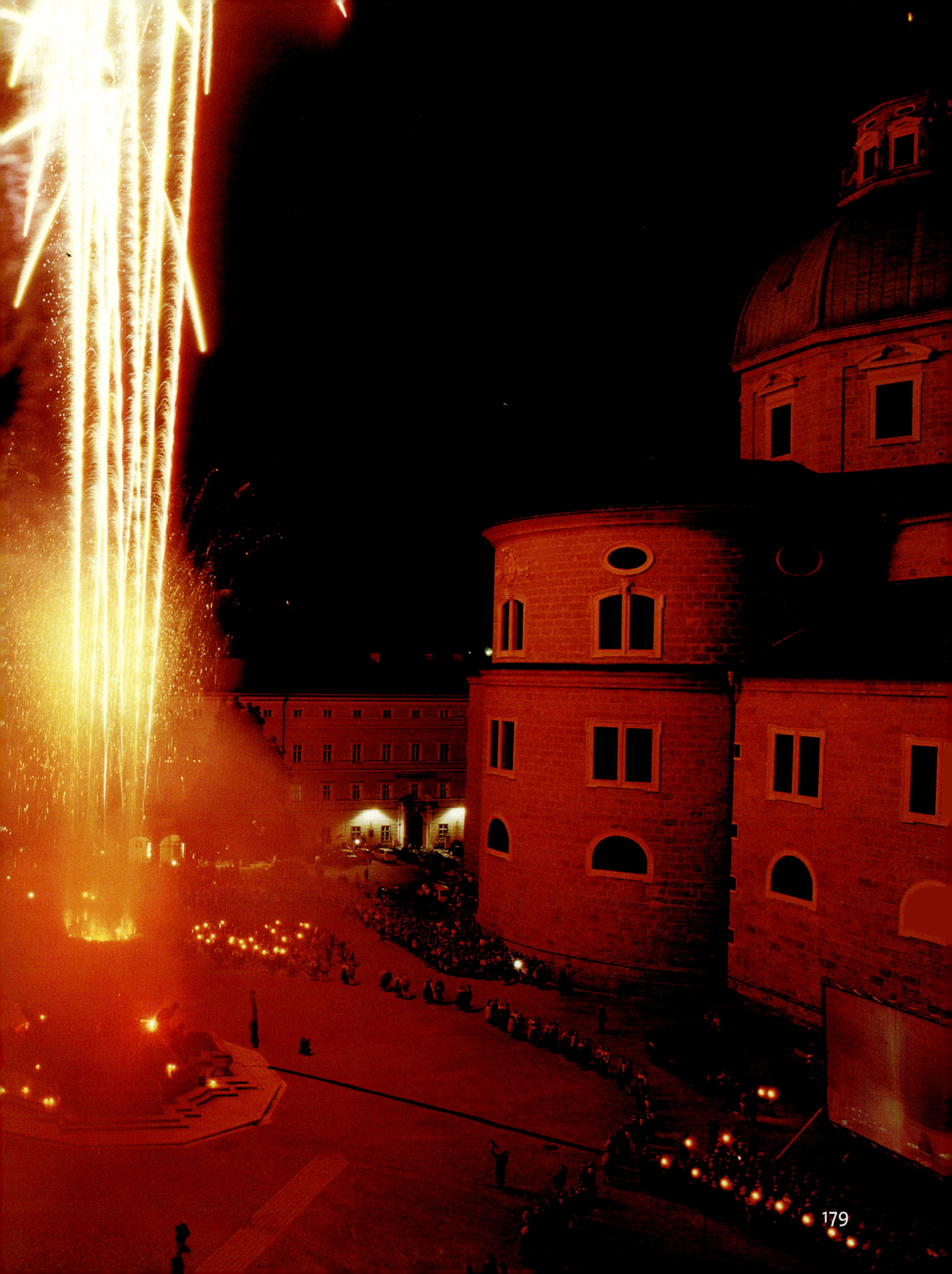

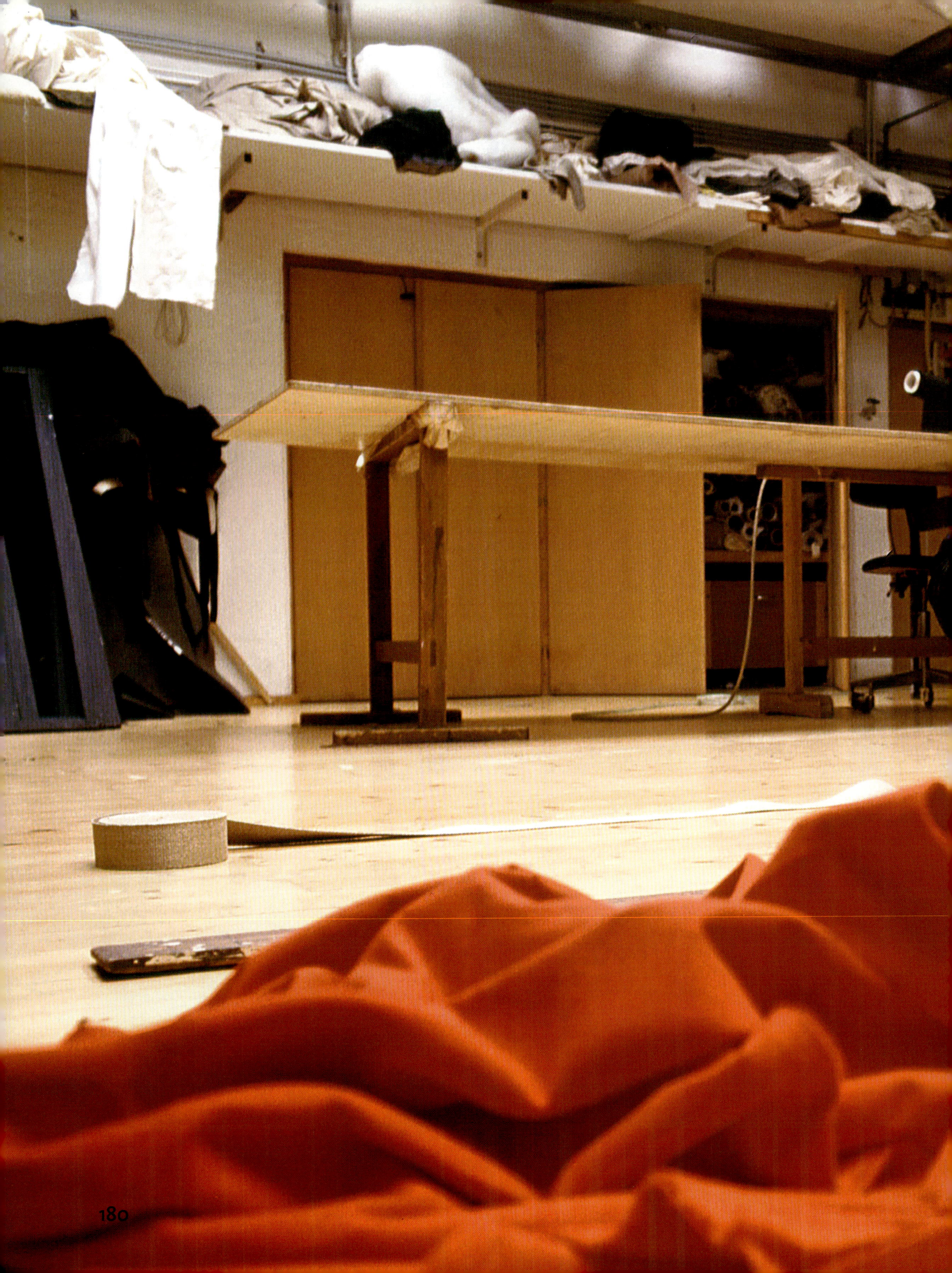

Die Salzburger Festspiele sind weitaus mehr als Sänger, Schauspieler, Dirigenten, Musiker, Regisseure und Bühnenbildner. Sie sind ein Ganzjahresbetrieb und bieten Arbeitsplätze für die unterschiedlichsten Handwerksberufe

The Salzburg Festival is much more than just singers, actors, conductors, musicians, directors and stage designers. It represents a year-round full-time job and employment for people from the most varied of trades

SALZBURGER SPIELSTÄTTEN

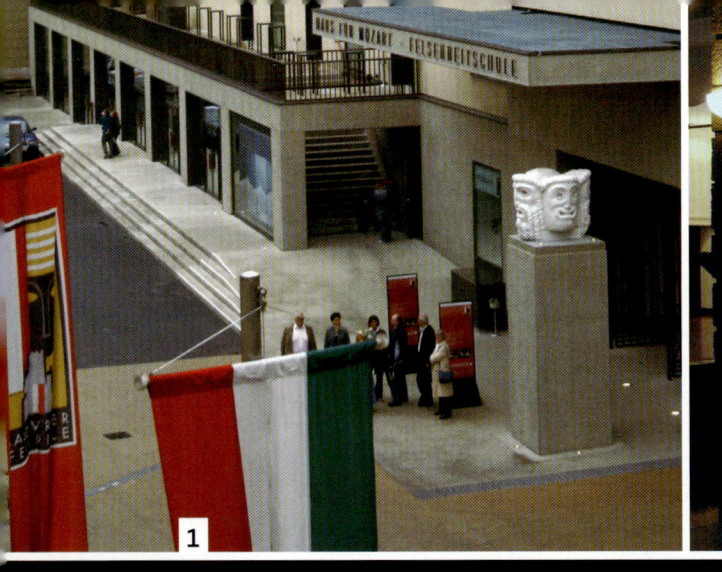

SALZBURG CONCERT VENUES

1 Haus für Mozart (ehemaliges Kleines Festspielhaus)
2 Das Foyer des Festspielhauses
3 Die Felsenreitschule
4 Der Karl-Böhm-Saal des Festspielhauses
5 Konzert im Innenhof der Salzburger Residenz

1 Haus für Mozart (formerly the Kleines Festspielhaus)
2 The foyer of the Festspielhaus
3 The Felsenreitschule equestrian school
4 The Karl-Böhm room in the Festspielhaus
5 Concert in the courtyard of the Salzburg Residenz

Während der Pfingstfeiertage wird in Salzburg die barocke Kunst in den Vordergrund gestellt. Mit den **Salzburger Pfingstfestspielen** geschieht dies auf höchstem musikalischen Niveau.

Den weltweiten Ruf als Kulturstadt verdankt Salzburg eindeutig den 1920 gegründeten **Salzburger Festspielen**. Sie setzen alljährlich in bewährter Verbindung von Tradition und Erneuerung Salzburg ins Zentrum des internationalen Kulturgeschehens. 212 Aufführungen an 40 Tagen und ein Kartenangebot von 242 000 Plätzen im Mozartjahr 2006 sowie ein Budgetvolumen von 44,9 Mio. Euro skizzieren die Dimension dieses Festivals. Seit Anbeginn gelingt es den Salzburger Festspielen, die international renommiertesten Dirigenten, Sänger, Schauspieler und Musiker nach Salzburg zu bringen und alljährlich den Festspielbezirk mit seinen Aufführungsstätten vom Domplatz über das neu errichtete Haus für Mozart, die Felsenreitschule bis zum Großen Festspielhaus zum Zentrum der Musik- und Theaterwelt zu erheben.

In bewährter Nachbarschaft gibt die Szene Salzburg im „republic" dem internationalen zeitgenössischen Tanz- und Theatergeschehen seit nunmehr 30 Jahren eine Bühne. Herausragende Tanzensembles aus allen Teilen der Welt waren und sind hier zu Gast, wobei im Laufe der Zeit sowohl Genregrenzen wie auch räumliche Festlegungen aufgehoben wurden und vor allem in den letzten Jahren eine künstlerische Eroberung des öffentlichen Raums stattgefunden hat.

Dem qualitätvollen Salzburger Kultur-Sommer folgt ein künstlerisch ereignisreicher Festival-Herbst. Seit nunmehr 11 Jahren sammeln sich internationale Jazzgrößen in der Salzburger Altstadt und bringen mit dem **Salzburger Jazz-Herbst** die Stadt zum Swingen. An die 100 Veranstaltungen jährlich – vom großen Festspielhaus bis zu den Plätzen der Altstadt – zeigen Salzburg in einem gänzlich „anderen" musikalischen Licht.

Ein Festival der ganz besonderen Art ist das **WinterFest** im Salzburger Volksgarten, eine alljährliche künstlerische Hommage an die Zirkuswelt, ihre Tradition und Gegenwart. Theater, Artistik, Pantomime und Illusionskunst in Verbindung mit kulinarischen Ereignissen machen dieses Festival zu einem außergewöhnlichen Ereignis im kulturellen Jahreskreis.

Traditionsreich endet der Festival-Reigen. Das Salzburger Adventsingen im Großen Festspielhaus kann auf eine über 60-jährige Geschichte zurückblicken. Diese vorweihnachtliche volkskulturelle Veranstaltung rund um das Thema Herbergsuche erreicht jährlich etwa 34 000 Zuschauer.

Salzburg's reputation in the world as a cultural city results without doubt from the **Salzburg Festival** founded in 1920. This festival thrusts Salzburg into the centre of the international calendar every year with a proven combination of tradition and renewal. 212 performances on 40 days, 242,000 tickets available in this the Mozart year 2006 and a budget of Euros 44.9 million bear witness to the dimensions of this festival. Ever since its inception the **Salzburg Festival** has managed to attract the best international conductors, singers, actors and musicians to Salzburg every year to put the city's venues – from the cathedral square to the newly built Mo-zart House, from the equestrian school to the Grand Festival Hall – in the spotlight of the world of music and theatre.

Salzburger JAZZ herbst 12 07

25. Oktober bis 4. November

Szene Salzburg has been using the "republic" to stage international contemporary dance and theatre for more than 30 years now. Outstanding dance ensembles from all corners of the globe perform here year after year, and over time both genre borders and spatial restrictions have been lifted, allowing an artistic revolution to take place among the public, especially in recent years.

The top-quality Salzburg summer of culture is followed by an artistically eventful festival-autumn. For the last 11 years, international jazz greats have

Mozarts Oper „Titus"
bei den
Salzburger Festspielen

Mozart's opera "Titus" at
the Salzburg Festivals

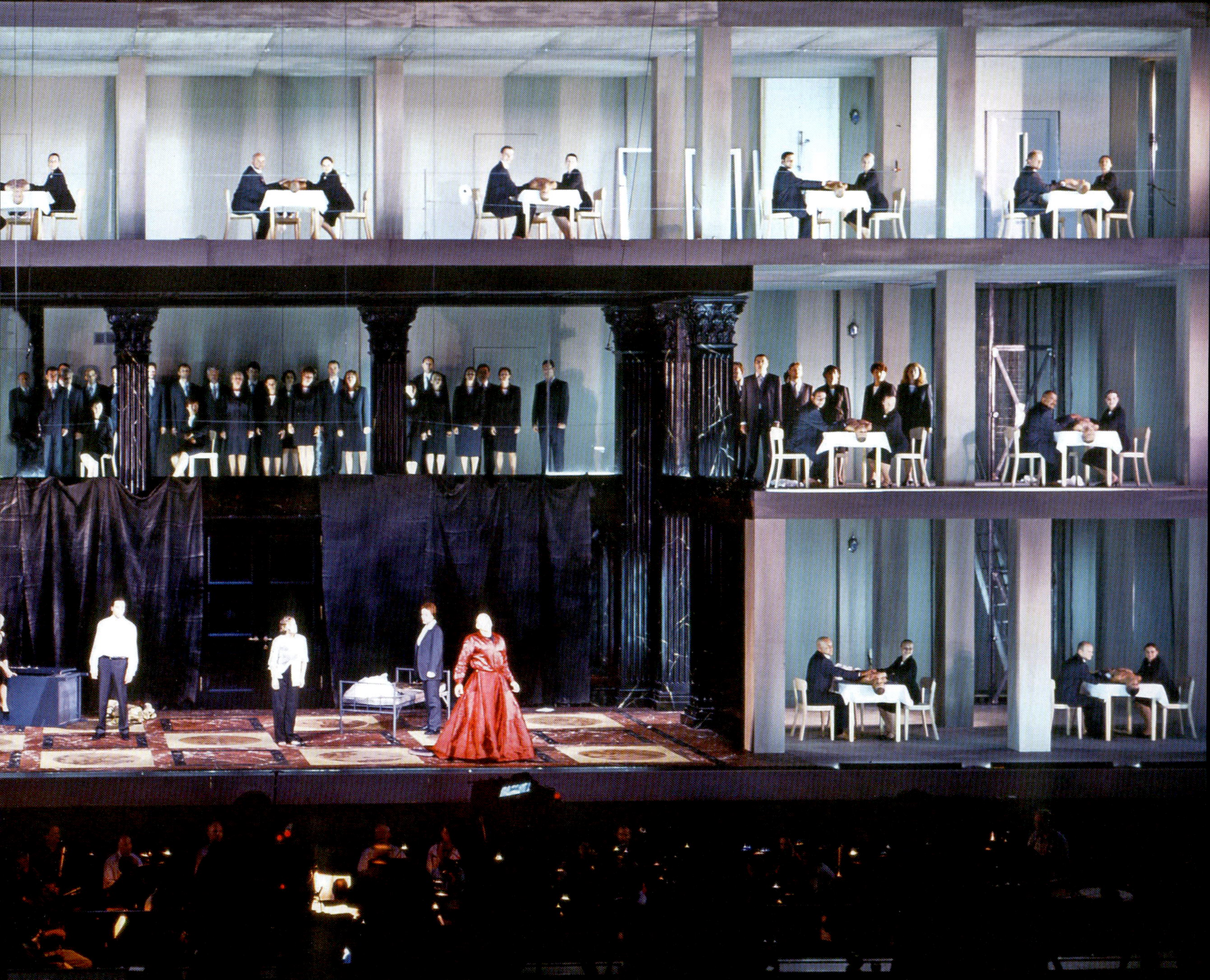

Die Salzburger Kulturszene

Auch wenn Salzburg mit ca. 150 000 Einwohnern eine vergleichsweise kleine Stadt ist, besticht sie durch ihr kulturelles Erbe und die Vielfalt des Angebots. Salzburg ist nicht nur die Stadt Mozarts, sondern kann auch außerhalb der musikalischen Sparte auf ein reichhaltiges Erbe und eine pulsierende Gegenwart verweisen.

Stefan Zweig erwählte 1919 Salzburg zu seinem Hauptwohnsitz, H.C. Artmann, Thomas Bernhard und Peter Handke sind prägende Literaten der Gegenwart, die hier arbeiteten und lebten.

Oskar Kokoschka gründete 1953 die Schule des Sehens als Internationale Sommerakademie für bildende Kunst, deren Tätigkeit nach wie vor alljährlich Schüler und Lehrende aus allen Teilen der Welt nach Salzburg bringt.

Seit den 1980er Jahren haben sich in der Stadt Salzburg im Rahmen eines „Kulturstättenkonzepts" neue Einrichtungen etabliert, die heute unverzichtbare Teile des Salzburger Kulturlebens darstellen.

So bietet beispielsweise das Salzburger Literaturhaus als Heimstätte der ansässigen Autoren und Literaturgruppen ein ganzjähriges Literaturprogramm, das sowohl einen Querschnitt der österreichischen und Salzburger Literaturszene als auch internationale zeitgenössische Literatur präsentiert.

Das Salzburger Rockhouse schafft für Salzburger Bands Proben- und Auftrittsmöglichkeiten, gleichzeitig ist es auch der lokale Veranstaltungs-

Flüchtlingsfest in der ARGEKultur

The Refugee Festival in the ARGEKultur

been coming to the historical centre of Salzburg for the **Autumn Jazz Festival Salzburg**, and making the old town swing. At around 100 shows a year, the music venues of Salzburg – from the Grand Festival Hall through to the various squares glow in a totally different light.

The **WinterFest** in the Salzburg Volksgarten is also a festival of a very special kind. It is an artistic homage to the world of the circus, its tradition and its present. Theatre, artistry, pantomime and illusionists join forces with culinary events to make this festival an extraordinary date on the cultural calendar.

The series of festivals ends in a traditional vein. The Salzburger Adventsingen in the Grand Festival Hall looks back upon over 60 years of history. Around 34,000 people experience this pre-Christmas cultural event on the theme of looking for a place to stay every year.

The cultural scene in Salzburg

Even if Salzburg is a relatively small city with only 150,000 inhabitants, it has an incomparable cultural heritage and an enormous range of things to do and see. Salzburg is not only the city of Mozart, it also boasts a proud history and a pulsating present day outside the field of music.

Stefan Zweig decided to make Salzburg his main place of residence in 1919. H.C. Artmann, Thomas Bernhard and Peter Handke are important contemporary literary names who lived and worked here.

In 1953, Oskar Kokoschka founded the Schule des Sehens (School of Seeing) as an international summer academy for the fine arts. It brings students and teachers from all around the world to Salzburg year after year.

Ever since the 1980s, new institutions have been establishing themselves in the city of Salzburg within the context of a cultural venue concept. Today, these locations represent an indispensable part of Salzburg's cultural vitality.

For example, the Salzburger Literaturhaus with its authors and literature groups offers a year-round literature programme that presents a good cross-section of Austrian and Salzburger literature and international contemporary literature.

The Salzburger Rockhouse provides practice rooms and gig opportunities for Salzburg's bands, while at the same time serving as the local venue for international and domestic pop and rock acts.

Opened in 2005, the ARGEKultur Nonntal, the second-largest open cultural centre in Austria, not only improves the infrastructure for the local initiatives, it also provides rehearsal and event opportunities for dance, theatre, cabaret and music groups.

Die Salzburger Sommerakademie: Hier lehren bedeutende internationale KünstlerInnen. Die Kurse sind weltweit begehrt und werden von Studentinnen und Studenten aus aller Herren Länder belegt. Die Akademie zeichnet sich durch ihre Offenheit gegenüber Nationalität, Alter, Geschlecht und kulturellen Hintergrund aus. Begleitet werden die Kurse durch hochkarätige Vorträge, Screenings, Diskussionen, Panels und Ausstellungen. Die Studios und Ateliers befinden sich auf der Festung Hohensalzburg, in den alten Salinen Hallein sowie im Marmorsteinbruch Fürstenbrunn

The Salzburg Summer Academy:
The teachers here are prominent international artists. The courses are coveted worldwide and filled with students from all nations. A feature of the Academy's admissions policy is its openness towards nationality, gender and cultural background. The courses are complemented by top-class presentations and lectures, screenings, discussions, panels and exhibitions. The studios are in Hohensalzburg fortress in the Alte Saline in Hallein and in the Fürstenbrunn marble quarry

Museum der Moderne Salzburg

Salzburg Museum of Modern Art

1–5 Die Münchner Architekten Friedrich, Hoff und Zwink haben das Museum der Moderne in Salzburg entworfen. Eröffnet wurde es im Jahr 2004 auf dem Mönchsberg. Die Struktur des Berges inspirierte die Architekten zum Bau eines monolithischen Blocks, deren Ausnehmungen viel Tageslicht in die Foyerzone bringen

6 Das Rupertinum in der Salzburger Innenstadt gehört ebenfalls zum Museum der Moderne

1–5 The Munich architects Friedrich, Hoff and Zwink designed the "Museum der Moderne" on the Mönchsberg in Salzburg, which was opened in 2004. The structure of the hill itself inspired the architects to construct a monolithic block, whose cut-outs flood the foyer with natural light

6 The Rupertinum in the inner city of Salzburg also belongs to the Museum der Moderne

ort für internationale und heimische Acts der Pop- und Rockkultur.

Mit der Neueröffnung der Räumlichkeiten für die ARGEKultur Nonntal im Jahr 2005, dem zweitgrößten offenen Kulturzentrum Österreichs, wurde nicht nur eine Infrastrukturverbesserung für die dort ansässigen Initiativen erreicht, sondern neue Probe- und Veranstaltungsräumlichkeiten für freie Gruppen aus den Bereichen Tanz, Theater, Kabarett und Musik geschaffen.

Das 2004 neu eröffnete Museum der Moderne mit dem Rupertinum, der Salzburger Kunstverein und die Galerie 5020 sind jene öffentlich geförderten Einrichtungen der bildenden Kunst, die sich der Präsentation und Vermittlung zeitgenössischer österreichischer und internationaler Kunst annehmen.

Eine Sonderstellung kommt der Galerie Fotohof zu, deren Tätigkeit weit über Salzburg und Österreich hinaus reicht und die neben der kontinuierlichen Ausstellungstätigkeit vor allem durch die hauseigene Bibliothek und durch Buchprojekte und Publikationen von sich Reden macht.

Salzburg verfügt auch über eine äußerst aktive Tanzszene, die mit dem Ausbildungszentrum SEAD (Salzburg Experimental Academy of Dance) und dem republic als Veranstaltungszentrum für zeitgenössischen Tanz und Theater auch international auf sich aufmerksam macht.

Die Musikstadt stellt ihre Kompetenz nicht nur während des Sommers unter Beweis. Das Mozarteum-Orchester, die Camerata Salzburg, die Junge Philharmonie Salzburg sind ebenso ganzjährig in der Festspielstadt tätig wie beispielsweise die Salzburger Bachgesellschaft oder die Salzburger Kulturvereinigung.

Dass Salzburg als Filmstadt Tradition hat, beweisen nicht nur Reminiszenzen aus der Vergangenheit. Eine neue Generation junger Salzburger Filmemacher kann sich gegenwärtig erfolgreich auf internationaler Ebene profilieren.

Im Bereich des Theaters bieten das Salzburger Landestheater als klassisches Dreispartenhaus, das Schauspielhaus, das TOI-Haus mit dem Schwerpunkt Jugend- und Kindertheater, das Kleine Theater und die vielen freien Theatergruppen ein ganzjährig attraktives Programm für einheimische und touristische Gäste.

Mit dem Salzburg Museum Carolino Augusteum, dem Barockmuseum, der Residenzgalerie und dem Dommuseum wird ein vielseitiges Angebot zu Geschichte und Kunstgeschichte von Stadt und Land Salzburg geboten.

Auch wenn ein Schwerpunkt des Kulturgeschehens auf musikalischem Sektor liegt – von den ca. 4 000 Veranstaltungen pro Jahr entfallen etwa 3 300 auf den Bereich Konzerte, Musik- und Sprech-

The new Museum of Modern Art that opened in 2004, the Salzburger Art Club and Galerie 5020 are publicly assisted fine art institutions devoted to presenting and marketing contemporary Austrian and international art.

Galerie Fotohof has its very own special place in the cultural life of Salzburg. Indeed, its activities go far beyond Salzburg and Austria, drawing a lot of attention to itself with its exhibitions, library, book projects and publications.

Salzburg also has an extremely active dance scene of international standard, with the Salzburg Experimental Academy of Dance and the republic – a performance venue for contemporary dance and theatre.

But the city of music doesn't show its worth only in summer. The Mozarteum Orchestra, the Camerata Salzburg and the Junge Philharmonie Salzburg are active all year in the city of festivals, as are other organisations such as the Salzburg Bach Association and the Salzburg Cultural Union.

Salzburg's reputation as a movie town is not only founded on reminiscences of a rich past either. A new generation of young Salzburg film makers is more than holding its own internationally.

The Salzburg State Theatre is a typical three-division theatre. With the Schauspielhaus, the TOI-Haus with its focus on youth and children's theatre, the Kleines Theater and many other theatre groups, it offers an attractive year-round programme for locals and tourists.

With the Salzburg Museum Carolino Augusteum, the Baroque museum, the Residence Gallery and the Cathedral Museum, the city has a varied

Salzburg hat eine aktive Tanzszene: Das Foto zeigt eine Probe im Ausbildungszentrum SEAD (Salzburg Experimental Academy of Dance)

Salzburg has a very active dance scene. The photo shows a rehearsal in the SEAD (Salzburg Experimental Academy of Dance)

theater – zeichnet sich die Salzburger Kulturszene durch Spartenvielfalt aus. Es gibt allein in der Stadt 800 aktive Kultureinrichtungen und -initiativen. Die genannten Veranstaltungen werden von über 850 000 Zuschauern besucht.

Auch im Bereich der Galerien, Museen und Sehenswürdigkeiten weist die Stadt Salzburg eine hohe Dichte auf. 66 Galerien und 17 Museen zeigen permanent Ausstellungen. Allein die Museen und Sehenswürdigkeiten verzeichnen etwa 3 Millionen Besucher pro Jahr.

Architektur und Weltkulturerbe

„Als geistliches Zentrum Mitteleuropas reicht die Bedeutung der ehemaligen fürsterzbischöflichen Residenzstadt Salzburg bis in die Frühzeit der abendländischen Kultur zurück. Die mit Mozart verbundene Musik und Festspieltradition Salzburgs ist eine weitere Dimension in der Bedeutung dieser Stadt." So lautet die Begründung der UNESCO anlässlich der 1996 erfolgten Eintragung der Altstadt von Salzburg in die Liste der UNESCO Weltkulturerbe-Stätten. Tatsächlich hat unter den Erzbischöfen Markus Sittikus und Paris Lodron die prägende bauliche und architektonische Stadtgestaltung mit Baumeistern wie Santiono Solari, Giovanni Antonio Daria, Gaspare Zuccalli und Fischer von Erlach stattgefunden. In dieser Zeit sind die Meisterwerke barocker Baukunst in Salzburg entstanden, in dieser Zeit wurde jenes besondere städtische Ambiente geschaffen, das auch heute noch jährlich tausende Besucher nach Salzburg lockt.

Die Stadt Salzburg schützt ihre ca. 1 500 erhaltenswerte Gebäude umfassende Altstadt durch ein vorbildliches Altstadterhaltungsgesetz, das seit 1967 in Kraft ist.

Dennoch wird der zeitgenössischen Architektur Platz eingeräumt, wie Beispiele aus der neueren Gegenwart (Makartsteg, Heizkraftwerk Mitte) beweisen.

Kultur als Wirtschafts- und Standortfaktor

Kultur, Tourismus und Wirtschaft sind in der Stadt Salzburg so verknüpft wie kaum in einer anderen Stadt.

Der kontinuierliche Ausbau und die Weiterentwicklung der kulturellen Infrastruktur – allein in den letzten Jahren wurden im Rahmen eines Kulturstätteninvestitions-Programmes 80 Mio. Euro in bestehende und neue Kultureinrichtungen investiert – die Ansiedlung international ausgerichteter Unternehmen im Umfeld der Kulturwirtschaft, die verstärkte Bindung internationaler Tagungen und Kongresse an die Stadt Salzburg wie auch die entspre-

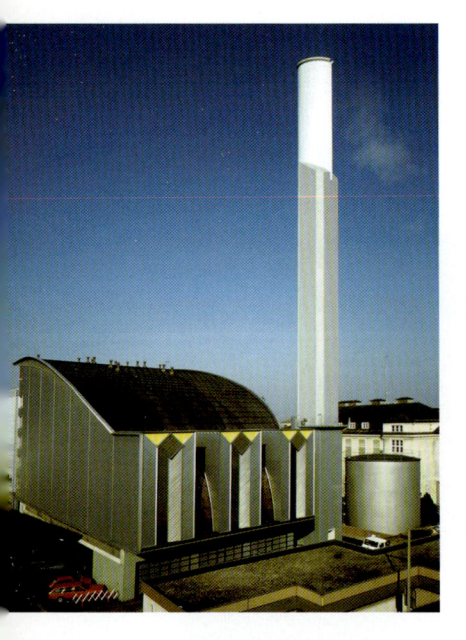

Das Heizkraftwerk Mitte in Salzburg

The cogeneration power plant in the middle of Salzburg

range of ways to learn about its history and the history of its art and that of the state of Salzburg.

Even if the cultural focus is undoubtedly on music – of the around 4,000 events taking place here per year, around 3,300 are concerts, plays or musicals – Salzburg's cultural life is nonetheless an example of cultural diversity. In the city alone there are 800 active cultural facilities and initiatives. More than 850,000 people attend the events mentioned here.

Salzburg also boasts a high density of galleries, museums and tourist sights. 66 galleries and 17 museums have permanent exhibits. And alone the museums and tourist sights attract around 3 million visitors a year.

Architecture and world cultural heritage

"As a spiritual centre of Central Europe, the importance of the former prince archbishop's residence Salzburg goes all the way back to the beginnings of the occidental culture. Salzburg's music and festival tradition based around Mozart is a further dimension of this city." This is how UNESCO substantiated the 1996 registration of Salzburg's old town centre in the list of UNESCO world cultural heritage sites. In fact it was during the rule of the archbishops Markus Sittikus and Paris Lodron that the city was given its predominant structural and architectural look, with builders the likes of Santiono Solari, Giovanni Antonio Daria, Gaspare Zuccalli and Fischer von Erlach. The masterpieces of Baroque architecture were built during this period and the special feel that the city exudes and that attracts so many thousands of visitors to Salzburg every year was born.

The city of Salzburg protects its inner city with its 1,500 or so listed buildings by way of an exemplary historical township maintenance law that has been in effect since 1967.

But nonetheless, contemporary architecture is also given its place here, as examples from the recent pas show (Makartsteg, Heizkraftwerk Mitte).

Culture as a commercial and location factor

Culture, tourism and economy are more closely interlinked in Salzburg than in almost any other town.

The continued development and expansion of the cultural infrastructure – Euros 80 million have been invested in existing and new cultural facilities in recent years – the establishment of internationally operating companies in the field of cultural economics, the strong loyalty of international con-

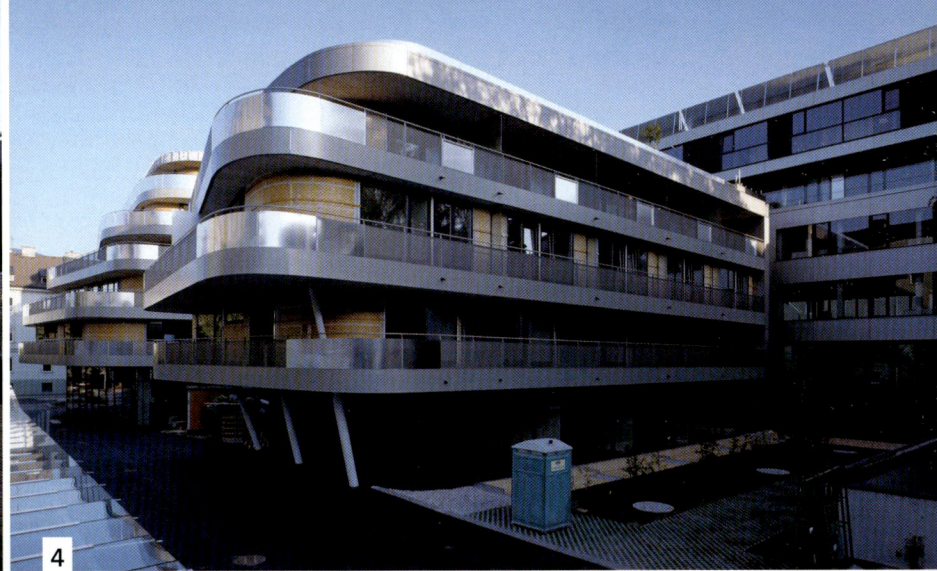

Zeitgenössische Architektur in Salzburg

Contemporary architecture in Salzburg

1–2 Der neue Makartsteg mit seiner markanten Krümmung eröffnet wechselnde Perspektiven auf die Stadt
3–4 Das Projekt Fallnhauser im Stadtteil Lehen ist ein Modell für die Integration neuer Wohn- und Arbeitsformen in einer vom Verfall bedrohten urbanen Landschaft
5 Bürogebäude an der Innsbrucker Bundesstraße
6 Von Leichtigkeit und Präzision bestimmt: die neue S-Bahn-Staion „Gnigl-Schwabenwirtsbrücke"
7 Wie ein großes Spielzeug wirkt der moderne Kindergarten Gebirgsjägerplatz Salzburg

1–2 The new Makartsteg bridge over the Salzach with its characteristic bend allows a variety of different views of the city
3–4 The Fallnhauser project in the Lehen district is a model for the integration of new forms of living and working in an urban landscape threatened by disrepair
5 Office building located Innsbrucker Bundesstrasse
6 Defined by lightness and precision: the new S-Bahn train station "Gnigl-Schwabenwirtsbrücke"
7 The highly modern kindergarten "Gebirgsjägerplatz Salzburg" gives the impression of being a gigantic children's toy

Theater, Tanz und Musik in Salzburg

Theatre, dance and music in Salzburg

1 Brechts „Dreigroschenoper" – Aufführung im Schauspielhaus Salzburg
2 „Die vierte Frau" – ein getanzter Krimi im Toihaus, Theater am Mirabellplatz mit seinem risiko- und experimentierbereiten Spielplan
3 Alljährlich kommen 40 000 Besucher zum Adventsingen ins Schauspielhaus
4 Szene aus Mozarts Zauberflöte im Salzburger Marionettentheater. Gegründet wurde es vor mehr als 90 Jahren und ist damit älter als die Festspiele

1 Brecht's "Threepenny Opera" – in the Schauspielhaus Salzburg theatre
2 "Die vierte Frau" (The Fourth Wife) – a thriller in dance in the Toihaus theatre at Mirabellplatz with its programme that likes to go out on a limb
3 40,000 people attend the Advent concert in the Schauspielhaus every year
4 A scene from Mozart's "Magic Flute" in the Salzburg Puppet Theatre, founded more than 90 years ago and thus even older than the Festival

chende Würdigung von Jubiläen – Mozart 2006, Herbert von Karajan 2008 – tragen erheblich zur Stärkung der wirtschaftlichen und kulturellen Kompetenz der Stadt bei.

So wurde der Nächtigungsrekord von 1,9 Mio. Nächtigungen aus dem Jahr 2005 bereits im ersten Halbjahr des diesjährigen Mozartjahres um 21,5 Prozent überschritten. Eine von den Salzburger Festspielen in Auftrag gegebene Studie über Besucherstruktur und Umwegrentabilität hat errechnet, dass durch die Festspiele ein Umsatzeffekt von 168 Mio. Euro pro Jahr und österreichweit ein Arbeits- bzw. Beschäftigungseffekt von bis zu 2 300 Arbeitsplätzen entsteht.

Zudem etablieren sich immer mehr Einrichtungen und Initiativen, die durch ihre Tätigkeit dazu beitragen, die kulturelle und wirtschaftliche Kompetenz des Zentralraumes Salzburg im Sinne einer Standortprofilierung zu verstärken. Insbesondere im Ausbildungsbereich, im Umfeld internationaler Tagungen und Kongresse sowie Messewesen werden neue, innovative Schwerpunkte gesetzt. Beispiele aus dem Kultursektor dafür sind die Aktivitäten des ICCM, eines international ausgerichteten Kompetenzzentrums für Managementausbildung, SEAD (Salzburg Experimental Academy of Dance) als einziges internationales Ausbildungszentrum für zeitgenössischen Tanz Westösterreichs oder die Aktivitäten der beiden Internationalen Sommerakademien für Musik und Bildende Kunst, die gemeinsam jährlich 1 300 ausgewählte Studierende während der Sommermonate nach Salzburg bringen.

Ebenso ist die Verankerung der alljährlichen Tagung der Preisträger des Alternativen Nobelpreises für Salzburg eine qualitative Bereicherung des kulturellen Spektrums und trägt zur thematischen Erweiterung des öffentlichen Diskurses bei.

Mit dem Bau der Salzburg-Arena, einer multifunktionalen Veranstaltungshalle für bis zu 6 700 Besucher, hat auch das Salzburger Messezentrum

ferences and congresses to the city of Salzburg and the appropriate celebration of anniversaries – Mozart 2006, Herbert von Karajan 2008 – make a great contribution to the city's vigorous commercial and cultural competence.

For example, the record number of 1.9 million overnight stays set in 2005 was already broken by 21.5% in the first half of this the Mozart year. A study of visitor structure and collateral earnings commissioned by the Salzburg Festival has found that the Festival generates total earnings of Euros 168 million per year and up to 2,300 jobs throughout Austria.

And in addition, more and more facilities and initiatives are being set up that help raise the cultural and commercial competence of central Salzburg by helping raise the region's profile. New, innovative focuses are arising, in particular in the field of education, international conferences and congresses. Some examples of this from the cultural sector are the activities of the ICCM, the International Competence Center for Management Training, the SEAD (Salzburg Experimental Academy of Dance), the only international training centre for contemporary dance in western Austria, and the two international summer academies for music and fine arts, that together attract 1,300 selected students to Salzburg every summer.

„Verkündigung" – ein Detail am Tor der Hoffnung von Ewald Mataré. Es ist eins der Bronzetore am Salzburger Dom

"Annunciation" – an element in the Gate of Hope by Ewald Mataré, one of the bronze gates of Salzburg Cathedral

Das Haus der Natur in Salzburg wurde 1924 von dem Zoologen Prof. Eduard Tratz gegründet und ist eines der führenden seiner Art in Europa. Zu den Besuchermagneten gehören die Weltraumhalle, die Saurierhalle und das Aquarium

The "Haus der Natur" in Salzburg was founded in 1924 by the zoologist Prof. Eduard Tratz and is one of the leaders of its kind in Europe. Among the big attractions are the Space Hall, the Dinosaur Hall and the aquarium

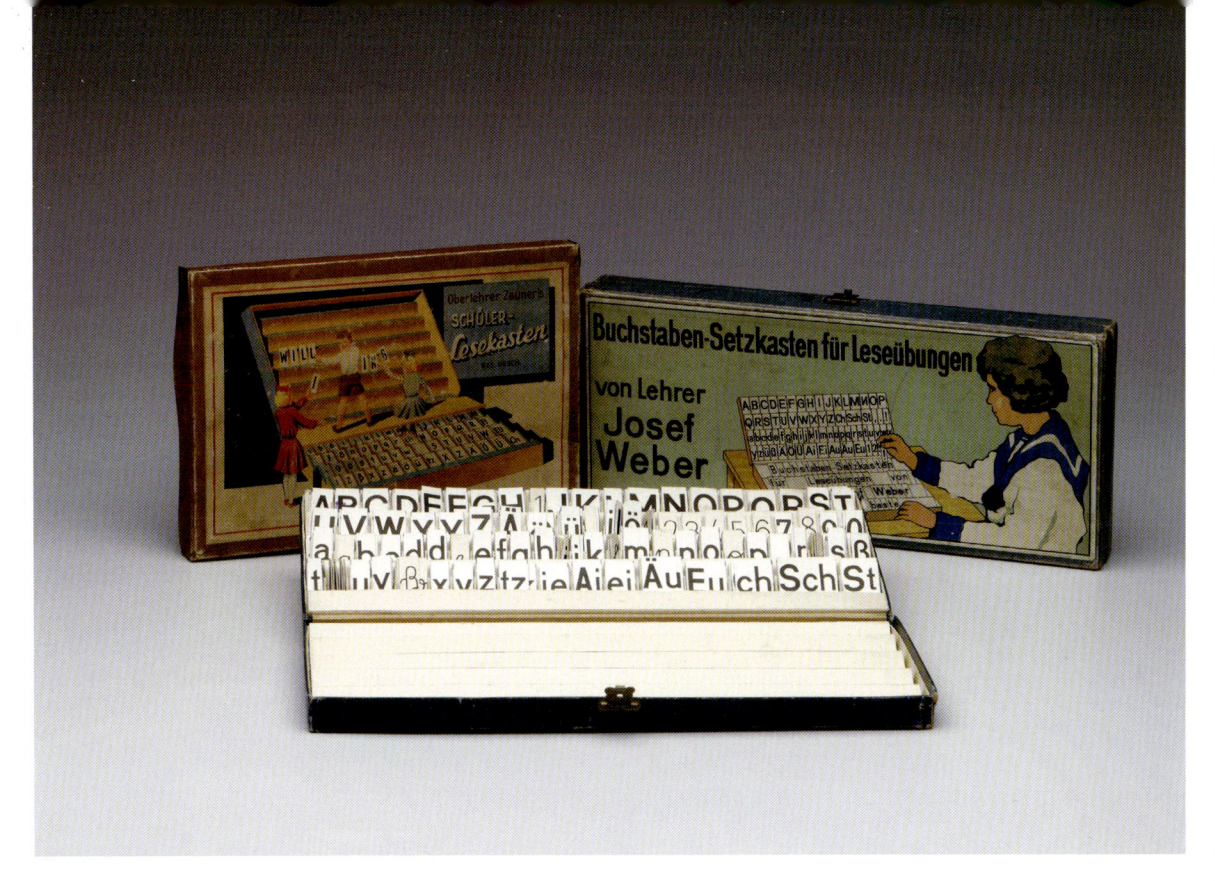

Im Spielzeugmuseum, einem Teil des Salzburger Museums Carolino Augusteum. Die Sonderausstellung zeigt Spielzeug von A wie Affe bis Z wie Zebra. Außerdem werden gezeigt: die Entwicklung der Schrift sowie eine Sammlung von Lesebüchern, Spielen und Videos rund um das ABC

In the Toy Museum; part of Salzburg's Carolino Augusteum museum. This special exhibition shows toys from A for ape to Z for zebra. It also shows how lettering was developed as well as a collection of books, games and videos all relating to the ABC

ein deutliches Signal gesetzt und eine Brücke zum Kulturveranstaltungsbereich geschlagen. Populärmusik, Klassik, Musical, spezielle Events jeder Art finden hier Möglichkeiten einer großformatigen Umsetzung.

Initiativen im Land Salzburg

Stadt und Land Salzburg verfügen über eine vielfältige, aktive und stark ausgeprägte Volkskultur. Chöre, Blasmusik, Volkstanz, Heimatvereine und Schützen leisten hervorragende Vereinsarbeit und bemühen sich stark um die Integration der Jugend. Allein im Land Salzburg gibt es über 40 Heimatmuseen und über 120 aktive Amateurtheaterbühnen.

Neben der volkskulturellen Schiene haben sich in den vergangenen 30 Jahren im Land Salzburg Kulturinitiativen entwickelt, die über den amateurhaften Beginn einen Weg der Entwicklung in die Professionalisierung eingeschlagen haben und heute als unverzichtbare Kultureinrichtungen identitätsstiftend und imagebildend für die Region wirken. So verfügen heute beispielsweise die Städte Hallein, Altenmarkt, Radtstadt, Oberndorf, Bad Gastein, Zell am See und Saalfelden über äußerst engagierte Kulturvereine, die ein vielfältiges Kunst- und Kulturprogramm für ihr Publikum produzieren. Gezählt sind es über 50 Kulturinitiativen, die mit 1 100 Veranstaltungen jährlich ein Publikum von etwa 280 000 Personen erreichen. ◄

Similarly, the annual conference of the winners of the Alternative Nobel Prize is an enrichment for Salzburg's cultural spectrum and contributes to the thematic expansion of public discussion.

By building the Salzburg Arena, a multifunctional hall for up to 6,700 people, the Salzburg Conference Centre has sent out an unmistakable signal, and constructed a bridge to the cultural event sector. Popular music, classic, musicals and special events of all kinds find their ideal stage here.

Initiatives in the Land of Salzburg

The city and state of Salzburg both have a varied, active and strongly defined culture. Choirs, brass bands, folk dance, traditional costume clubs and shooting clubs do great work and put a lot of work into integrating youth. In the state of Salzburg alone there are more than 40 traditional museums and 120 amateur theatres.

In addition to the folk culture side of things, other cultural initiatives have also been founded over the last 30 years in the state of Salzburg that have developed from humble amateur beginnings into professional institutions that are indispensable for the identity and image of the region. The cities of Hallein, Altenmarkt, Radtstadt, Oberndorf, Bad Gastein, Zell am See and Saalfelden, for example, have very active cultural clubs and produce a varied art and culture programme for their audiences. There are more than 50 cultural initiatives that attract around 280,000 people to 1,100 events every year. ◄

Mag. Inge Brodil-Kuhn
Generalsekretärin „Mozart 2006 Salzburg"

Dr. Andrea Blöchl-Köstner
PR/Öffentlichkeitsarbeit „Mozart 2006 Salzburg"

Das Mozart-Jahr 2006 in Salzburg

The Mozart Year 2006 in Salzburg

Salzburg verdankt W.A. Mozart seinen internationalen kulturellen Ruhm. Salzburg war, ist und wird immer die Mozart-Stadt bleiben. Hier kam er am 27. Januar 1756 zur Welt, hier verbrachte er seine prägenden Kinder- und Jugendjahre, hier bildete sich das „Wunder Mozart" (Goethe) heran. 2006 präsentierte sich Salzburg der Weltöffentlichkeit einmal mehr als Ort der Begegnung, des künstlerischen Austausches und als Bühne für Mozarts Werk.

Anlässlich des 250. Geburtstages von W.A. Mozart bot Salzburg ein facettenreiches Veranstaltungsprogramm zwischen Tradition und Moderne, an aufregenden neuen und an bekannten Orten. Im Zusammenspiel mit den Kultureinrichtungen und Künstler/innen entstanden Spannungsbögen zwischen Mozarts Musik und zeitgenössischen Klängen, zwischen Operninszenierungen und Installationen im Stadtraum, zwischen sakraler Musik und kreativen Jugendprojekten. Konzertreihen und Festivals präsentierten außergewöhnliche Mozart-Interpretationen, bauten „Wege zu Mozart" und eröffneten „Dialoge" zu anderen Klang- und Kunstsprachen.

Nur in Salzburg war es möglich, alle Bühnenwerke Mozarts innerhalb nur weniger Wochen szenisch zu erleben. Mit „Mozart 22" haben die Salzburger Festspiele Musikgeschichte geschrieben, und sie können sich zudem über die zweithöchste Besucherzahl ihrer Geschichte freuen. Die Internationale Stiftung Mozarteum hat mit der Mozartwoche und mit der neuen (und weiterführenden) Reihe „Dialoge" Maßstäbe für die Zukunft gesetzt.

Mozarts Geburtshaus und Wohnhaus warteten mit Sonderausstellungen und Neupräsentationen auf. Die ganzjährige Ausstellung „Viva!MOZART" in der Neuen Residenz begeisterte das Publikum durch interaktive Präsentationsformen und mit wertvollen internationalen Exponaten. „Zwischen Himmel und Erde" im Dommuseum legte den Schwerpunkt auf Mozarts kirchenmusikalisches Werk und war ideale Ergänzung zu den eindrucksvollen Ausstellungen im Jubiläumsjahr, die zusammen von rund 850 000 Menschen besucht wurden.

Als besonderes Ziel der Programmplanung galt es, Kindern und Jugendlichen die Begegnung mit dem Genius Loci zu erleichtern. Ob Musik, Tanz oder Theater, Bildende Kunst oder Film, Radiobeiträge oder Workshops – alle Projekte fanden großen Anklang und setzten nachhaltige Impulse für die kommenden Jahre.

Zwei neue Festivals der zeitgenössischen Kunst wurden zeitlich in das Gesamtprogramm eingebettet. Das internationale Festival „Kontracom" im Frühsommer brachte international renommierte Künstler/innen nach Salzburg, die sich bewusst mit der Identität des jeweiligen Ortes ihrer Intervention

Salzburg owes W.A. Mozart its international cultural fame. Salzburg was, is and will always be the Mozart town. He was born here on 27 January 1756. He spent his childhood and youth here. This is where the "wonder Mozart" (Goethe) grew up. In 2006, Salzburg presented itself to the world once again as a place of encounters, of artistic interaction, and as a stage for Mozart's oeuvre.

On the occasion of Mozart's 250th birthday, Salzburg offered a multi-faceted programme of events between the traditional and the modern, of exciting new and well-known venues. Together with the cultural organisations and artists, a bridge was formed between Mozart's compositions and contemporary music, opera and art installations in the city, sacral music and creative youth projects. Concert series and festivals presented extraordinary Mozart interpretations, built "paths to Mozart" and opened up dialogues with other sound and artistic languages.

Only in Salzburg was it possible to experience all the stage works of Mozart within the space of just a few weeks. The Salzburg Festival wrote music history with "Mozart 22" and was rewarded with the second highest attendance in the Festival's history. The International Mozarteum Foundation has set new standards for the future with the Mozart Week and the new (and continuing) "Dialogues" series.

The house where Mozart was born and the one where he lived were equipped with special exhibitions and new presentations. The permanent exhibition "Viva!MOZART" in the Neue Residenz impressed its visitors with interactive presentations and prized international exhibits. "Between Heaven and Earth" in the Cathedral Museum focused on Mozart's ecclesiastical works and was the ideal complement to the impressive exhibitions held in the anniversary year, and that were seen by around 850,000 people.

The special goal of the programme was to help children and young people find a connection to the Genius Loci. Whether music, dance or theatre, fine art or film, radio or workshops – all the projects were a huge popular success and built a strong foundation for the years to come.

Two new festivals of contemporary art have been included in the programme. The international festival "Kontracom" in early summer brought internationally renowned artists to Salzburg, who took a close look at the identity of their respective homes. This was followed by heated debates on the value of contemporary art in the public arena. In autumn, the "OFFMozart" festival filled the free scene in Salzburg with concerts, exhibitions, performances and theatre projects, all of which were shown for the first time here.

Im Herzen Salzburgs, in der Getreidegasse, steht jenes Haus des Salzburger Handelsherrn und Spezereiwarenhändlers Johann Lorenz Hagenauer (1712-1792), das der junge „Hochfürstl. Salzburg'sche Kammermusikus Leopold Mozart mit seiner Ehefrau Anna Maria Walburga im Jahre 1747 bezog. 26 Jahre bewohnte die Familie Mozart eine aus Küche, Kabinett, Wohn-, Schlaf- (Geburtszimmer Mozarts) und Arbeitszimmer bestehende Wohnung im 3. Stock. Hier wurden ihre sieben Kinder geboren, von denen nur zwei das Kindesalter überlebten: 1751 Maria Anna Walburga („Nannerl") und am 27. Januar 1756 „Johannes Chrysostomus Wolfgang Theophilus" (Wolfgang Amadeus)

Right in the heart of Salzburg, in the little lane called Getreidegasse, stands the little apartment building belonging to the Salzburg trader and spicery dealer Johann Lorenz Hagenauer (1712-1792) that the young Court chamber musician Leopold Mozart moved into with his wife Anna Maria Walburga in 1747. For 26 years the Mozart family occupied the little flat on the third floor, consisting of a kitchen, closet, living room, bedroom (in which Wolfgang was born) and study. All of their seven children were born here, of which only two survived infancy: Maria Anna Walburga ("Nannerl") born 1751 and Johannes Chrysostomus Wolfgang Theophilus (Wolfgang Amadeus) born on 27th January 1756

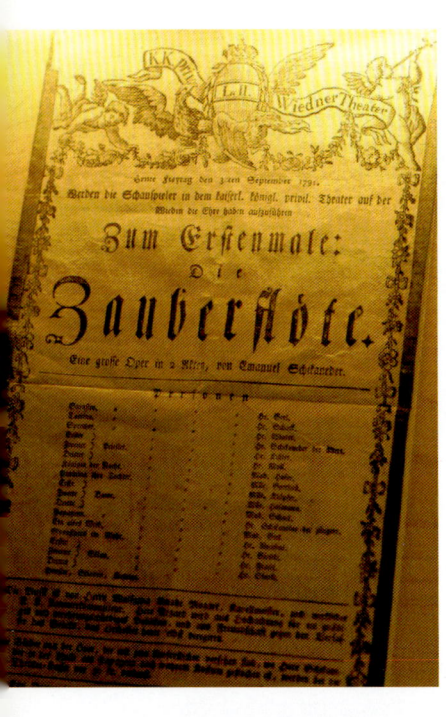

Die Zauberflöte (KV 620), Mozarts wohl berühmteste Oper, wurde 1791 uraufgeführt. Damals war der Komponist gerade einmal 25 Jahre alt. Das Libretto stammt von Emmanuel Schikaneder

The Magic Flute (Köchel number 620), probably Mozart's most famous opera, premiered in 1791 when the composer was just 25 years old. The libretto is from Emmanuel Schikaneder

201

Sebastiani Friedhof – das Grab von Konstanze und Leopold Mozart

Mozarts Geburtshaus (27. Januar 1756)

Sebastiani cemetery – the grave of Konstanze and Leopold Mozart

The house where Mozart was born (27 January, 1756)

auseinandersetzten. Es folgten heftige Diskussionen über den Stellenwert zeitgenössischer bildender Kunst im öffentlichen Raum. Im Herbst bot das Festival „OFFMozart" der freien Szene Salzburg mit Konzerten, Ausstellungen, Performances und Theaterprojekten ausschließlich Ur- und Erstaufführungen.

Besondere internationale Aufmerksamkeit im Jubiläumsjahr zog der im Rahmen der österreichischen EU-Präsidentschaft ausgerichtete Kongress „The Sound of Europe" auf sich, der hochkarätige Persönlichkeiten aus Kunst, Politik und Medien nach Salzburg brachte. Ein vom Land Salzburg hoch dotierter „Internationaler Kompositionspreis" wurde im Mozart-Jahr erstmals und wird in Folge alle drei Jahre verliehen. Als große Chance für den musikalischen Nachwuchs gilt auch der anerkannte Internationale Mozartwettbewerb, der alle drei bis vier Jahre ausgerichtet wird. Im Mozart-Jahr galt er der Sparte „Gesang" und Teilnehmer/innen aus 33 Nationen präsentierten einer hochkarätigen Jury ihr Können. Zudem war Salzburg einmal mehr Begegnungsstätte und Gastgeber für eine Vielzahl von Teilnehmer/innen bei themenbezogenen wissenschaftlichen Tagungen und Kongressen. So trafen sich in der Mozart-Stadt im Herbst beispielsweise über 1 200 Musikpädagogen und -pädagoginnen aus ganz Europa.

Darüber hinaus haben Land und Stadt Salzburg gemeinsam mit dem Bund umfangreiche bauliche

The congress "The Sound of Europe" held within the framework of Austria's EU presidency attracted very special international attention in the anniversary year. It brought top personalities from the fields of art, politics and media to Salzburg. A highly endowed "International Composition Prize" from the state of Salzburg was awarded for the first time in the Mozart Year and will be bestowed on talented young composers every three years. Another great opportunity for young musicians is the globally recognized International Mozart Competition, which is held every three or four years. In the Mozart Year, the competition was about voice, and participants from 33 nations presented their vocal talents to a top-class jury. In addition, Salzburg was once again the place of encounter for and host to numerous visitors at various scientific conferences, such as, for example, the more than 1,200 music teachers that came to Mozart's home town from all over Europe in autumn to discuss their calling.

And on top of all this, both the state and the city of Salzburg have made extensive edificial investments in Salzburg's cultural venues together with the national government. The large university auditorium (an authentic Mozart concert venue) was reopened in 2005 after a redesign of several years duration, followed by the "Haus für Mozart", which was inaugurated in July 2006 with Mozart's opera "The Marriage of Figaro". Students and teachers also had reason to celebrate: new constructions

Investitionen und Verbesserungen in Salzburgs Kulturstätten getätigt. Die Große Universitätsaula (ein authentischer Mozart-Spielort) wurde bereits im Jahr 2005 nach mehrjähriger Adaptierung wieder eröffnet, gefolgt vom „Haus für Mozart", das im Juli 2006 mit Mozarts Oper „Le Nozze di Figaro" eingeweiht wurde. Über enorme Verbesserungen können sich auch Student/innen und Lehrende freuen, die durch den Neubau der Universität Mozarteum und des Salzburger Musikum nun über zeitgemäße Ausbildungsstätten verfügen.

Hunderte internationale Journalisten berichteten während des gesamten Jahres über und aus Salzburg. Das Festkonzert zu Mozarts Geburtstag am 27. Jänner wurde weltweit ausgestrahlt, an die 11 000 dokumentierte Presseberichte, hohe Zugriffsraten auf den Websites und eine Vielzahl an Anfragen aus aller Welt belegen einmal mehr das große Interesse am Mozart-Jahr – und die von den Tourismusorganisationen genannte Zielsetzung wurde mit 18 Prozent Besucherzuwachs in der Stadt Salzburg nicht nur erreicht, sondern weit übertroffen.

Zum Ausklang des Mozart-Jahres 2006 wurde das Großprojekt „NMA online" der Internationalen Stiftung Mozarteum und des Packard Humanities Institutes ins Internet gestellt. Es basiert auf der „Neuen Mozart-Ausgabe", der wissenschaftlichen Gesamtausgabe, die von Musikwissenschaftern aus aller Welt in den letzten 50 Jahren erarbeitet wurde. Die Zielsetzung: Mozarts Werk allen Menschen auf der Welt kostenlos zugänglich zu machen. Die Nachfrage überstieg alle Erwartungen: Binnen der ersten 12 Stunden nach Freischaltung wurden weltweit über 400 000 Suchanfragen gestellt und innerhalb einer Woche waren es bereits 20 Millionen.

Der Auftrag eines Abschlussberichts steht mit den befragten Ziffern und Zahlen nahezu diametral der Botschaft eines Mozart-Jahres gegenüber. Die wahre Bedeutung liegt vielmehr darin, dass ein Gedenkjahr in vielerlei Hinsicht eine Entdeckungsreise sein soll – zu Begegnungen mit dem großen Komponisten W.A. Mozart und mit dem kreativen Potenzial seiner Heimatstadt. Am Beginn des Salzburger Mozart-Jahres 2006 stand die herausragende Eröffnungsrede von Nikolaus Harnoncourt, der die Kunst und mit ihr die Musik als wesentlichen Bestandteil des menschlichen Lebens bezeichnete, als Gegengewicht zum Praktischen, zum Nützlichen, zum Verwertbaren... Die Musik ist ein unerklärliches Zaubergeschenk, eine magische Sprache. Und: ...wenn so ein Besinnungsjahr trotz alledem einen Sinn haben soll, dann müssen wir hören – hören – hören – und können dann vielleicht einen kleinen Teil der Botschaft verstehen. Mozart braucht unsere Ehrungen nicht – wir brauchen ihn und seinen aufwühlenden Sturmwind. So ein Jahr ist in Wirklichkeit unsere Chance. ◄

at the Mozarteum University and the Salzburger Musikum mean that these in-stitutions now have state-of-the-art learning facilities.

Hundreds of international journalists reported on and from Salzburg throughout the year. The festival concert on Mozart's birthday on the 27th of January was broadcast worldwide, 11,000 documented press articles, high hit rates on the websites and numerous inquiries from across the globe show the international interest that the Mozart Year attracted – and the goal of 18 percent more tourists visiting Salzburg that the tourism organisations set themselves was not only achieved but easily surpassed.

As the Mozart Year 2006 was coming to a close, the major project "NMA online" of the international foundation Mozarteum and the Packard Humanities Institute went on-line. It is based on the "New Mozart Edition", the complete works put together by music experts from all over the world the last 50 years. The objective was to make Mozart's works available for free to everyone in the world. And demand exceeded all expectations: there were well over 400,000 hits in the first 12 hours, and 20 million in the first week.

The idea of writing a final report with the facts and figures stands almost diametrically opposed to the message that a Mozart Year is out to get across. For the real significance lies in a commemorative journey of discovery, in inciting an encounter with the great composer W.A. Mozart and the creative potential of his home town. At the beginning of Salzburg's Mozart Year 2006 was the exceptional opening speech by Nikolaus Harnoncourt, who referred to art and music as a major component of human life, as a counterweight to the practical, the expedient, the utilisable. ...Music is an inexplicable gift, a magical language, and, if a year of commemoration such as this has to have a purpose, then that purpose must be to listen – listen – listen – and then perhaps we will be able to understand part of the message. Mozart doesn't need our tributes – we need him and his effervescent storm wind. A year like this is, in actual fact, our great privilege. ◄

Im Jahre 1880 wurde die öffentliche Musikschule Mozarteum gegründet und heißt seit 1998 Universität Mozarteum Salzburg. Sie gewährt neben Ausbildungen für Streich- und Blasinstrumente, Zupf- und Schlaginstrumente in den Bereichen Konzertfach und Musikpädagogik auch eine solide und renommierte Ausbildung für Schauspiel. Das Hauptgebäude des Mozarteums steht heute in der Neustadt im alten Borromäum nahe dem Mirabellgarten in der Rainerstraße, wieder eröffnet nach umfangreichen Renovierungsarbeiten im Jahre 2006

In 1880 the public school of music known as the Mozarteum was founded, renamed as the Universität Mozarteum Salzburg in 1998. As well as teaching strings and wind, plucked strings and percussion instruments for concert musicians and teaching, it also provides a highly thought of course of training for actors. The main building of the Mozarteum is today in Neustadt in the former Borromäum near the Mirabell Garden in Rainerstrasse. It was reopened after extensive renovation work in 2006

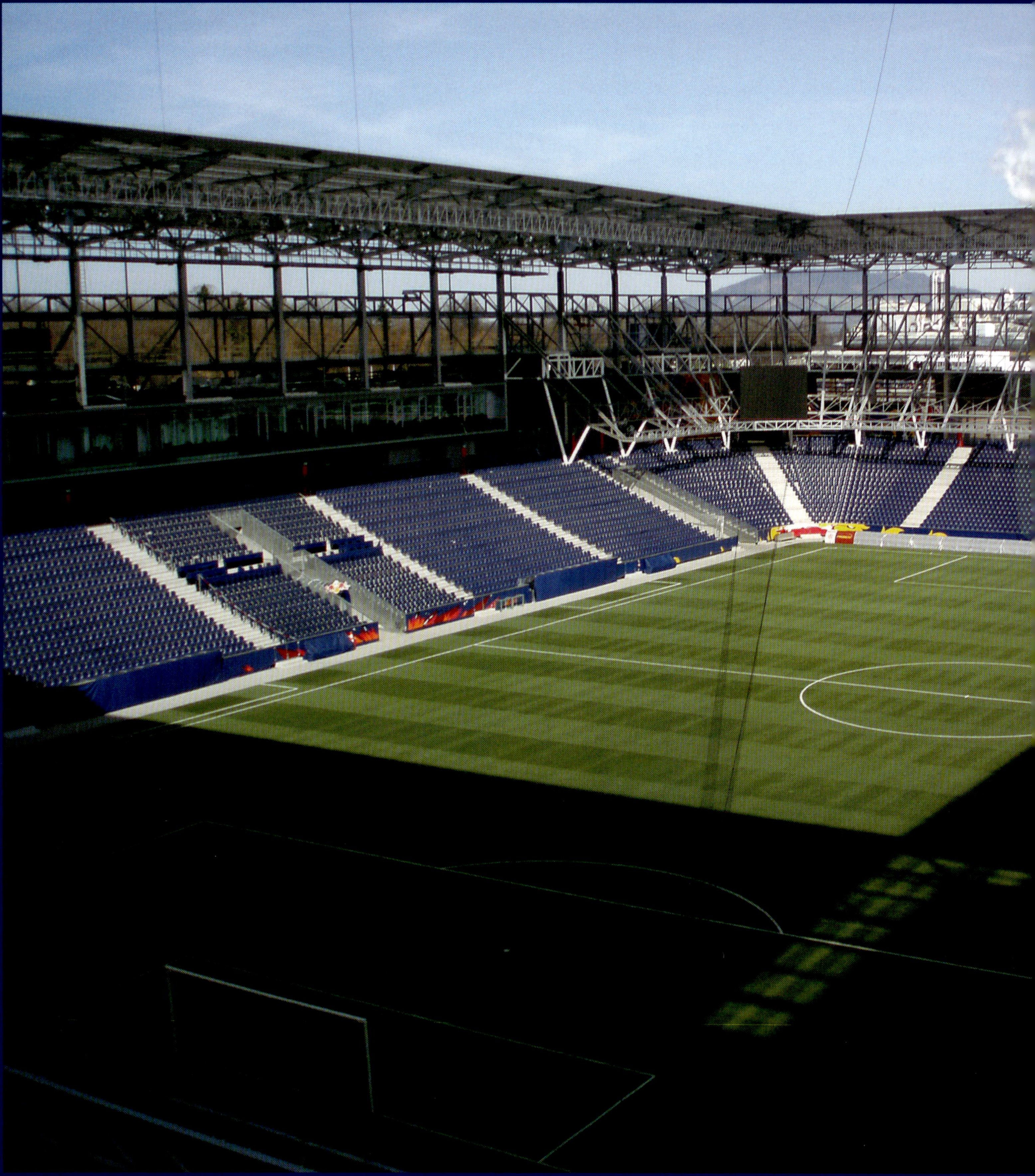

Prof. Joachim Glaser
Sportjournalist

Salzburg und der Sport

Salzburg and Sports

Obwohl sie schon fünf Knieoperationen hinter sich hat, gehört Marlies Schild aus Saalfelden zur absoluten Weltklasse und ist die beste Slalomläuferin der Gegenwart

Hermann Maier aus Flachau ist schon zu Lebzeiten eine Legende des österreichischen Skisportes. Er ist einer von zehn Salzburger Olympiasiegern

Despite five knee operations Marlies Schild from Saalfelden belongs to the world's skiing elite and is the best slalom specialist of our time

Hermann Maier from Flachau is a living Austrian skiing legend. He is one of the ten Salzburg Olympic Games gold medallists

Es ist sicher Zufall, dass die drei wichtigsten Termine in der rund 150-jährigen Geschichte des Salzburger Sportes auf den engen Zeitraum von wenig mehr als 20 Monaten zusammengedrängt sind: Die Radweltmeisterschaften im September 2006, die Entscheidung des Internationalen Olympischen Komitees (IOC) über den erhofften Zuschlag für die Olympischen Winterspiele 2014 im Juli 2007 und die Spiele der Fußball-Europameisterschaft im Juni 2008. Ansonsten aber hat der Weltsport hierzulande noch nicht Station gemacht, sieht man vom Skisport ab, der eine von Tourismus und Skiindustrie geprägte exklusive Ausnahme darstellt.

Zweimal war das Land Salzburg Gastgeber alpiner Skiweltmeisterschaften (1954 in Bad Gastein, 1991 in Saalbach-Hinterglemm), und Dutzende von großen Skirennen wurden ausgetragen, doch mit den eingangs erwähnten globalen Anlässen werden ganz andere Dimensionen erreicht. Spiegelt diese exklusive Ausnahme aber auch das „Sportland Salzburg" realitätsbezogen wider? Darf man Nachhaltigkeit erwarten, oder versinkt der Salzburger Sport anschließend wieder in seinen gemütlichen Alltag?

Im „Sportland Salzburg" leben statistisch gesehen auf jedem Quadratkilometer 35 Sportler, besser gesagt, sportlich Interessierte und Organisierte. Die nahezu 1000 Sportvereine melden nämlich erstaunliche 250 000 Mitglieder. Wer nun glaubt, das sei eine solide Basis für den Spitzensport, der irrt. Denn der Hochleistungssport ist auf nur ganz weni-

It is of course a coincidence that the three most important dates in the 150-year history of sports in Salzburg fall within the space of 20 months: the cycling world championships in September 2006, the International Olympic Committee's (IOC) decision on who will host the 2014 Winter Games in July 2007 and the European Cup of soccer in June 2008. Apart from this Salzburg is not really a home of world sports, apart from alpine skiing of course, which is an exclusive exception that connects tourism and a thriving sporting industry.

The state of Salzburg has hosted two alpine skiing world championships (1954 in Bad Gastein, 1991 in Saalbach-Hinterglemm) and dozens of major races, but the global dimensions of the events named above attain entirely new heights. Is this unique circumstance a true reflection of sports in Salzburg? Can we expect a lasting effect, or will Salzburg's sport fall back into its cosy everyday trot when it is all over?

Statistically speaking there are 35 sportspeople on every square kilometre of land in Salzburg – that is, people interested in sports and registered in organised clubs. The almost 1,000 sports clubs here report an astonishing 250,000 members. But if you think that is a good basis for top sport, you are mistaken. Because professional sport is restricted here to a very small number of disciplines and hasn't really come out of the starting blocks for some years. The great exception to this rule are the skiers, who have brought forth numerous Olympic

ge Disziplinen beschränkt und kommt seit Jahren nicht recht vom Fleck. Die große Ausnahme sind die Skisportler mit ihren zahlreichen Olympiasiegern und Weltmeistern, von Sepp Bradl über Annemarie Moser-Pröll, Petra Kronberger, Thomas Stangassinger bis Hermann Maier, Alexandra Meissnitzer, Alois Stadlober, Wolfgang Rottmann bis hin zu Michael Walchhofer, Manuela Riegler, Felix Gottwald und Michael Gruber. Dazu dürfen sich noch Fußball und Eishockey das Mäntelchen des Spitzensportes umhängen, hier darf dank des enormen Engagements von Red Bull von einer Renaissance gesprochen werden; im Fußball wird nach den drei Titeln 1994, 1995 und 1997 unter dem seit Sommer 2006 wirkenden italienischen Meistermacher Giovanni Trapattoni erneut der Anschluss an die europäische Elite versucht, im Eishockey hofft man nach zahllosen Anläufen auf die Nummer eins in Österreich.

Interessant ist, dass das Binnenland Salzburg schon immer hervorragende Segler hatte: Hubert Raudaschl ist mit zehn olympischen Teilnahmen internationaler Rekordmann und Legende zugleich, Roman Hagara und Hans-Peter Steinacher schafften mit dem schnellen Tornado zweimal hintereinander den Olympiasieg. Alles in allem regiert aber die Eigeninitiative, wofür der Judokämpfer Ludwig Paischer als Paradebeispiel steht. Dass die Spitze minimal bleibt, ist bei einem Sportbudget, das nur 0,35% des Landeshaushaltes ausmacht, auch kein Wunder. Dennoch: 177 Salzburger und Salzburgerinnen waren seit 1932 bei Olympischen Spielen am Start und holten 44 Medaillen in die Heimat. Weshalb bewirbt sich ein speziell im Winter (mit 7 000 Hektar ausgewiesenen Skipisten) ziemlich ausgereiztes Bundesland wie Salzburg um Olympische Spiele? Sicher nicht des Sportes wegen, weil neben dem Skilauf keinerlei Ansätze für eine Orientierung in Richtung Hochleistungsniveau erkennbar sind, weder auf dem Eis noch in der Bob- und Schlittenbahn. Demnach darf man die Triebfeder ausschließlich jenen Orten zuschreiben, in denen der alpine Skilauf zuhause ist – was nicht unbedingt mit Skirennsport zu tun hat. Und deshalb auch hat die Bevölkerung Salzburgs, vor allem die in der Landeshauptstadt, mit der Akzeptanz des olympischen Gedankens so ihre Probleme – denn dort wird nach Olympia so gut wie nichts bleiben, ausgenommen vielleicht ein Eisstadion.

Die bisher zweimal gescheiterten Olympia-Befürworter können jetzt zurecht auf ein gutes Sportstättenkonzept verweisen, konnten zugleich aber die Vorteile und Pluspunkte gegenüber den Skeptikern nicht zufriedenstellend und ausreichend kommunizieren, keine hundertprozentig positive Stimmung erzeugen – Sport ist auch Emotion. Bei der Bewerbung für 2006 war Salzburg innerösterreichisch über den Mitbewerber Kärnten gestolpert,

and world champions, from Sepp Bradl to Annemarie Moser-Pröll, Petra Kronberger, Thomas Stangassinger to Hermann Maier, Alexandra Meissnitzer, Alois Stadlober, Wolfgang Rottmann and on through to Michael Walchhofer, Manuela Riegler, Felix Gottwald and Michael Gruber. Then there are soccer and ice hockey that can claim to be in the top ranks of sport here. Thanks to the enormous generosity and commitment of Red Bull, one could even speak of a renaissance; in soccer, after winning three national titles in 1994, 1995 and 1997, a new attack is being made on the top of the table and into the European elite with the new Italian coach Giovanni Trapattoni. In ice hockey we are hoping to win the Austrian league again after innumerable failed efforts in the past.

Interestingly enough, landlocked Salzburg has always produced excellent sailors: Hubert Raudaschl is our international record holder and legend with ten Olympic Games behind him. Roman Hagara and Hans-Peter Steinacher won Gold twice in a row with their fast Tornado. All in all, however, personal initiative is required here, for which judoka Ludwig Paischer is a perfect example. And it is no wonder that the air is thin at the top, with a sports budget that only accounts for 0.35% of the state expenditure. But nonetheless, 177 Salzburgers have competed at the Olympic Games since 1932, and they have brought no less than 44 medals home with them. So why is a state like Salzburg, which is pretty close to its limit already, especially in winter (with 7,000 hectares of designated ski runs), applying to hold the Olympic Games? It can't be because of the sport itself, because besides skiing, not even the beginnings of an orientation towards high sporting goals can be recognised here, neither on the ice nor on the luge and bob runs. So it can only be assumed that the impetus for this event comes from those places where alpine skiing is at home – which doesn't necessarily have anything to do with ski racing. And this is why the people of Salzburg, in particular those in the state capital, have their issues with accepting the Olympic idea, because there, virtually nothing will remain after Olympia's visit, except perhaps an ice-skating stadium.

Mit 14 Medaillen bei Olympischen Spielen und Weltmeisterschaften ist der Nordische Kombinierer Felix Gottwald aus Zell am See Österreichs erfolgreichster Skisportler

With 14 medals won at Olympic Games and world championships the Nordic Combined competitor Felix Gottwald from Zell am See is Austria's winningest skiier

Am 20. Mai 2007 durfte sich der italienische Startrainer Giovanni Trapattoni über seinen 22. Meistertitel freuen, den ersten mit Red Bull Salzburg

Nach zehn Jahren Pause ist der österreichische Meistertitel im Fußball wieder nach Salzburg zurückgekehrt. Statt Austria heißt der Klub jetzt Red Bull

The Italian star coach Giovanni Trapattoni celebrated his 22nd league championship on 20 May 2007, and his first with Red Bull Salzburg

After a ten-year absence the Austrian league trophy has returned to Salzburg. The winning club is now called Red Bull and no longer Austria though

---

für 2010 waren die ausländischen Hürden zu hoch, hatte man das Lobbying unterschätzt und zu sehr die kulturelle Karte gespielt; die Abstimmungsniederlage in Prag war blamabel und schmerzlich zugleich. Der dritte Anlauf lebt von einem stark gestrafften Sportstättenkonzept mit den Eckpfeilern Landeshauptstadt (Eissport, Zeremonien), Schönau am Königssee (Bob und Rodeln), Bischofshofen (Springen), Altenmarkt, Flachau und Radstadt (Alpiner Skilauf, Langlauf, Snowboard, Freestyle).

Holprig und von Rückschlägen gezeichnet war der Auftakt zu dieser dritten Salzburger Olympia-Bewerbung; die über das regionale Schmalspurdenken hinaus notwendige Professionalität kehrte erst im Sommer 2006 ein, als Fedor Radmann die Zügel in die Hand nahm, also jener „Netzwerker", der neben Franz Beckenbauer den größten Anteil daran hatte, dass die Fußball-Weltmeisterschaft 2006 an Deutschland vergeben wurde. Zehn Monate werkelte der umtriebige Bayer, der einstens in Salzburg die Schulbank gedrückt hat, an der Bewerbung, am 22. januar 2007 – 164 Tage vor dem IOC-Entscheid – warf er das Handtuch – „gesundheitliche Gründe" wurden offiziell genannt.

Zuvor musste Radmann zahlreiche Stolpersteine aus dem Weg räumen. Die erbetene Ausfallshaf-

The twice-failed Olympia advocates can now rightfully claim to have an excellent concept for the sporting venues, but they have not been able to adequately communicate the advantages and benefits of such an event to the sceptics. After all, sport is emotion, and they have not managed to generate a 100% positive sentiment. In the application for 2006, Salzburg stumbled and fell behind its fellow Austrian candidate Kärnten. For 2010 the international hurdles were too high, with Salzburg underestimating the lobbying and relying too much on the cultural trump; the vote in Prague was painful and embarrassing. The third attempt now lives from its much tighter sporting venue concept based on the state capital (ice sports, ceremonies), Schönau am Königssee (bobsled and luge), Bischofshofen (ski jumping), Altenmarkt, Flachau and Radstadt (alpine skiing, cross country, snowboard, freestyle).

The start to this third Salzburg Olympia candidacy was bumpy and marked with setbacks. The necessary professionalism didn't overcome the regional conservatism until the summer of 2006, as Fedor Radmann took up the reins. Radmann was the networker who, next to Franz Beckenbauer, played the biggest part in Germany for being the venue

tung durch den Bund ließ Monate auf sich warten, und wie ein Keulenschlag wirkte die dürre Mitteilung des IOC (sie wurde in Salzburg selbst vier Monate geheimgehalten), dass die Fernsehgelder bei weitem nicht so fließen werden wie vom IOC in Aussicht gestellt – da spielt es keine Rolle, ob es nun 150 oder gar 400 Millionen Euro weniger sind (weil die TV-Präsenz der Winterspiele eben stark zurückgegangen ist). Guter Rat war – im wahrsten Sinn des Wortes – teuer und wurde von allen Seiten erteilt, nicht unbedingt im Sinne der Betreiber – eine Folge mangelnder Kommunikation nach außen. Dazu gilt es die speziell aus dem Nachbarland Tirol kommenden Nadelstiche abzuwehren (oder nicht ernst zu nehmen). Mit dem Sparstift wurde „fünf Minuten vor zwölf" die für den regionalen Frieden notwendige Rettungsaktion eingeleitet. Ein Durchführungsbudget von ursprünglich 1,33 Milliarden Euro handstreichartig auf 734 Millionen Euro zu reduzieren und das Investitionsbudget mit 148 Millionen Euro zu fixieren, kann freilich nur eins heißen: Entweder war Haushalt Nummer eins aufgebläht oder entspricht Haushalt Nummer zwei nur der halben Wahrheit. Was wird nun leiden? Die Sportstätten, das Personal, die Organisation? Sicher kann bei den Sportstätten eingespart werden, denn

of the 2006 Soccer World Cup tournament. This busy Bavarian, who many years ago went to school in Salzburg, worked on the bid for 10 months. On 22 January 2007, 164 days before the IOC decision, he had to throw in the towel, officially for health reasons.

There were many hurdles and stumbling blocks that he had to eliminate before he did. The requested contingent liability from the national government took months to be issued, and the meagre report from the IOC (which was kept under wraps in Salzburg for four months) came like a bolt from the blue, stating that the TV rights wouldn't generate nearly as much as the IOC originally planned – it makes no difference whether it is 150 or 400 million euros less (because the TV interest in the Winter Games has diminished drastically). Everyone offered their two cents, but not always to the benefit of the operators – a consequence of poor outward communication. On top of that there were the niggling pinpricks coming from in particular the neighbouring state of Tyrol, which had to be defended against (or not taken seriously). At the last minute the necessary rescue campaign for the regional peace was started. An original implementation budget of Euro 1.33 billion was struck down to Euro

Die Eishockey-Mannschaft der Red Bulls hatte beim Gewinn der ersten österreichischen Meisterschaft ein paar Wochen Vorsprung vor den Ball spielenden Kollegen

The Red Bulls ice hockey team beat its kicking colleagues to its first Austrian championship by a few weeks

Roman Hagara und Hans-Peter Steinacher schafften mit dem schnellen Tornado zweimal hintereinander den Olympiasieg

Roman Hagara and Hans-Peter Steinacher caused a sensation by winning the Olympic gold medal twice in a row with their speedy Tornado

es ist nicht einzusehen, moderne Einrichtungen etwa für Biathlon und Eisschnelllauf, wie sie im benachbarten Bayern bestehen und die mit dem Auto von Salzburg aus in einer halben Stunde erreichbar sind, nicht zu nützen – dieser Einsparungseffekt wird ohnehin hinter vorgehaltener Hand diskutiert, und ein Wörtchen werden nach einem eventuellen Zuschlag auch noch die internationalen Fachverbände mitreden.

Eher gering dürfte das Einsparungspozential beim Personal (bis zu 20 000 Personen sollen freiwillig helfen, kosten aber unter dem Strich auch genug) und bei der Abwicklung der Wettkämpfe sein. Sehr gerne wird der Begriff der Umwegrentabilität in die Waagschale geworfen (strapaziert), ebenso der Wertschöpfungseffekt, der im Falle Olympia bei 800 Millionen Euro liegen soll.

Weit niedriger lag dieser Wert bei den Radweltmeisterschaften im September 2006, die ein durchaus positiver Testlauf für Olympia und Fußball-Euro 2008 gewesen sind. Zu den Radrennen kamen von der Polizei geschätzte 300 000 Besucher, die von bis zu 34 Fernsehkameras eingefangenen Bilder erreichten bei einer ge-samten Übertragungszeit von 342 Stunden beachtliche 307 Millionen Fernsehzuschauer. Auch bei dieser ersten wirklich großen Veranstaltung in Salzburg, deren Dimension viele Ent-

734 million and the investment budget set at Euro 148 million, which can mean only one thing: either budget number one was too extravagant or budget number two only tells half the story. What will suffer? The sporting venues, the staff, the organisation? Of course money can be saved in the sporting venues. For example it makes no sense not to use the modern facilities for biathlon and speed skating that exist less than half an hour's drive from Salzburg in neighbouring Bavaria – one saving that is being quietly discussed in the wings. And if Salzburg is chosen, the international associations will certainly have their say in the matter.

The savings potential among the personnel is probably fairly limited (up to 20,000 people are supposed to help as volunteers, but cost enough as it is) as is the case in the organisation of the events. The term "indirect profitability" is being thrown around a lot (perhaps too much), as is "value added effect", which is claimed to amount to euro 800 million for Olympic Games.

This figure was much lower for the cycling world championships in September 2006, which were a highly successful test run for Olympia and soccer's Euro 2008. The police estimate that 300,000 people came to see the races in all. The TV pictures, captured by up to 34 cameras, reached a

scheidungsträger bis zuletzt nicht wirklich einzuschätzen wussten, wurde auf die zusätzlichen Übernachtungen hingewiesen, bei der Euro 2008 sollen es für die drei Spiele sogar mehr als 100 000 sein – also auch hier wird in erster Linie an der Wirtschaftsschraube gedreht. Das mag auch ganz im Sinne jener Unternehmen sein, die den Namen Salzburgs in Zusammenhang mit Sport zum Teil schon seit vielen Jahren in die Welt hinaustragen. Stellvertretend seien die Skifabrikanten, Zulieferfirmen für den Motorsport inklusive der Formel 1 und Hersteller von mittlerweile weltweit vertriebenen Zutrittssystemen in Stadien und Skiarenen genannt. Zum positiven Image des „Sportlandes Salzburg" gehören schließlich noch zwei im Halleiner Stadtteil Rif angesiedelte Einrichtungen: das Landessportzentrum, dessen Infrastruktur österreichweit einzigartig ist, und das in der Sportforschung tätige Christian Doppler-Labor der Universität Salzburg. Sie alle haben einen Stellenwert, den man sich für das Gros der mehr als 50 anerkannten Sportarten in Salzburg wünscht. ◄

respectable 307 million viewers with a total transmission time of 342 hours. Here too, at this first really major event in Salzburg, the dimensions of which many decision-makers didn't really recognize until the last minute, the number of additional overnight stays was pointed out. At Euro 2008 the three games are intended to give rise to 100,000 stays, so the financial aspect is key. And this may be just the right medicine for those companies who have carried the name Salzburg out into the sporting world for so many years now. There are the ski makers, motor sport suppliers, including Formula 1, and the manufacturers of stadium admission systems that are now marketed worldwide. After all, two facilities based in the Hallein district of Rif are an important factor in the positive image of "sporting state Salzburg": the State Sports Centre, which is one of its kind in Austria, and the Christian Doppler Laboratory of Salzburg University that is active in sports research. These all have a significance that we would wish for all of the more than 50 recognised sports in Salzburg. ◄

Östlich der Festspielstadt Salzburg liegt der Salzburgring. Errichtet wurde er im Jahr 1968 auf einem 42 Hektar großen Areal. Nach einjähriger Bauzeit erfolgte im September 1969 die Eröffnung mit einem kombinierten Auto- und Motorradrennen. 1970 wurde der erste „Große Preis von Österreich" für Motorräder durchgeführt, und ein Jahr später fand der erste FIM-Motorrad-Weltmeisterschaftslauf statt

To the east of the Festival city Salzburg lies the Salzburgring race track. It was built in 1968 on a 42 hectare property. After being a year in the making, it was then opened in September 1969 with a combined automobile and motorbike race. The first Austrian Grand Prix for motorcycles was then held on it in 1970, followed a year later by the first FIM motorcycle world championship

VORSTELLUNGSENDE

„Dies Österreich ist eine **kleine Welt,** in der die große ihre Probe hält. Und waltet erst bei uns das **Gleichgewicht,** dann wird's auch in der andern wieder Licht."

Christian Friedrich Hebbel, am 26. Februar 1862, bei einem Prolog zur Feier des Jahrestages der Februarverfassung

Anhang
Appendix

Unternehmen
Enterprises

Nachstehende Unternehmen haben das Zustandekommen dieses Buches in dankenswerter Weise gefördert.

The following companies have supported the realization of this book which is much appreciated.

ALPINE Mayreder Bau GmbH
Salzburg
Seite/page 76/77
www.alpine.at

Böhm Schweißtechnik GmbH
Salzburg
Seite/page 79
Tel: +43 662-87 00 29-0

Fürst Developments GmbH
Salzburg
Seite/page 62/63
www.fuerstdevelopments.com

IFK Ges.m.b.H. & Co. KG
Salzburg
Seite/page 89
www.ifk.at
www.freshfx.at

KATHREIN Vertriebs-Ges.m.b.H
Salzburg
Seite/page 85
www.kathrein-gmbh.at

Gebrüder Limmert AG
Salzburg
Seite/page 65
www.limmert.com

Palfinger AG
Salzburg
Seite/page 75
www.palfinger.com

Privatinvest Bank AG
Salzburg
Seite/page 67
www.privatinvest.com

Salzburger Flughafen GmbH
Salzburg
Seite/page 90-93
www.salzburg-airport.com

Scotts Celaflor Handelsges.mbH
Salzburg
Seite/page 68/69
www.scotts.at

Stieglbrauerei zu Salzburg GmbH
Salzburg
Seite/page 127
www.stiegl.at

Stiftskeller St. Peter
Salzburg
Seite/page 134/135
www.haslauer.at

Synthes Österreich GmbH
Salzburg
Seite/page 109
www.synthes.com

System Standbau Ges.m.b.H.
Salzburg
Seite/page 86/87
www.systemstandbau.at
www.systemstandbau.eu
www.expoxx.at

Hotel Weisses Rössl GmbH
St. Wolfgang
Seite/page 168/169
www.weissesroessl.at

W&H Dentalwerk Bürmoos GmbH
Bürmoos
Seite/page 83
www.wh.com

Wirtschaftskammer Salzburg
Salzburg
Seite/page 94-99
www.wko.at/sbg

Fotografen
Photographers

Gemeinde Adnet
Seite 56

ARGEkultur
Seite 186

Altstadt Salzburg Marketing Ges.m.b.H.
Seite 82, 130 links

Archiv Grohag
Seite 54 Nr. 1, 2, 3

Bergbahnen Lungau GesmbH
Seite 52

Büro für Public Relations
der Universität Salzburg
Seite 60

Café Bazar
Seite 126 Nr. 5

Demel Salzburg
Seite 126 Nr. 7

Heinz-Peter Deska
Seite 45 Nr. 6

Dommuseum, Josef Kral
Seite 193

Eisriesenwelt Werfen
Umschlag Rückseite 3. Bild v. rechts,
Seite 48 Nr. 5

Karl Forster
Seite 182 Nr. 1, 2 und 4

Konditorei Fürst
Umschlag Rückseite 1. Bild v. rechts,
Seite 18/19

Fuschlsee Tourismus GmbH
Umschlag Rückseite 2. Bild v. rechts,
Seite 45 Nr. 1

Gasteiner Kur-, Reha- und Heilstollen-
betriebsgesmbH
Seite 48 Nr. 2, 170, 171

Golfclub Lungau
Seite 51 Nr. 1, 166 Nr. 2

Architekturbüro HALLE 1,
Foto: Gebhard Sengmüller
Seite 73, 191

Haus der Natur
Seite 194

Hotel Sacher Salzburg
Seite 133 Nr. 11

Internationale Sommerakademie
für Bildende Kunst in Salzburg
Seite 32/33, 187

Internationale Stiftung Mozarteum (ISM)
Seite 22/23, 196/197

Katschbergbahnen GmbH
Seite 51 Nr. 2

Atelier Thomas Klinger, München
Umschlag großes Bild, Innentitel,
Seite 6: 1. und 2. Bild von oben, Seite 7:
3. Bild von oben, 14/15, 20/21, 30/31, 36/37,
38/39, 40, 45 Nr. 2 und 3, 46, 53, 112/113, 115,
116/117, 118/119, 121, 122, 124/125, 126 Nr. 1, 2,
3, 4 und 6, 128/29, 130/131 Mitte, 136/137,
138/139, 140/141, 142/143, 144, 146/147,
148/149, 150/151, 152/153, 160/161, 174/175,
177, 178/179, 180/181, 184/185, 199, 200/201,
202, 203, 212

Geschw. Lanz Trachtenmoden GmbH
Seite 28/29

magazin Salzburg
Seite 81, 133 Nr. 9 und 10

Magistrat der Stadt Salzburg
Seite 112 oben

MdM (Museum der Moderne) Salzburg
Umschlag vorne 2. Bild v. rechts
(Simone Rosenberg)
Seite 123, 188 Nr. 5
Seite 133 Nr. 1 (Daniel Gebhart)
Seite 188 Nr. 1 und 4 (Daniel Gebhart)

Fotografen
Photographers

Seite 188 Nr. 2 und 3 (Simone Rosenberg)
Seite 188 Nr. 6 (Werner Reichl)

Palfinger AG
Umschlag vorne 1. Bild v. rechts

Mag. Herbert Podlipnik
Seite 145

RED BULL PHOTOFILES
Seite 7: 4. Bild von oben, 133 Nr. 2, 208, 209

Reed Exhibitions
Seite 71

Restaurant Esszimmer
Seite 132, 133 Nr. 6, 7 und 8

Restaurant Riedenburg Salzburg
Seite 133 Nr. 3, 4 und 5

Sailing Team Hagara Steinacher
Seite 210 (Foto: Sabine König)

Salzburg AG
Seite 190

Salzburger Burgen & Schlösser
Seite 48 Nr. 1, 51 Nr. 3

Salzburger Festspiele Archiv
Seite 34/35, 182 Nr. 5

SalzburgerLand Tourismus Ges.m.b.H.
Umschlag vorne 4. Bild von rechts
Seite 45 Nr. 5 und 7, 47, 48 Nr. 3 und 4, 55, 162, 163, 164, 166 Nr. 3 und 4, 167, 173, 198

Salzburg Museum
Seite 195 links (Rupert Poschacher)
Seite 195 rechts (Hermann Seidl)

Salzburgring (IGMS)
Seite 211

Frank Schäfer, München
Seite 26/27

Schauspielhaus Salzburg
Seite 192 Nr. 1

Schmittenhöhebahn AG
Seite 160 links

Schubert & Franzke
Seite 6: 3. Bild von oben, 58/59

SEAD Salzburg
Seite 189

Shutterstock, Inc.
Seite 7: 1. Bild von oben, 24/25, 41, 42/43, 45 Nr. 4, 49, 110/111, 158/159, 165, 166 Nr. 1

SLSV (Salzburger Landes-Skiverband)
Seite 207

Spiess Foto Tirol
Seite 206

SWS Stadion Salzburg Wals-Siezenheim
Seite 204/205

Tauern Touristik GmbH
Seite 54 Nr. 4, 57

toihaus Andreas Hauch
Seite 192 Nr. 2

Tourismus Salzburg GmbH
Umschlag vorne 3. Bild v. rechts,
Seite 7: 2. Bild von oben, 16/17, 61, 120, 126 Nr. 8, 130 rechts, 182 Nr. 3, 192 Nr. 3 und 4

Universität Salzburg
Seite 74, 78, 100/101, 102, 103, 104, 105, 106, 107, 108

viennaentertainment
Seite 183

Wirtschaftskammer Salzburg
Seite 6: 4. Bild von oben, 94/95, 96, 97, 98

Alle Porträtfotos wurden von den jeweiligen Autoren zur Verfügung gestellt.

Portrait photos were provided by the authors.